DIOGENES
OF OENOANDA

The Fragments

UNIVERSITY OF HULL PUBLICATIONS

DIOGENES
OF OENOANDA

The Fragments

A TRANSLATION AND COMMENTARY

BY

C. W. CHILTON

Published for the UNIVERSITY OF HULL *by*

OXFORD UNIVERSITY PRESS

LONDON NEW YORK TORONTO

1971

Oxford University Press, Ely House, London W. 1

GLASGOW NEW YORK TORONTO MELBOURNE WELLINGTON
CAPE TOWN IBADAN NAIROBI DAR ES SALAAM LUSAKA ADDIS ABABA
DELHI BOMBAY CALCUTTA MADRAS KARACHI LAHORE DACCA
KUALA LUMPUR SINGAPORE HONG KONG TOKYO

ISBN 0 19 713416 5

PRINTED IN GREAT BRITAIN
AT THE UNIVERSITY PRESS, OXFORD
BY VIVIAN RIDLER
PRINTER TO THE UNIVERSITY

FOR

HOWARD AND PENELOPE

CONTENTS

PLATES

PREFACE

THIS work deals with the remains of a unique inscription set up in a remote part of Lycia around A.D. 200 to proclaim to all and sundry the doctrines and message of Epicurus. The text on which it is based is, by kind permission of the publishers, that of my Teubner edition *Diogenis Oenoandensis Fragmenta* (Leipzig, 1967), where will be found text, critical apparatus, bibliography, and indices. This book can be regarded as a companion volume to that edition. It contains a translation of the fragments, an amplified introduction, and a commentary dealing both with the readings adopted and also with the philosophic and linguistic content of the fragments; in this, the longer part of the book, it has been my object to save the reader trouble by fairly full quotations, since not all of the references are readily accessible.

I have at the same time taken the opportunity to include certain background material, such as illustrations, which would not have been appropriate in the text.

The original versions of both this book and the text to which it refers first saw the light of day as a doctoral thesis submitted to the University of Hull in 1963. Acknowledgements for help received in the preparation of the text for publication have already been made in that work (though I should like to take this opportunity of recording my appreciation of the scholarship and skill of Dr. Reimar Müller who saw it through the press for B. G. Teubner); it is now my pleasant duty to offer public thanks for help received in the revision and preparation of this instalment.

How much I owe to earlier scholars who have written on Diogenes in German or Italian will be evident from the commentary. Two of my colleagues in the Department of Classics here, Professor A. F. Norman and Mr. J. C. G. Strachan, have given me enlightenment and valuable advice on a number of

points of interpretation and elucidation, while Professor J. B. Skemp has read the whole typescript and most generously found the time to suggest improvements to all parts of the work. My debt to him is particularly heavy.

Finally, I must not fail to thank the Publications Committee of the University of Hull who undertook the expense of publication, Mrs. Katharine Peacock who began, and Miss Heather Thompson who completed, the typing of a most difficult manuscript, and Mr. Dean of the Department of Geography who drew the map.

C. W. C.

Hull
February 1971

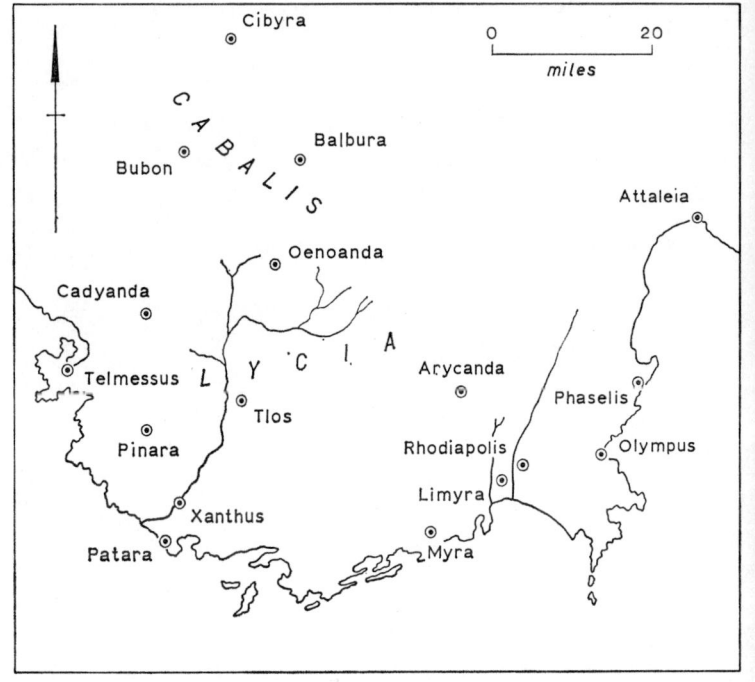

A map of *Lycia and the Cabalis,* based by permission of Messrs. John Murray on one in *An Account of a Journey through Lycia* by Sir Charles Fellows (1841).

INTRODUCTION

Lycia and the Cabalis

LYCIA is the name given in classical times to that portion of south-western Turkey where the coastline projects into the sea opposite to Rhodes—the area roughly south of a line drawn from Fethiye (Telmessus) to Antalya (Attaleia). It is largely mountainous country but from the earliest times it was well wooded and not infertile. The original Lycians were not Greek. They had their own alphabet and language, which persisted until the time of Alexander the Great, and thanks to their national spirit, and to their willingness to co-operate with one another in some kind of federal league, they were able to resist Greek settlement and colonization. They were subdued by the Persians in the sixth century, but retained their national character and native princes under that empire. Towards the end of Persian power in Asia Minor they came under the rule of Mausolus, satrap of Caria; their native dynasties disappeared, but they retained a large measure of independence and there was a considerable number of self-governing towns in the country, the largest being, as before, Xanthus, or Arna as the Lycians themselves called it.

The coming of Alexander meant, of course, a change of overlord. On his death Lycia was assigned to Antigonus, but soon afterwards passed to the Ptolemies of Egypt and remained a vassal of theirs throughout the major part of the third century. It was during this century that the Lycian language was finally supplanted by Greek, and the Lycians themselves began to consider themselves, and to be considered, as part of the Greek world.

Conquered by Antiochus the Great of Syria in 197 B.C., they were given by the Romans, when they had defeated Antiochus, to Rhodes—all except Telmessus, which went to Eumenes of Pergamum—but so harsh was Rhodian rule that the Lycians constantly revolted, until in 169 the Roman Senate declared

them free. From then on the country was governed by a revived Lycian League, which appears to have had a constitution far in advance of anything achieved by the Greeks of this or any other period. It was based on the idea of proportional representation. According to Strabo (xiv. 3. 2–3) there were 23 cities with the vote, the largest having three votes in the federal assembly, intermediate ones two, and the smallest one. The assembly elected the Lyciarch and other officers, deliberated on matters of foreign policy, and fixed the contributions of individual cities to taxes and, no doubt, to the federal armed forces also, in proportion to the number of votes the cities possessed. A. H. M. Jones, however, (*Cities of the Eastern Roman Provinces*, p. 104) considers that there must have been many more than the 23 cities mentioned by Strabo and suggests that probably groups of small cities shared one vote between them. The total number could well have been as high as 70.

Oenoanda was not originally a member of this league; in fact its founders can hardly have been Lycians at all. It lay in the central portion of the high ground on the northern border of Lycia, in the area called Cabalis or Cabalia. The Cabalians, according to Strabo (xiii. 4. 16), were said to be Solymi, a people who appear as enemies of the Lycians in Homer's story of Bellerophon in *Iliad* vi. Herodotus accounts for this by a tradition (i. 173) that they once held the whole of Lycia but were driven into the northern mountains by Sarpedon, who came from Crete in heroic times. It may well be true that the historic Lycians were originally an immigrant people, non-Greek and probably non-Cretan also, but there can be no doubt that the Cabalians were different from them in origin and language. Besides this we find them on their first appearance in history under the domination of a Lydian colony, Cibyra. In 189 B.C. this city was under a prince named Moagetes (Livy xxxviii. 14 describes how he was compelled to pay 100 talents to the Roman Cn. Manlius); before long it became head of a tetrapolis by the inclusion of Oenoanda, Bubon, and Balbura. Cibyra retained this position until 84 B.C. when, after the first Mithridatic war, Murena suppressed the dynasty, broke up the confederacy, and

added Bubon, Balbura, and almost certainly Oenoanda, also, to
the Lycian League.

This is the first mention of Oenoanda in history; we are not, however, entirely without information about it before it was joined
to Cibyra; there are two pieces of non-literary evidence, a coin
and the city walls. The coin, the only one in the B.M. collection
bearing the city's name (*BMC Lycia*, p. 73), is assigned to the early
second century B.C. and therefore must pre-date its absorption
by Cibyra, and perhaps point to an earlier period of independence. The city's walls, parts of which still stand, firmly and
beautifully built, suggested to W. Ruge (*R.E.*, s.v. Oenoanda)
that it may have been part of the dominions of Pergamum in the
time of Eumenes II (197–159 B.C.)—possibly acquired by him
under the treaty of Apamea (188 B.C.) at the same time as the
port of Telmessus. On the other hand it is possible that the
Oenoandans imported Pergamene masons to build their defences. They did, however, as we have seen, become part of
a Cibyratic confederacy during the mid or late second century,
and on its dissolution, members of the Lycian League; not very
loyal ones, it would seem, as Oenoandans assisted Brutus in the
siege and capture of the capital, Xanthus, in 42 (Appian, *Civil
War* iv. 79). As a punishment for this the city appears to have
been expelled; Pliny at least includes it in the province of Galatia
(*N.H.* v. 147), but in Vespasian's reorganization of Asia Minor
Oenoanda, with Bubon and Balbura, was reincorporated in the
enlarged province of Lycia–Pamphylia and rejoined the league,
into which it was soon completely and finally assimilated.

The Lycian League

The Lycian League had, of course, lost all real independence
years before, but it evidently remained very important within its
own borders and seems to have enjoyed a greater degree of self-
government than was normally allowed to provincial assemblies
in the Roman east. We know a great deal about its organization
and its officials,[1] knowledge derived mainly from the many

---

[1] The best account known to me is Magie, *Roman Rule in Asia Minor*, pp. 530 ff.

honorific inscriptions which still survive scattered about the ruins of its cities. I illustrate one such still to be seen at Oenoanda (Plate VI).

There were many cities, none very large (the six most important were Xanthus, Patara, Pinara, Tlos, Myra, and Olympus) but even those of moderate size enjoyed the normal appurtenances of urban life in the Graeco-Roman east—magistrates, boule, demos, agora, theatre—and for a century and a half after Vespasian appear to have been thriving and prosperous communities. Some of their citizens acquired great wealth, which they were prepared to spend liberally on public service and public benefactions in the hope of achieving the high position of Lyciarch or Chief Priest of the Augusti—positions which were clearly much sought after among the provincial aristocracy. These aristocrats, often, though not always, bearing Roman names, had frequently won Roman citizenship, bestowed either by Claudius or a later provincial governor, and occasionally became themselves, or had descendants who became, Roman senators and high-ranking Imperial officials. The one best known to us for his liberality was Opramoas of Rhodiapolis, who between A.D. 140 and 143 made gifts of perhaps 500,000 denarii to repair earthquake damage in 28 of the towns of Lycia as well as numerous other benefactions. Another, whose lineage is recorded on stone, was C. Licinnius Longus, grandson of C. Licinnius Musaeus, Lyciarch and Chief Priest of the Augusti probably under Nero, himself Lyciarch and Chief Priest, and the ancestor of senators and consulars. His gifts included 10,000 denarii to Myra, 50,000 to Tlos, and an endowment for yearly presents to a number of his fellow citizens. During these years of prosperity, before the disasters of the third century, such men as these spent their fortunes endowing valuable contests, presenting public buildings to their cities, and distributing money to the people. Oenoanda was one of the smaller cities of Lycia—she seems to have been one of the cities not to trouble to issue federal coins, though Bubon did—but she was fortunate to number C. Licinnius Longus among her citizens, and it is extremely probable, as we shall see, that our Diogenes was a member of the same family.

The Author

The evidence for this belief is to be found in *I.G.R.* iii. 500 (n. 60 HK, published in *Denkschrift Akad. Wien* xlv (1897), 41 ff.). This is a long inscription setting out the genealogy of 'Licinnia Flavilla and her kinsman Diogenes' over seven generations. It has been the subject of a study by Miss Shelagh Jameson in *Anatolian Studies* xvi (1966), 125–37; in this she brings out that Licinnia and Diogenes belonged to two branches of one of the most distinguished Lycian families of early Imperial times, a third branch of which included a number of Roman senators and even, in the second half of the second century, consuls. The other two branches were content with local honours but were by no means obscure— they included the C. Licinnius Musaeus mentioned above, who obtained the citizenship under Nero and, of course, his grandson C. Licinnius Longus. Another of Musaeus' descendants is named Flavianus Diogenes. This man's high birth does indeed appear to be all on his mother's side; his father, Simonides, son of Diogenes, was not himself a Roman citizen. Nevertheless, it is probable that Simonides had an ancestor of some eminence also; it is almost certain that he was descended from the Moles, son of Diogenes, who, although a citizen of Oenoanda, was priest of the temple of Caesar at Xanthus during the reign of Augustus (*O.G.I.S.* ii. 555).

But, whatever his ancestry in the male line, this Flavianus Diogenes is the most likely candidate to be the Diogenes referred to in the title to the inscription. The only other bearer of the name is his son Diogenes Eirenaeus, but if Flavianus was born between A.D. 150 and 160, and Licinnia herself as early as 115,[1] and if the inscription was set up in her lifetime, as Heberdey and Kalinka maintained (*Denkschrift Akad. Wien* xliii (1896), then Eirenaeus would be a little young to have achieved the distinction worthy of such a mention. Why Flavianus should be so singled out it is difficult to say. He had been Lyciarch, it is true, but, as has been said above, a number of his maternal relations, contemporaries of his, had held high office in the Imperial

---

[1] I am indebted to Miss Jameson for these dates.

service; Sulpicius Justus, for instance, another descendant of Licinnius Musaeus, was proconsul of Lycia–Pamphylia at some time between 193 and 211. Even so Licinnia does appear to have chosen Flavianus for the honour of appearing with herself at the head of this great family tree, and the suggestion, made first by Grilli in his 1960 edition of the fragments, that this Diogenes compiled and set up the inscription which is our subject is very attractive. The dates fit—both inscriptions can be dated to the end of the second or beginning of the third century—and our Diogenes must have been a man of wealth and standing in the city. Perhaps it was his fame as a philosopher, or his generosity, which persuaded Licinnia to name him in preference to the proconsul. There are indeed objections which may be brought against this identification:

1. The genealogy we have been discussing is not complete. It seems to have had eight columns but the extant text breaks off in col. VI. There may then have been other bearers of the name Diogenes in later generations, but the arguments against Eirenaeus would apply even more forcibly to them.
2. Our Diogenes may be someone quite unconnected with Licinnia; it is not an uncommon name. In that case we know nothing about him except what he tells us himself. Nevertheless Grilli's suggestion still seems very convincing.

About A.D. 200, then, Flavianus Diogenes—or his namesake—decided to erect a lengthy inscription setting out the message of Epicurus. He was ageing (fr. 2 II), near to death, he thinks, as a result of severe stomach-trouble (fr. 50), but had been a lifelong adherent of Epicurean philosophy with friends, no doubt fellow Epicureans, in Athens, Thebes, Chalcis, and Rhodes (frs. 15, 16, 51). There is, incidentally, no evidence to show that he had ever been in charge of an Epicurean school in Rhodes as suggested by Philippson, who mentions that Philodemus testifies to the existence of such a school in his time (*Rhet.* 1. p. 89, col. LII and p. 90, col. LIII). Diogenes is much more likely to have been a wealthy amateur of philosophy like Seneca. However, spurred on by a wish to bring the message of salvation

to all who passed by in the market-place, fellow citizens and strangers, both those already living and those not yet born (fr. 2 IV–VI), he decided to 'use this colonnade' to set out his message. Where this colonnade stood will be considered in a moment, but it must have been a prominent feature of the city. The suggestion that it flanked a basilica depends on a restoration of fr. 51, but is not inherently unlikely. He must then have had to obtain permission from the magistrates and town council to carve his message on the wall—and it was a long message, extending for over 40 m. and three or four columns high. But the council evidently gave this permission, though he nowhere says so. It is, of course, possible that he built the whole colonnade himself as a present for the town—a gift similar to the stoa of Attalus in Athens. Such an act of generosity would have been by no means unusual at this time, and Diogenes might well have been inclined towards it by his desire to set up his inscription in as public a place as possible, but again we have no means of knowing whether or not this was what happened.

So Diogenes had his message inscribed on stone in his native city and there for perhaps 150 years or more it stayed. As a document from the Graeco-Roman world it is unique. These are fragments of a vast 'wayside pulpit' and nothing like it has survived elsewhere; indeed it is highly probable that nothing like it ever existed. But philosophic handbooks in themselves were common enough in the early centuries of the Roman Empire. This was an age when most educated people and great numbers of the not so educated interested themselves in moral philosophy, and more or less loosely attached themselves to some sect. Of these sects the two most influential were the Stoics and the Epicureans. Stoicism appealed more to the western, Romanized, part of the Mediterranean world, but Epicureanism had many adherents all over the Empire, and it may not be inappropriate to summarize what we know of its fortunes during these years. It will show that Diogenes was probably not an isolated phenomenon, and that even the remoter towns of Asia Minor could, and almost certainly would, have had their Epicurean communities.

The Epicurean School in Imperial Times

Of the influence of Epicureanism in the last years of Republican Rome there is no need to say very much. Its doctrines, especially on physics, had been set out in one of the greatest works of Latin literature, the *De rerum natura* of Lucretius, and expounded in the pamphlets of the Greek Philodemus of Gadara who was a protégé of the noble L. Calpurnius Piso. Many prominent Romans openly acknowledged their adherence to Epicurus—Cassius and Cicero's friend Atticus are but two of them. Such a state of affairs need not cause surprise; in a century marked by continuing political instability and occasional civil war, men were bound to be attracted to a creed which taught that everyone could, and should, achieve a life of untroubled tranquillity and that no divine power had any influence over human affairs for good or evil. When Cicero towards the end of his life turned to the writing of philosophic works, it was principally with the object of examining and refuting the doctrines of Epicurus.

De Witt in his *Epicurus and his Philosophy* (Univ. of Minnesota, 1954), p. 345, says that as a result of Cicero's efforts 'Epicureanism was discredited both socially and politically' and 'forced to become anonymous'. This would seem to be a little too sweeping. Certainly the regime of Augustus, masquerading as a revived Republic, would not take kindly to such apparently selfish and irreligious teachings, but one at least of its official propagandists, Horace, makes no secret of his leanings towards them and there is sufficient evidence, such as, for example, the numbers of statues and busts of Epicurus that survive, to show that Epicureanism was by no means stifled during the first century A.D.

If this is true of Rome and Italy it is even truer of the Greek East. The Garden remained as the headquarters of the School and head followed head in a continuous succession. The *Suda* has a brief life of Epicurus in which it says: 'His school lasted 227 years until the first Caesar, during which there were 14 heads' (καὶ διέμεινεν ἡ αὐτοῦ σχολὴ ἕως Καίσαρος τοῦ πρώτου ἔτη σκζ̄, ἐν οἷς διάδοχοι αὐτῆς ἐγένοντο ῑδ)—or, reckoning from the death of the Founder in 270 B.C., to 44 B.C. But this is clearly only a quotation from a writer of that time; the succession went on

much longer than that. Diogenes Laertius, who most likely lived in the early third century A.D., writes (x. 9) that while all other schools had more or less died out, the Epicurean still went on for ever with a numberless succession of heads (ἥ τε διαδοχή, πασῶν σχεδὸν ἐκλιπουσῶν τῶν ἄλλων, ἐσαεὶ διαμένουσα καὶ νηρίθμους ἀρχὰς ἀπολύουσα . . .). The final comment is no doubt an exaggeration, but the succession was clearly still very secure in A.D. 121 when Trajan's widow Plotina, herself a member of the sect, petitioned Hadrian to vary the rules governing the appointment to the headship of the School. By this time, apparently, it was obligatory for the head to be a Roman citizen, which obviously restricted the choice open to heads when they came to nominate their successors, and also that of the members of the school if they wished to exercise their privilege of substituting another name for that found in the late head's will. Hadrian granted this request and the letters were recorded in an inscription (Dessau, *Inscr. Lat. Sel.* no. 7784).

Other evidence for the continuing vigour of the school in the first century A.D. is provided by the *Acts of the Apostles* 17. 18 (where some of the Epicurean and Stoic philosophers talked with Paul in Athens) and the writings of Plutarch, who was born, most probably, in A.D. 47. Ten of the moral essays listed in the Catalogue of Lamprias are on anti-Epicurean themes and three of them are extant, the *Non posse suaviter* ('You cannot live a pleasant life if you follow Epicurus'), written probably about the end of the first century, the *Adversus Colotem* ('Reply to Colotes'), which seems to date from about the same time since it is dedicated to L. Herennius Saturninus who was proconsul of Achaia in 98–9, and the short essay *An recte dictum*, which asks whether the Epicurean tag 'Live unknown' (λάθε βιώσας) is good advice or not. The date of this is uncertain (cf. Loeb edn. of the *Moralia*, xiv, p. 319).

Plutarch's *De superstitione* on the other hand, which may have been written rather earlier than the end of the century, is notably tolerant of the (basically Epicurean) refusal to believe in malevolent deities. Atheism is better than such superstitition, he says. But for the most thorough-going belief in the strength of

Epicureanism in this century, especially in the Greek East, we must revert to Paul—or rather to another book by N. W. De Witt, *St. Paul and Epicurus* (Univ. of Minnesota, 1954). De Witt believes that Paul was 'by early education an Epicurean', and that a great deal of the argumentation, and much of the language, in the Epistles was derived from and deliberately directed against Epicurean doctrine. This was because, De Witt thinks, Paul knew that there were Epicurean communities in almost all the towns and cities he visited on his missionary journeys, and that the chief opposition to his teaching came from these communities. His thesis is not entirely convincing; many of his assertions are impossible of proof, and some of the allusions to Epicurean doctrine which he finds in the Epistles are very difficult to recognize, but one cannot doubt that there were Epicurean communities in many of these towns, communities which Paul might well have hoped to convert. As De Witt points out, Colossae is only 50 miles north of Oenoanda.

In the second century the evidence for the continuing and indeed increased vigour of the sect is widespread and convincing. The parent school in Athens received another mark of Imperial favour, as we shall see, and it is clear that Epicureans remained a numerous and influential community, especially in Asia Minor. The second century was, of course, the era of the Antonines, that Golden Age of peace, prosperity, and intellectual revival so highly praised by Gibbon, but there is another reason for the significant increase in the number of Epicureans during these years. It was also an age in which people longed for a religion to believe in, and were ready in their need to turn to any kind of outlandish faith or superstition (cf. Usener, *Epicurea*, pp. lxxiii seqq.). The one sect which consistently opposed superstition and would have nothing to do with the oracle-mongers was the Epicurean; the Stoics, through their belief in Providence, had been forced to compromise long ago, and even the best of them could at times be taken in by charlatans as when Marcus Aurelius, at the bidding of an oracle of Alexander of Abonuteichus, had two lions thrown into the Danube before beginning his war against the Marcomanni and Quadi. The result, says

Lucian (*Alexander the False Prophet* 48), was that the lions were killed by the barbarians with clubs while the Romans lost 20,000 men and were driven back into Italy. It is not surprising that in this age many sensible people turned to Epicurus as the 'man who was truly saintly and divine in his nature, the man who alone knew what was right and true and passed it on, the liberator of all who came to him' (ἀνδρὶ ὡς ἀληθῶς ἱερῷ καὶ θεσπεσίῳ τὴν φύσιν καὶ μόνῳ μετ' ἀληθείας τὰ καλὰ ἐγνωκότι καὶ παραδεδωκότι καὶ ἐλευθερωτῇ τῶν ὁμιλησάντων αὐτῷ γενομένῳ—Lucian, op. cit. 61).

Lucian again (*Eunuchus* 3), with Philostratus (*Lives of the Sophists* 566), is our authority for the mark of imperial favour shown to the School when Marcus Aurelius endowed at least one and probably two chairs in it, doing the same for the Academics, Peripatetics, and Stoics, and assigned the choice of the actual incumbents to Herodes Atticus (A.D. 103–79). The popularity of the sect itself is proved by many references to it, some favourable, the majority critical. Diogenes Laertius was convinced of its superiority to all other systems and concludes his philosophic history with the life of Epicurus. Lucian shows how Epicureans proved themselves the chief opponents of superstition and so incurred the hostility and hatred of such men as Alexander. At a mystic celebration which the latter organized in Athens he began with a proclamation, 'If any atheist or Christian or Epicurean has come here to spy on the rites let him leave', and taught the crowd to chant 'Epicureans, out' in reply to his 'Christians, out' (*Alexander* 38). The followers of Plato, Chrysippus, and Pythagoras, says Lucian (op. cit. 25), were his friends, but he waged a truceless war against Epicurus (ὅλως δὲ ἄσπονδος καὶ ἀκήρυκτος αὐτῷ ὁ πόλεμος πρὸς Ἐπίκουρον ἦν).

Other authors bear witness to the continuing attraction of Epicureanism. Galen (A.D. 130–c. 200) in a catalogue of his own works (*De libris suis* 17) lists eight titles of an anti-Epicurean trend; two books, for instance, Περὶ τοῦ κατ' Ἐπίκουρον εὐδαίμονος καὶ μακαρίου βίου; two Περὶ τῆς κατ' Ἐπίκουρον ἀμαυροῦ ἡδονῆς, etc. Eusebius (*Praep. Ev.* 14. 5) quotes a passage from the second-century Numenius in which he compares the School of

Epicurus to a true harmonious state with one common mind and purpose, 'of which there were and are and, as it seems, will be enthusiastic followers' (ἔοικέ τε ἡ Ἐπικούρου διατριβὴ πολιτείᾳ τινὶ ἀληθεῖ, ἀστασιαστοτάτῃ, κοινὸν ἕνα νοῦν, μίαν γνώμην ἐχούσῃ. ἀφ' ἧς ἦσαν καὶ εἰσὶ καί, ὡς ἔοικεν, ἔσονται φιλακόλουθοι). In a later chapter of the same work (*P.E.* 14. 21) he quotes another second-century philosopher, Aristocles, as saying that he must argue against the doctrine that pleasure and pain are springs of choice and avoidance because 'even now the Epicureans say something like this' (ἔτι γέ τοι καὶ νῦν τοιαῦτά τινα λέγουσιν οἱ περὶ τὸν Ἐπίκουρον), and in other writers of about the same time whose works have survived such as Alexander of Aphrodisias, Apuleius, and Athenaeus many references to the doctrines of Epicurus can be found. It was at the end of this century, or possibly at the beginning of the third, that Diogenes set up his inscription in Oenoanda—itself the most convincing evidence possible that Epicureanism, far from being a spent force, or a study for academics only, was still in his day a vigorous, living influence at least among some sections of society in Greece and Asia Minor.

It continued to flourish in the third century, as we can tell by the growing number of attacks upon it in the works of Christian writers. In the days of Alexander of Abonuteichus Christians and Epicureans had been allies, but such an alliance, temporary as it was and dictated by outside pressures, obviously could not last. The denial by Epicurus of any divine order or interest in the world of men was anathema to Christians; in their eyes he was the arch-enemy of religion, and the frequence and violence of their attacks upon him and his doctrines is a measure of their continuing influence. Arnobius the Elder (early third century) criticizes him, displaying a wide acquaintance with Lucretius, Eusebius (*P.E.* 14. 23-7) includes a long attack on Epicurean Physics from the pen of Dionysius, bishop of Alexandria in the mid third century, Tertullian snipes at him, and Lactantius, Arnobius' pupil, who was born about A.D. 250 and published his *Divine Institutes* probably in the reign of Constantine, devotes many pages of Book iii to arguing against the ethical doctrine; he admits (17. 2) that it has always been much better known than

that of the other sects. Finally, to go back a little in time, there is the evidence of Origen, who died soon after 250. Towards the end of his life he published an elaborate rebuttal of a searching attack on Christianity written by a certain Celsus; it is one of the best of the early defences of the new religion, but for our purposes the interesting thing is how often he tried to condemn his opponent as an Epicurean, although it is obvious from the text that Celsus was nothing of the kind. We should not exaggerate the importance of this. 'Epicurean' for Origen seems to be little more than a 'dirty word', roughly equivalent to 'atheist', but his use of the term is significant in the context of contemporary Christian writings.

In the end it was the triumph of Christianity and its recognition by Constantine which brought the Epicurean sect to an end. By the middle of the fourth century it was dying or dead; Julian seems pleased to be able to say in his *Letter to a Priest* (301 c), written probably in 362, 'Let us not admit Epicurean or Sceptic talk, for by now the gods have deservedly destroyed them so that most of their works have disappeared' (μήτε 'Επικούρειος εἰσίτω λόγος μήτε Πυρρώνειος· ἤδη μὲν γὰρ καλῶς ποιοῦντες οἱ θεοὶ καὶ ἀνηρήκασιν, ὥστε ἐπιλείπειν καὶ τὰ πλεῖστα τῶν βιβλίων)—though this does not prevent him quoting Epicurus on occasion (e.g. *Oration* vi, 195 b, *Letter to Themistius* 255 b). Nevertheless, the school itself was quite finished by the end of the fourth century; Augustine twice dwells on the fact in his *Letter to Dioscorus* CXVIII. ii. 12 and ii. 21 (Goldbacher): '. . . since there is no longer any warmth in the ashes of even the Stoics and Epicureans', he says (ii. 12), 'to give life to any spark against the Christian faith' (*quando iam ne ipsorum quidem . . . Stoicorum aut Epicureorum cineres caleant unde aliqua contra fidem Christianam scintilla excitetur*).

So, about a century and a half after it was set up, the message of Diogenes, which he put up with such feelings of benevolence towards citizens and strangers alike, came to be regarded as both useless and sacrilegious, and before long, it would appear, the very wall on which it was inscribed was destroyed. When its fragments were discovered in the nineteenth century it was noticed with surprise that so few turned up in the area where

the stoa must have stood, and that most of the blocks were found to have been built into other structures in a different part of the city.

The Purpose of the Work

When Diogenes began his work all this was, of course, in the future. He believed that his inscription would stand for centuries as a statement of the only teaching which could bring peace and happiness to all mankind. As devoted to the Master as Lucretius had been two centuries before, Diogenes in his turn determined to give as full and convincing an exposition as he could of the message of salvation. His inscription, therefore, was made up of several parts. The two most important, and much the longest, were the Physics and the Ethics. This would have been obligatory for him, as it was for Lucretius. The Epicurean must first set out his view of the world—that it, and everything on it, is a chance creation of atoms and space, fortuitously formed and destined at some time to break up, neither process depending in any way on divine intervention, for although gods exist they are not concerned with terrestrial affairs—and then he must deduce from this what man, a creature of a day, must do to achieve peace of mind while he lives. For the student there was also a preliminary course on psychology, epistemology, and the rules of scientific reasoning (the *Canonice*, as Epicurus called it), but this would be inappropriate in a work of popularization, and so there was no separate treatment of it here.

Of the Physics little has survived, but there is enough to show that it followed the usual Epicurean line, with frequent refutations of Stoic doctrine, as is the case in Lucretius also; it seems that Diogenes split it into two parts, the Physics proper and a separate treatise on the doctrine that our world is not unique but merely one of an unlimited number. The Ethics, as we shall see, is most heavily represented in the surviving fragments, though it probably was not the biggest part of the original. In addition to his statement of the doctrine, based of course on Epicurean authorities, Diogenes inscribed beneath it a continuous band of the Principal Doctrines of Epicurus himself and, elsewhere on the

wall, a collection of other ethical maxims whose origin we do not know. This was clearly to Diogenes the most important part of his message and the one he was most anxious should be read. But there were other, shorter, sections which he must have felt would cheer the converted or convince the waverers. We have fragments, pathetically few and badly damaged, of a diatribe on Old Age; its arguments, so far as we can see, are very similar to those in Cicero's *De senectute* and perhaps Diogenes put this up for his own consolation as well as for the instruction of the people. And then there was a 'Letter to Mother'. This will be discussed fully later, but it seems almost certain to have been a copy of one of Epicurus' own letters. Why Diogenes should have wished to have this carved on stone nearly five hundred years after Epicurus' death, we cannot say for certain, but the most likely explanation is that it was one of a collection of the Master's letters (we know there were such collections) which showed how attractive a character he was and at the same time brought out a point of the Epicurean doctrine on dreams and visions. There are also a few fragments of a personal nature—a part of Diogenes' will, of his instructions about the erection of the work, and so on.

The purpose of the whole is plain—to show the reader how, thanks to Epicurus, he can achieve peace of mind by banishing groundless fears, to rehearse for him the physical doctrines which show why these fears are groundless, and to encourage him not to be despondent when his time of life nears its end. It must be a matter for regret that Diogenes' message had such a short life, and that so little of it has come to light in modern times.

Rediscovery

The exploration of Lycia began in the early 1800s but the site of Oenoanda was still unknown to Sir Charles Fellows, who toured the area in 1838 and 1840. It was finally identified in October 1841 by Messrs. Hoskyn and Forbes, who were attached to H.M. Surveying Ship *Beacon* (Mr. Forbes as naturalist); and then, when the *Beacon* returned to Lycia in January 1842 to remove the antiquities which Fellows had discovered at Xanthus, Mr. Forbes and Lieut. Spratt R.N., the assistant surveyor, joined

with a clergyman-antiquarian, the Revd. E. T. Daniell, to spend
some months exploring the area. Mr. Daniell unfortunately died
of malaria, but the survivors published the account of their
journey in 1847, and in it we have our earliest description of the
city, together with the plan reproduced in this book (Plate II).

Their description takes up only three pages (*Travels in Lycia* i.
273–5) and is worth quoting in full:

May 13th.—About two miles from the konak, on the opposite side
of the river, are the ruins of Oenoanda. The city was built on the
extremity of a spur of the Massicytus. To reach it we crossed over
a high stone bridge, and ascended by an ancient road leading up
the hill from its western side. On the ascent we passed many sarcophagi, and a small group of badly cut rock-tombs resembling those
at Termessus, and evidently of a late date. There were also many
tablets rudely sculptured on the face of the rock. On one of them was
a representation of two open hands. The lids of one of the sarcophagi
were ornamented with crouching lions, and their ends by the emblem
of the shield and sword as at Balbura. The walls of the city are on one
side in good preservation, and of admirable construction. They are
built of blocks of limestone, in some places polygonal, in others forming
regular courses, and always accurately fitting. The summit of the wall
has projecting and sloping eaves; and there are square towers at intervals, with narrow doors, windows, and loop-holes. One of these, with
the wall by it, we found to be thirty feet high. This had an arched
gateway, a window opening townwards, and a doorway only two feet
wide, leading outwards. Over the gate were two inscribed tablets,
but so defaced as to be almost illegible. The first part of this wall runs
across a low neck or ridge, where the city was most easily accessible.
In places where the sides of the mountain are very precipitous, there
are no traces of defences. Near the tower described is a fallen monument or mausoleum, round the basement of which there was a long
inscription, as on the monument at Rhodiapolis. This we had not
time to copy. The upper part of the hill, where the principal public
edifices stood, is covered with ruins. These are so buried in woods of
cedar, that it was only by ascending the trees we could make out the
relative positions of the buildings, so as to construct the accompanying
plan. Nearly in the centre of this part of the city was a flagged court
or square, surrounded by pedestals,—this was most probably the
Agora. The pedestals are all inscribed, and on one of them was the
name of the town. Surrounding the Agora were several large and
handsome buildings, portions of which are still standing. Fragments
of highly ornamented pediments and columns lie strewed about in

abundance. The capitals of some of the latter are Corinthian, a few Doric, others Ionic; one of the buildings has its front adorned with Ionic pilasters. Most of the remains are indicative of Roman times. When Mr. Hoskyn and Mr. Forbes visited this site during the previous autumn, they found no theatre. Convinced, however, that a city so important must have had one, we made a scrutinizing search among the thickets, and at length came upon a theatre, built in a hollow of the hill, and so buried among trees and bushes, that we had passed by it many times before we came upon it. It is one hundred and forty-four feet in diameter, and has fifteen rows of seats not separated by a diazoma. The area is large in proportion to the size of the building, and the proscenium very perfect. Most of the seats are remarkable for not being channelled and depressed at the back part, as is usually the case. The summit of the hill was a fortified acropolis, and is excavated in parts to form large reservoirs for water. From it, there is a very fine view over the yailahs and down towards the head of the valley of the Xanthus, to which there is a road passing under the ruins and entering near the Dey's-bridge.

Thereafter various travellers visited the site and copied the inscriptions to be found on the overturned pedestals and elsewhere, but nothing unusual was reported until in 1884 two French scholars, Holleaux and Cousin, discovered five fragments which clearly came from an inscription setting out Epicurean doctrine. These are in my edition fr. 2 II–VI; fr. 6; fr. 10 I–IV; fr. 15; and fr. 28 I–III.

The next year Cousin and Diehl found 22 more pieces of the same inscription and in 1889 Cousin alone unearthed 38 more. By this time he felt able to publish his findings, which he did in the organ of the French School at Athens, the *Bulletin de Correspondance Hellénique*, for 1892. In spite of the time he had taken over it, this was not a very accurate or very informative piece of work. It gave merely a copy of the text of the inscription, in capitals, with a general description of the appearance of the stones and, usually, where they were found, but no measurements, either of stones or lettering. A transcript was added, but few restorations attempted.

Cousin had noticed that the lettering was not all of equal size, but the main difference which struck him was that some fragments had 14 lines to a column while others had 15; he

concluded that in the original a row of 14-line columns had stood above a row of 15-line columns, both rows looking like an unrolled papyrus, and that the whole work had been in the form of a Letter to Antipater. He therefore begins with fr. 15, after the fragment of Diogenes' name (fr. 54).

This publication caused great excitement in the academic world, at least on the Continent. In the same year Gomperz published some critical notes on it, while Usener, the editor of *Epicurea* (1887), republished the whole text with many acute emendations and restorations in *Rheinisches Museum*. The next year, 1893, H. van Herwerden, in a paper which seems to have escaped the notice of all subsequent editors, also published a large number of penetrating observations on Cousin's text, often agreeing with Usener though apparently without knowledge of Usener's work. All these scholars were, however, handicapped by the inaccuracy of much of Cousin's copying, as was proved when, at Usener's suggestion, the Austrians Heberdey and Kalinka went to Oenoanda in 1895. They spent several weeks there, concentrating their search on the 'flagged platform with pedestals' of Spratt's plan (D), at many points stripping the walls (which in places were still 1·5 metres high) to the ground in the hope of finding inscribed stones, since Cousin had found many of his fragments built into other structures; but they had little success there. They did, however, find again most, though not all, of Cousin's discoveries and 24 more fragments of varying size, reread the whole work, and published their results in *B.C.H.* for 1897. This is a much more satisfactory text. They gave careful facsimile drawings (to a scale of 12/100) of all the stones they saw (cf. for example the illustration to fr. 58), together with measurements of both stones and lettering, and it is on their work that all subsequent study of Diogenes has depended.

As has been seen, the fragments were not discovered in any one particular spot. The first to be found were scattered in the northern part of the town, as were most of those unearthed in the three subsequent expeditions, the most fruitful source being the obtuse-angled wall running north and east from the C on Spratt's plan. Cousin noted that many of the blocks had been

built into this wall, or into foundations near it, with the inscribed face inwards. He found others in various ruins to the north and south of this wall and a few in the ruins round the 'flagged platform' on which Heberdey and Kalinka (or, for brevity, HK) concentrated. They found only three pieces there, but had more success in the area already explored by Cousin, i.e. north and south of the 'Great Wall', as they called it (Plate III). It would certainly seem likely that Diogenes' inscription did not last undisturbed for long before it was demolished and dispersed.

Nevertheless, there is little doubt about its original site. From the first it was accepted that the most likely place for the stoa on the walls of which it was set up was Spratt's 'flagged platform' (D). It is a level, rectangular courtyard measuring 54 by 27 yards (approx.), with two steps running the length of the long sides, and we have the evidence of the plan, supported by HK, that rows of columns had originally enclosed it on those sides. Both Spratt and Cousin thought it might have been the agora of the city; HK doubted this, preferring to place the agora in Spratt's area B, but Ruge is inclined to return to the older view and acquaintance with the site supports him. No other part of the city, which is quite small, would so well fulfil the functions of an agora and, if this identification is correct, it would be the ideal place for Diogenes to have his message inscribed when, near the close of his life, he decided from a feeling of benevolence to all men, fellow citizens and strangers alike, to 'set forth in public the remedies which bring salvation'.

Today the stones are still lying where they were left by HK. Some are fairly well preserved, others are now weather-beaten and worn. Until recent years few visitors found their way to the site. Professor G. E. Bean was there in 1952 and I am indebted to him for the photograph of fr. 41 (Plate IV). Miss Freya Stark mentions a visit in her *Alexander's Path* (1954) and observes that a 'pillared square overgrown with trees was perhaps a market with pedestals all round it, its space still flagged and smooth' (p. 199), but when I went there in 1962 I believe that I was the first to go looking for Diogenes since HK left him in 1895.

It is a rather rough 40-mile journey from the port of Fethiye

to the village of Incealiler, followed by a long climb up a hill to the ruins. After crossing what seem to be the remains of an aqueduct, one passes through the city wall at about point F on Spratt's plan. This wall, and the tower which projects from it, still stand to a considerable height. Then, in a few minutes, the 'flagged area' is reached. Its pillars are no longer standing, and trees and shrubs have sprouted between the stones, but the pedestals of vanished honorific statues are still there, and I reproduce one well-preserved inscription (Plates V and VI).

A little further north is the Great Wall, around which most of the known fragments of the inscription were found, and where they are still lying.

It has always seemed possible that a new, thorough investigation of the ruins would reveal more of Diogenes' work. The Epicurean scholar Vogliano wrote to Grilli after the publication of the latter's 1950 commentary, saying that he was sure that 'time in its further destruction of the remains of the town has brought to light new stones of the inscription'. This possibility would seem to be made stronger by the remoteness of the site and the absence of any buildings to which the stones might have been transferred—there is no sign of them in Incealiler. Now at last what Grilli (*Praefazione*, p. 7) called a 'vain and unrealizable hope' may be realized. Mr. M. F. Smith went to Oenoanda in the summer of 1969 to review the extant stones (which he found had been in general very accurately recorded by HK) and actually succeeded in finding four new fragments. He has published these in *Am. J. Arch.* lxxiv, no. 1 (January 1970); we must hope that this is only a beginning and that more will be unearthed in future expeditions.

The Text

There can be little doubt that whatever additions are made to it, HK's 1897 text will always be basic for the study of Diogenes—this is at once archetype and *editio princeps*. It superseded Cousin (and Usener), and their discovery of fragments with a larger lettering than any known to Cousin (except the title) ruled out his idea that the inscription had originally consisted of only two

bands of text. HK arranged their text in order of diminishing size of script, beginning with the block with the largest lettering (the title, fr. 54) and ending with the 15-line fragments (the ethical discourse). This results in the fragments falling into more or less homogeneous groups, as can be seen from the Index Numerorum in the text. The division of the work into sections, however, is the work of William, who edited it for Teubner in 1907. On the basis of internal and external evidence (cf. my Praefatio, p. viii) he arranged the fragments into six sections, i.e.:

A. Diogenis De Natura Rerum Liber.
B. Diogenis De Innumerabilitate Mundorum Epistula ad Antipatrum.
C. Diogenis Disputatio Ethica.
D. Epicuri Sententiae.
E. Diogenis Oenoandensis Scripta Privata.
F. Diogenis De Senectute Liber.

This division has now become more or less canonical, and only slight modifications are to be found in Grilli and the present Teubner edition. The principal change I have made in the latter has been to re-unite the pieces of the 15th line with the ethical fragments to which they originally belonged (cf. Praef., pp. xii–xiii).

For the size of the lettering (uncials), the peculiarities in it, the rules of word-division, and the types of punctuation used cf. Praefatio, pp. viii–ix. (Note that ει is used for ῑ.) It might be added that the curved παραγραφή (∼) is used to mark the end of lengthy parentheses only. The number of letters per line varies but the average is 16–18—there is more on this in the next section and, where it is important, in the commentary. The mistakes of the lapicide, or lapicides, were few and not serious. There is sometimes confusion between H and N (cf. 8 II 11 and III 9), and at 8 II 7 occurs one of the two examples of dittography—the other is at 14 I 5. C seems to be a mistake for O at 45. 1 and to have been omitted at 30. 8, but apparent confusion between Λ and A, and between C and Є is usually the result of wear on the stone rather than an error in the cutting. All such errors—

they amount to fewer than 20—are noticed as they occur in the apparatus and, if necessary, the commentary.

The stone on which the inscription is carved is limestone. The blocks, which are sometimes square, sometimes oblong, with, as a rule, bevelled edges, vary greatly in thickness. The least tall ones, i.e. those at the top of the wall, average about 30 cm. in thickness (though there is the occasional one of 77 cm.); those of the Physics—which I take to be the second course up (cf. below, pp. xlii–iii)—vary between 26 and 44 cm., but in the tallest blocks (the Ethics) variation can be as great as between 23 cm. and 77 cm.

The Arrangement of the Inscription

After Cousin's theory, which had to be abandoned, William was the first to consider the question of how the inscription had been set out on the wall, or walls, of the stoa in which it was inscribed. He noticed that the complete blocks recorded by HK fell into four groups according to height. These groups are (cf. Praef., p. ix):

(a) 56–65 cm. (Max. 62 cm. in W but he overlooked fr. 25)
(b) 46–50 cm.
(c) 37–41 cm.
(d) 33–5 cm.

One stone 43 cm. high (HK 17, fr. 65) must be included in (b), since apart from height it is similar in every respect to the other fragments of the diatribe on Old Age. The blocks in groups (a) and (b) are, with certain exceptions, inscribed in smaller letters (i.e. 1·5–2 cm. high); those in (c) and (d) are all in larger (i.e. 2·5–3 cm.). The distribution of the blocks among the groups is set out in Praefatio, p. ix (the numbers given to the stones by HK are used because frequently a fragment consists of two or more stones), but it may be convenient to indicate here the parts of the work to be found in each category.

The tallest group, that is (a), consists mainly of the remains of the Ethical Treatise. This consists of 14-line columns, with a 15th line which is in fact a band in slightly larger lettering running

INTRODUCTION xxxvii

continuously below the columns and containing a selection of the
Principal Doctrines of Epicurus. The presence of this band is in-
valuable. It helps us to assess how much of the treatise is missing,
although the order of the Doctrines found here is not that used
by Diogenes Laertius and parts of one or two doctrines otherwise
unknown are included. Incidentally, the presence of this 15th
line enables us to assign to this section HK 72 (fr. 33) although
it is only the lower part of a block There are as a rule 15–18
letters to the line and an occasional gap between words, but in
general punctuation is indicated by straight παραγραφαί on the
left.

This group also includes:

1. The title to the Ethical Treatise (fr. 23).
2. A short Letter to Antipater on the Innumerability of the
   Worlds (frs. 15–22). This has no 15th line but possesses
   παραγραφαί.
3. Some other maxims of varying length inscribed on single
   stones, maxims which may not be the work of Epicurus himself
   (frs. 40–8).

The second tallest group, (b), consists of:

1. The remains of the Physical Treatise (frs. 3–14). The columns
   are again of 14 lines, with roughly the same number of letters
   per line as in the Ethics. Gaps between words are more frequent here and there are no παραγραφαί. There is, of course,
   no 15th line.
2. A kind of general introduction in 14-line columns (frs. 1 and
   2). This has a number of gaps between words but a few
   παραγραφαί also.
3. Seven stones in larger lettering with a scored border along
   the bottom and what are clearly only the lower five lines of
   columns from a treatise on Old Age (these are now frs. 56, 60,
   63, 65, 66, and the lower parts of frs. 58 and 61).
4. Part of Diogenes' will—one block in larger lettering (fr. 50).
5. Part of a letter, also in larger lettering, which seems to concern
   the erection of the inscription (fr. 51).

The other two groups are much less numerous. Group (*c*) has only eight stones in it. One (fr. 49) must be part of another general introduction; it has nine lines of 14 letters with a margin above and on the left. Two (frs. 57 and 64) seem to have consisted of two columns (or parts of columns) of eight lines of varying length with no margins either above or below: yet another (fr. 62) has seven lines without margins. These three from their content would seem to belong to the treatise on Old Age. Finally, there are four blocks (frs. 52–3) containing the whole or parts of seven ten-line columns which make up the Letter to Mother. These again have nothing that one can describe as a margin either at top or bottom. There are between 15 and 18 letters per column.

Compared with this rather puzzling group the last of all, (*d*), consists of the least tall stones, few in number, and is easy to place. One (fr. 54) has most of what was once Diogenes' name in very large letters. The other three stones in this group are the upper halves of ten-line columns from the treatise on Old Age (frs. 55, 58, 61).

This group clearly stood at the top of the inscription. Fr. 54 may have been part of the title to the diatribe on Old Age, as William thought; but it may equally well have been a general heading to the whole work, standing in the middle of the highest course. The other three stones in this group must also have stood at the top and if the pairs of stones in frs. 58 and 61 are correctly joined, as seems very likely, then it is tempting to assume that the diatribe on Old Age was inscribed on pairs of blocks with a scored border along the bottom, each pair stretching down for a distance of 80 cm. from its top. Unfortunately it is not easy to see how frs. 57, 64, and 62 from group (*c*), which from internal evidence form part of the diatribe, can be made to fit into this arrangement. Fr. 57, for instance, has eight lines, and is only 37 cm. tall; fr. 64 is similar; fr. 62 is the same height but has only seven lines; none of these stones has a border above or below.

This difficulty does not seem to have worried William. He placed the diatribe together in the top right-hand corner of his suggested arrangement (p. xlvii), does not mention the scored

border, and assumed that the varying heights of the stones could be explained by the necessity to even out irregularities lower down. But it did worry Philippson (cf. Praef., p. xi) and he proposed inserting these three blocks between upper and lower blocks such as make up frs. 58 and 61. That this could in fact be done is shown in TAB II of my edition but it would result in 18-line columns extending for 120 cm. down three courses of stones. This seems unlikely, and Grilli rejected it. In 1950 he suggested that the inscription might have been on two walls of the stoa, with the pairs of stones on one wall and the single ones from groups (b) and (c) in the upper courses of the other. In his 1960 edition, however, he reverted to the single-wall theory and suggested that the solution to the problem might be that these three blocks (i.e. frs. 57, 64, and 62) are narrower because they stood under the beams which supported the roof of the stoa and that below them must have been other stones with two or three lines of text and the scored border. This is possible, but must be recognized as pure surmise. In fact, the only safe conclusion to be drawn from this discussion is that no conclusion is possible. If these fragments do all form part of a treatise on Old Age—and they certainly seem to—then we do not have sufficient evidence to determine how they were fitted together, or answer the question why some have a distinctive border and others do not.

It may be convenient here to consider the possible allocation of the remaining stones of group (c). Three, as we have seen, belong to the diatribe on Old Age. Another is fr. 49; this is part of an introduction, either to the whole work, as Philippson thought, or to some new portion apart from the Physics and Ethics, as William thought—it refers to Diogenes' kindly feeling for strangers and to the treatises on Physics and Ethics. But since its lettering is bigger, and it speaks of the physical and ethical treatises inscribed *below*, it must have stood in at least the third course from the bottom, on a level, probably, with the lower part of the treatise on Old Age. The remaining four blocks make up the Letter to Mother (frs. 52 and 53); three of these are 41 cm. high, the fourth is 38 cm., they are all inscribed in similar

(larger) lettering, and must also have stood in the same range as the previous stone.

This is W's arrangement (cf. p. xlvii). At the same time he adds to this range the fragment of Diogenes' will (fr. 50) and the Letter to Friends (fr. 51). These are in fact taller stones (47 cm. and 49 cm.) but they have the larger lettering (in 11 and 10 lines of text respectively) and their subject-matter suggests that they should go closely with fr. 49. It is worth noting that their additional height is partly due to a blank margin, 7 cm. and 10 cm. high, along the bottom of the stone. If this margin is ignored the amount of stone inscribed is almost exactly the same as in the Letter to Mother, which also has 10-line columns. One obvious result of W's arrangement is that the top of the inscription is not at a uniform height; for though most of it extends over only three courses, the diatribe on Old Age reaches into a fourth and stands up higher on the right-hand side. Grilli did not like this and felt that the top would have been uniform; he also believed that the scored border, about 10 cm. high, probably ran the whole length of the inscription between second and third courses (cf. the sketch of the two arrangements at p. xlvii).

This latter suggestion has its attractions; it would certainly produce a more harmonious result than W's. Unfortunately it must be recognized once again as pure speculation. It implies that below the Will, the Letter to Mother, and the fragments of introductory material stood other stones uninscribed, apparently, except for the 10 cm. margin—stones of which no fragment has survived. This seems a great deal to assume. W's projecting section is perhaps less aesthetically pleasing but what reason is there to suppose that the inscription was one harmonious rectangle? The upper stones in larger lettering, i.e. groups (c) and (d), are so much less numerous, and their subject-matter so limited, that it is impossible to believe that the higher part of the inscription, i.e. that standing above the Physics and Ethics, could have been anything like as extensive as the lower two courses.

These lower courses present fewer problems. One, group (b), consists basically of the physical treatise, the other, group (a), of the Ethics. The peculiarity of the former group is that it

contains stones with 14-line columns in smaller lettering but also stones which have the larger letters and sometimes as few as five lines of text. These are the lower halves of columns from the diatribe on Old Age already referred to; it is almost certain, as we have seen, that they stood in the next course above, together with Diogenes' will and the Letter to Friends which are the other stones in this group with similar, larger, lettering. It may be theoretically possible to construct a scheme whereby all the stones in this group can be fitted in on the same level as the 14-line columns of the Physics, but the result is an extraordinary hotch-potch—some columns have five lines, others 14, some have small letters, others large, some have a broad scored border along the bottom, others have nothing; such a scheme is quite unacceptable. This being so, we must assume that this course included nothing but the Physics and the Foreword—most probably a general introduction to the Physics and Ethics combined (for a fuller discussion see below, pp. 26-7).

We are now left with the tallest stones. Most of them, as mentioned above, belong to the Ethics and except for the title have the distinctive 15th line; they range from 56 to 62 cm. in height with one of 65 cm. (fr. 25). Two other sections of the work are usually included in this group—the *Sententiae Variae* (Various Maxims), because the only two complete blocks among them are 58 and 57 cm. high, and the Letter to Antipater, with stones ranging from 56 to 59 cm. For the former of these two groups to stand in this course would be entirely appropriate; they are additional maxims which may or may not be by Epicurus himself but whatever their authorship they would go naturally with the 15th line, which consists, as has been said, of a selection of Epicurus' Principal Doctrines. One note of caution, however, must be sounded here—it is not certain that all the stones in this section *were* of a similar height; for instance fr. 45 *may* have stood no more than 40 cm. high (cf. Praef., p. x) and have differed from the other maxims in other respects. It follows that we must admit the possibility that these maxims did not all stand in the same course but were divided between the two lower ones. The Letter to Antipater, however, must have stood together—it is

a homogeneous group of stones on a single topic. The only possible difficulty with this is that it naturally belongs to the Physical Treatise and might have been expected to be inscribed with it. The arguments against such an arrangement are two:

1. The height of the stones—no stone in the Physics is higher than 49 cm., no stone in the Letter is lower than 56 cm. and the average is nearer 59 cm.
2. The Letter is liberally punctuated with παραγραφαί, which are not used at all in the Physics and in only two columns of the Foreword.

For these reasons it has been generally accepted that this Letter stood on the same level as the Ethics, and there seems no good reason to reject this opinion, especially if we believe that the Physics was originally the longest section in the work and might easily have spread over more than one course.

There exists, then, substantial agreement as to the contents of these two lower courses: one contained the Ethics, the Letter to Antipater, and (possibly) the Various Maxims, the other the Foreword and the Physics. William and Grilli differ, however, on which of these stood above the other. W assumed that the tallest, i.e. the Ethics etc., would be at the bottom and the Physics etc. above, but Grilli disagreed with this in both 1950 commentary and 1960 edition. For the reasons set out on Praef., p. xii he considers that the Physics stood at the bottom of the inscribed area with the Ethics above. Briefly these reasons are that the Physical columns have nothing below to separate them from the material underneath as Old Age has its scored border and the Ethical treatise its 15th line—he considers therefore that they should rest on the uninscribed lower part of the wall. He finds support for this theory in the different methods of punctuation used in the different parts of the work; the Physics—at eye level—uses only spaces between words; the Ethics and Letter to Antipater have παραγραφαί; while the Old Age etc., being 3 metres or more from the ground, revert to larger spaces. This is also Epicurus' order of teaching and the order in which since W the various parts of the work have been printed.

Grilli may indeed be right; certainly there is insufficient evidence to prove him wrong. But objections can be urged against his view. One is that his argument from the scored border below the diatribe on Old Age is largely invalidated unless it can be proved (as it cannot) that this border ran across the entire width of the inscription; another, perhaps minor one, is that spaces between words do occur in the Ethics also. But the really serious objections are, first, that it upsets the natural order of descending height in the stones by inserting a course of the tallest stones, group (*a*), in between groups (*b*) and (*c*), both of which are noticeably less tall. We must remember that the stoa was built before Diogenes had his message carved upon it; is it reasonable to suppose that the masons in building the upper part of the wall, i.e. from 1·5 to about 2·5 metres, put in a whole row of stones all higher than the course below it? Secondly, with this arrangement the running band of Principal Doctrines will cut right across the inscription between the first and second courses. It is much more natural, and much more in keeping with Epicurean veneration of the Master, to suppose that this ribbon of doctrine was the basis and foundation of the whole work.

In its general outlines, then, W's arrangement seems to agree best with the external and internal evidence of the surviving portions of the inscription. Assuming that it was carved on one wall only minor adjustments can be accepted with any conviction. Of course, it *may* have been divided between two walls of the stoa—as G suggested in 1950—but if this were so it is quite impossible on the evidence available to say how the work was divided, and which portions were on which wall. As has been seen, this is no solution to the most puzzling problem of all—the presence of differing blocks and varying column lengths in the diatribe on Old Age. This, however, does not mean that W's arrangement has to be accepted in its entirety. For instance, if we accept his placing of the Letter to Antipater on the left of the Ethics (as a kind of appendix and conclusion to the Physics) it is by no means so certain that the Various Maxims stood all at the same level on the right. If the last portion of the Ethics is completely missing, as seems to be the case, it would be

surprising if maxims which followed the end of the Ethics have survived. This suggests that these maxims may also have stood on the left—or even, as has been proposed earlier, been distributed between other parts of the work.

The Total Length of the Inscription and its Location

It may now be possible to amplify a little the short note appearing on pp. xiii and xiv of the Praefatio. We have seen that by counting the number of letters missing from the ribbon of Principal Doctrines running below the Ethics it is possible to deduce with a fair degree of accuracy the number of columns lost from that treatise. We have the remains of 43 cols. and it would seem that about 80 more are missing; this gives a rough total of 120 columns for the section. We know from HK's facsimile of nos. 66–7 (fr. 26) that 4 columns of Ethics measured 1·30 metres; 120 columns would therefore extend for 39 metres. In addition, it seems likely that the Letter to Antipater stood at the side of the Ethics; we have 2·96 metres of this letter, this clearly being only part of the original length. William, as seen above, would put the *Sententiae Variae* in the same course—2·55 metres of these are extant. These figures total 44·51 metres. We can then say that in all probability, wherever the *Sententiae Variae* stood, the length of the lowest course of the inscription was at least 45 metres and perhaps rather more. It is reasonable to suppose that the central course, the Physics, was of the same length; the two upper courses, which seem to have been added later, may not have extended so far.

This is a considerable length (though Usener suggested originally that the work had probably extended for about 40 metres) and it must inevitably raise the question whether the building which is usually identified as Diogenes' stoa could have had walls of this length. We have seen above that ever since the first publication of the inscription it was thought that Spratt and Forbes's 'flagged platform with pedestals' (D on the plan) was the most likely place for this stoa, but unfortunately neither Cousin nor HK, although the latter accepted this identification, gave any measurements and Spratt–Forbes's plan is on too small

a scale for accurate deductions. It was, then, part of the purpose of my visit to Oenoanda in 1962 to measure the ground plan of this 'flagged platform' in the centre of the city. If my observations were accurate—and there is a vast quantity of debris lying everywhere (in particular the ruins of a temple, presumably Spratt's E, cover the eastern end of the area)—the length of the long side is a little over 49 metres. This would allow sufficient room for the inscription, even arranged as W suggests, to be inscribed on one wall. As to its height, if we assume that the bottom of the lowest course was 4½ ft. from the ground and the maximum height of the inscribed stones is *c.* 180 cm. (about 6 feet), then the height of the wall must have been at least 10½ ft. and the uppermost band some way above eye-level. The evidence of HK proves that the inscription did not begin lower, since when they saw the site parts of the walls were still standing to a height of 1·5 metres, but none of the stones was inscribed.

Conclusion

The inscription of Diogenes must indeed have been a wonderful sight when it was first carved—120 or more columns of text stretching for over 40 m., with another parallel range of the same length above, and still more material above that. One wonders how many of his fellow citizens paused to read it from end to end —and what impression it made on them when they did. We have only a mutilated fraction of his work today, but even so we can form a clear picture of the old man who had it inscribed nearly 1800 years ago.

He was a genuine amateur of the philosophy of Epicurus and a passionate believer in the value of its message, to the propagation of which he devoted a great deal of time and money. He is not an original thinker, but Epicureans never were; their sole aim was to pass on the teachings of the Master. However, his knowledge of those teachings is wide; less than half of his inscription is left and yet we have references, and accurate references, to most of the basic doctrines, often supported by arguments and proofs not found elsewhere. As to the teachings of other schools his knowledge of the pre-Socratics is full enough

for his purposes and his supposed mistake about Aristotle in fr. 4 may not be a mistake after all. Writing as he did in the second century A.D., a great deal of his time had, of course, to be spent combating the Stoics; this he does with success especially in frs. 7 and 27.

The impression he gives is that of a kindly old man who can show both acuteness of mind and flashes of sardonic humour. He is imbued with the cosmopolitanism of his age and anxious to help both fellow citizens and the strangers in their midst. If at times his style is rather garrulous and repetitive this is confined to the introductory passages—which have survived almost intact whereas vitally important passages of, for instance, the Physics are lost. Elsewhere the argumentation is reasonably concise, and expressed in good, clear Greek; this is none the worse for being the Greek of the early centuries A.D. with an admixture of words from the κοινή (a feature to be found even in Epicurus himself), while the occasional occurrence of words not found earlier anywhere else (e.g. κασωτός, εὐσύγκριτος) rather adds to its interest. Our author has, of course, been through the usual rhetorical education of upper-class members of Graeco-Roman society and this has left its mark in a sometimes tortuous word-order, the avoidance of hiatus, and an attention to the rhythm at the ends of clauses (on this see Grilli's article in *Parola del Passato*, fasc. 71, 1960). But these are minor peculiarities and do not seriously detract from the value of this unique document from a remote corner of the Roman world. The pity is that so little of it has been preserved.

Suggested Arrangement of Fragments

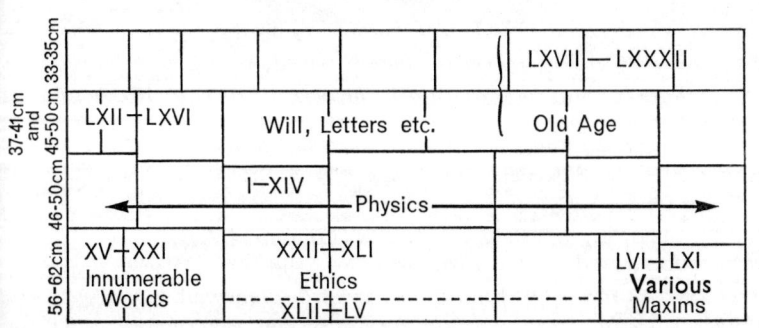

William

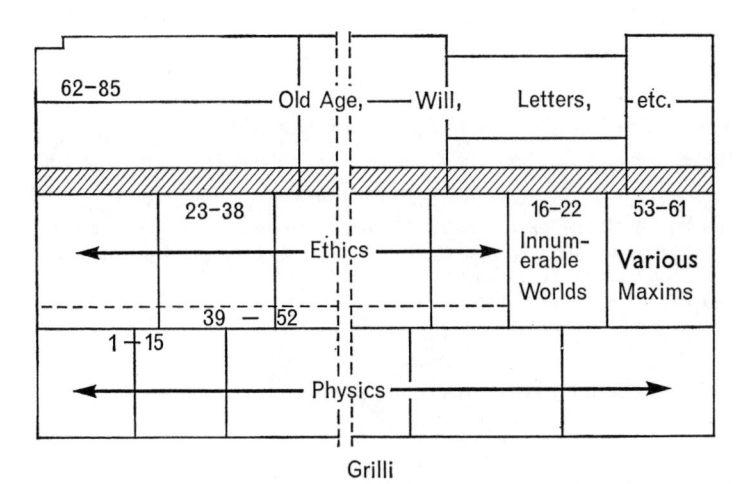

Grilli

(Based on the plan in his 1960 edition)

Selected Additions to the Bibliography

BAILEY, C., *Epicurus. The Extant Remains* (Oxford, 1926).

—— *T. Lucreti Cari De Rerum Natura* (Oxford, 1947).

DE WITT, N. W., *Epicurus and his Philosophy* (Univ. of Minnesota, 1954).

—— *St. Paul and Epicurus* (Univ. of Minnesota, 1954).

ERNOUT, A., and ROBIN, L., *Lucrèce, De Rerum Natura* (2nd edn., Paris, Budé, 1962).

FARRINGTON, B., *The Faith of Epicurus* (London, 1967).

FESTUGIÈRE, A.-J., *Épicure et ses dieux* (2nd edn., Paris, Presses Universitaires, 1968; Eng. trans., Oxford, Blackwell, 1955).

JONES, A. H. M., *Cities of the Eastern Roman Provinces* (Oxford, 1937).

KIRK, G. S., and RAVEN, J. E. *The Presocratic Philosophers* (Cambridge, 1957). (KR)

MAGIE, D., *Roman Rule in Asia Minor* (Princeton, 1950).

PANICHAS, G. A., *Epicurus* (New York, TWAS, 1967).

SMITH, M. F., *Observations on the Text of Diogenes of Oenoanda* (Hermathena, no. CX, 1970, pp. 52–78).

SPRATT, T. A. B., and FORBES, E., *Travels in Lycia, Milyas, and the Cibyratis* (London, 1847).

WALDEN, J. W. H., *The Universities of Ancient Greece* (London, 1913).

Corrigenda to the text

xvi l. 3: for Barrigazzi *read* Barigazzi; for fr. 25 *read* 24.

3 App. crit. to fr. 1 III: for Castiglione *read* Castiglioni.

11 Fr. 6 heading: for 20 *read* 19.

105 τίκτω: for 68 I 8 *read* 57 I 8.

Addenda to the text

39 App. crit. to fr. 24 III: *add* cf. p. 69 enarrationis.

51 App. crit. to fr. 28 V: *add* cf. p. 78 enarrationis.

B

TRANSLATION

Foreword

(Seeing those who follow the empty opinions of the soul and do I
not listen to the body) bringing against the soul its . . . and just
accusations, that it is harassed and maltreated by it as it ought
not to be, and dragged by it into things that are not necessary;
for the body's wants, I maintain, are slight and easy to procure,
and the soul too can live happily by sharing in their enjoyment,
whereas the ambitions of the soul are great and hard to satisfy, II
and, as well as being no help to nature, do in fact bring dangers
with them—seeing these men, therefore, (to make my point
again) living in this condition I grieved over their manner of
existence and wept at the waste of time, and considered it the
duty of a good man so far as it is in my power (to assist) those
among them who are endowed with sense . . . (This then is the III
first reason for my writing. I assert that the groundless fear of
death has a powerful grip on most of us, but that which produces
true contentment and joy is not theatres and . . . and baths . . .
and unguents; all these things we have left to the masses . . .

. . . and not least that I may refute those who attempt to abuse Fr. 2 I
philosophy saying that it cannot be of any use.) But acting thus
instead of meddling in politics I say these things through my
inscription as though I were present, trying to show that the
natural good—I mean peace of mind—is the same for one and
all. And so having revealed the second reason for my work it is II
(now) time to mention how serious my purpose is and to describe
its nature. For standing now at the sunset of my life through old
age and all but on the point of departing this life with a cheerful
song for the fullness of . . . I wanted at this moment to help men III
of sense without being cut off beforehand. Now if only one man
or two or three or four or five or six or as many more than that
as you wish—but not too many—were in an evil plight I would do IV
all in my power, even calling on them one by one, to give them

the best advice. But since, as I have asserted, the great majority are all in common, as in a time of plague, sick with false opinions about things—and their numbers are growing even bigger (for through copying each other one catches the sickness from another

V like sheep) ; and since it is right that I should help also those who will come after me (for they too are mine even if they are not yet born) as well as being a kindly act to give assistance to the strangers living amongst us ; since then the assistance from my work concerns a greater number I wished by making use of this

VI colonnade to set forth in public the remedies which bring salvation, remedies of which I would say in a word that all kinds have been revealed. The fears that gripped us without reason I have abolished, as to pains some I have utterly eradicated, those that are natural I have reduced to quite small measure, making their severity infinitesimal . . .

A. *The Physical Treatise*

FRAGMENTS 3 AND 4

Some philosophers, and especially those of the Socratic school, say that the study of nature and worrying about things up above is superfluous, and they do not condescend to spend time on such things.

(Others do not dare to say outright that we should not study

Fr. 4 I nature), being ashamed to make this statement, but they employ another method of getting rid of it. For when they allege that things are incomprehensible, what else are they saying but that we should not study nature? For who would choose to search

II for something he will never find? Aristotle, therefore, and those who follow the same line as Aristotle say that nothing can be scientifically known; things are always in flux and because of the swiftness of the flow they escape our apprehension. We for our part accept the flux itself but do not agree that it is so swift that at no time can the nature of each thing be grasped by per-

III ception. For indeed the very people who hold this opinion would themselves be unable to say the kind of thing they do say, that

at one time this is white and that is black, at another neither is
this white nor that black, if they had not known beforehand the
nature of white and black. And to those others who practise
'suspension of judgement', whose 'things clear' . . .

FRAGMENT 5

And we will explain the nature of those entities which are I
called the elements of things, existing as they do from the beginning and being indestructible and yet productive of things; but
first we will dispose of the opinions of others. Now Heraclitus
of Ephesus said that fire was elementary, Thales of Miletus water,
Diogenes of Apollonia and Anaximenes air, Empedocles of II
Acragas both fire and air and water and earth, Anaxagoras of
Clazomenae the homoeomeries of each thing, and those from
the Stoa matter and God. Democritus of Abdera did well to
speak of 'indivisible natures', but since he went wrong about
them in certain respects he will be considered among our opinions. III
Now, however, we will criticize the men just mentioned, not
arguing against them in a contentious spirit but wishing the
truth to be preserved, and we will start with Heraclitus since he
has been the first to be ranged against us. You are wrong,
Heraclitus, to say that fire is elementary. It is not indestructible
since we see it perishing, nor can it generate things . . .

FRAGMENT 6

. . . (nor suppose that) it cannot (go further than) the end be- II
cause it knows it (to be the end). But Democritus also made a
mistake unworthy of himself when he said that only the atoms
really exist in objects, all the rest merely existing by convention.
For according to your argument, Democritus, far from discover-
ing the truth we shall not even be able to live, being unable to
guard ourselves either against fire or slaughter or . . .   III

FRAGMENT 7

. . . Images (? in sleep) are not then empty figments of the I
imagination, as the Stoics claim. For indeed if they call them

empty for the reason that although they do have a bodily nature yet it is extremely thin and does not impinge on the senses, then the
II expression they employ is wrong since these too, thin as they are, should have been called 'makers of visible shapes'. But if they are so thin that they do not have a bodily nature at all—which is what they really want to say rather than the former—how can the empty be depicted if it does not even exist? Images do indeed
III have a thin constitution and one that has escaped our sight . . .

FRAGMENT 8

I (The stars have their orbits but not the same orbit.) All move on their own courses but some meet one another and others do not. And some pursue a perpendicular course up to a certain point, others an oblique one, like the sun and the moon; others rotate where they are, like the Bear. Again some move in a high orbit and some in a low one. Now most people are quite ignorant of
II this; at least they assume the sun to be as low as it appears to be, whereas it is not as low as that, for if it were the earth and all things upon it must have caught fire. It is its appearance (?), therefore, which we see low in the sky and not the sun itself; but this is by the way.

Let us now speak about risings and settings and matters con-
III nected with them, first making this point, that it is rash for the inquirer into obscure subjects, if he sees a number of possible explanations, to pronounce categorically about only one. Such is the method of a soothsayer rather than a wise man; to say that all explanations are possible but this one is more convincing than that is correct. It is therefore possible that the sun is a kind of
IV coal-like circle, very thin, which is lifted up by the winds and sustains the role of a source (of heat), some fire going out from it and other fire flowing into it from the entire universe in small coagulations because of its multifarious composition. And so by itself it is sufficient for the universe . . .

FRAGMENT 9

. . . how the human frame emerged throughout the earth, wet or muddy as it was, is shown by our present argument. So, being

sprung from the earth in embryonic shape, some kind of strength inherent in nature . . .

FRAGMENT 10

(As time went on?) fleeing from the wintry weather they came I to devise houses and, as a result of the wrappings which they made for their bodies, covering them with leaves or plants or skins— for they were already killing animals—they thought of clothes, not flexible (textile?) as yet but thick (felt?) perhaps, or of some kind or other. And then the passage of time put into their minds, II or the minds of those who came after them, the loom also. So neither for these skills nor for any other do we need to bring in Athena or some other god; they all arose from their needs and chance happenings combined with time.

And for the sounds of speech also—I mean the nouns and verbs of which men born from earth first made utterance—do not III let us introduce Hermes as an instructor as some do—that is obviously idle talk—nor let us believe those philosophers who say that names were given to things by prescription and teaching so that men might have symbols of them for the sake of easy IV communication one with another. The idea is absurd, in fact it is more absurd than any absurdity as well as being quite impossible that anyone should bring together so many multitudes being only one himself—for as yet there were no . . . nor even letters where there were no sounds; for as to these . . . to bring V them together (by?) word of command—and after bringing them together that he should instruct them like a schoolmaster, taking hold of a (stick) and touching each thing should say as he did so, 'This is to be called *stone*, and this *wood*, and this *man*, or *dog* . . .'

FRAGMENT 11

(. . . perished, and the noblest men like Anaxagoras they per- I secute. Therefore it will be made clear that it is not we who do away with the gods but other people. And it was Diagoras the Melian, in the exposition of his doctrine in Eudemus, who

asserted that there are no gods, bitterly attacking those who think
II otherwise.) And Protagoras of Abdera in effect held the same
opinion as Diagoras but used different words so as to avoid its
excessive boldness. He said that he did not know whether gods
exist, which is the same as saying that he knew they did not.
For if he did oppose to his first statement 'I certainly do not know
III that they do not exist', (it is clear that he is more or less trying
to make an excuse so as not to seem to be doing away with the
gods entirely; but since he said that it was uncertain whether
gods exist or not, in fact he is obviously doing the same as if,
having said that he did not know whether they exist, he had
stopped there. The view he propounded, then, is, as I say, the
same, or has the same force, as the formers.)

FRAGMENT 14

I (Gladly have I followed your) sayings on death and you have
persuaded me to laugh it to scorn. I am not in the least afraid
because of the Tityuses and Tantaluses that some people depict
in the underworld, nor does the decay of the body make me
shudder, bearing in mind that destruction of the body causes
no displeasure when the soul has perished; nor does anything
else upset me . . .

B. *Diogenes of Oenoanda: On the Innumerability of the Worlds*

FRAGMENT 15

I Diogenes to Antipater, greetings. Many are the indications of
your keenness which you have given me, Antipater, both in your
letters sent to me recently and when I saw you before, heartily
embracing philosophy, in which you, if anyone, enjoy a life of
supreme happiness amidst the best of studies. It is for this very
II reason that I am most anxious to meet again you in particular
and our other friends in Athens, Chalcis, and Thebes, and I
imagine that you all feel the same. This present letter, however,

I am writing to you now from Rhodes, having left my own country not long ago at the beginning of winter . . .

FRAGMENT 16

(But since the future is uncertain) because of the fickleness and I uncertainty in human affairs and also because of my age, I have sent you the treatise on the innumerability of the worlds as you asked me to do. And in this matter you have been fortunate, for before the arrival of your letter Theodoridas of Lindos, a companion of ours not unknown to you, who is just beginning the study of philosophy, was engaged on the same topic, and this II subject has been made clearer as a result of both of us working on it together. For our mutual agreements and contradictions, and our questionings also, made the inquiry after the object of our search more precise. I have therefore sent to you, Antipater, an account of that discourse so that it may be the same III as if you were here yourself, agreeing—as I did—with some of Theodoridas' views, criticizing others, and asking questions as well. This was the kind of way in which we began: 'Diogenes,' Theodoridas said, 'that the doctrine laid down by Epicurus about the innumerability of the worlds is true . . .'

FRAGMENT 18

I laugh with derision especially when I learn from you the arguments you have reported to us from those who allege . . . arguments which do away with the entire universe . . .

FRAGMENT 19

. . . Therefore, the indivisible natures being assumed by us to be I limited in number, and for the reasons we have given being II unable to coagulate—for since they were formed no other natures have as yet arisen to surround their multitude, support them from below, and bring them together from the sides—how are they to generate things, separate as they are from one another? So not even this world would exist. For if they were limited they could not have come together.

FRAGMENT 20

I ... let us make a defence of our theory ... saying: 'Gentlemen, ... you cannot explain either the earth or the infinite. Do you limit the earth by the circle of the heaven above ... and begin-
II ning from there extend it to infinity into the zone below, disregarding equally all laymen and philosophers who think that the earth is circled by the stars above and below—driving the sun outside the universe to the sides and bringing it back again from the sides—or do you not say this, but that a single earth...?

c. *The Ethical Treatise*

FRAGMENT 23

Diogenes of Oenoanda, on feelings and actions . . ., an epitome.

FRAGMENT 24

I Many people pursue philosophy for the sake of (wealth or reputation) as though they will obtain these things from private persons or kings who have come to believe that philosophy is some great and costly possession. But we have not hastened to undertake the same study so that any of the above rewards should
II come to us also, but so that we may be happy, gaining possession of the end and purpose of life sought by nature. And what this end is, and that neither wealth can provide it, nor political reputation, nor kingship, nor a life of luxury, nor a rich table, nor the pleasures of exquisite love affairs, nor anything else, but
III only philosophy, (this we will now show, putting before you the whole matter. For this treatise we have prepared not for our own sakes but for yours, fellow citizens, to benefit you and serve as a fitting introduction to the argument here.)

PRINCIPAL DOCTRINE I

The blessed and indestructible being is neither troubled itself nor does it cause trouble to another, and so it is not subject to feelings of anger or partiality; all that belongs to weakness.

FRAGMENT 25

... (if) time (allows). And this we have devised with the object I
that even while sitting at home it might be possible for us to set
forward the benefits of philosophy not to (all men here...)
Furthermore we did this not least for the sake of those who are II
called strangers though they are not really so. With regard to
the several divisions of the earth one has one country and one
another, but if we look at the entire compass of this world there
is one country for all, the whole earth, and one home, the world.

Now I am not rushing any of you into accepting without
thought and consideration that what is said is true—I have made III
no dogmatic statements—but look at everything from all angles
and consider it in company with me. One thing only I ask, as I
did just now, that you do not look at what is written after the
fashion of passers-by, or in a spirit of carelessness and boredom,
paying only fickle attention to one section after another and
passing on ...

PRINCIPAL DOCTRINE 2

Death is nothing to us, for that which has been dissolved into its
elements has no sensation and that which has no sensation is
nothing to us.

FRAGMENT 26

... (this opinion [criticism?] being) as ill-natured as the previous I
one. I will speak of their stupidity in a moment, but first about
virtues and pleasure. If, gentlemen, the matter in dispute between these men and ourselves were an inquiry into what is
productive of happiness, and they had wanted to say that it is
the virtues, which is indeed the truth, there would be no need to
do anything but agree with them and leave it at that. But since, II
as I say, the question is not what is productive of happiness but
what is happiness itself, and what it is which our nature in its
innermost being desires, then I say both now and always, crying
aloud to Greek and foreigner, that it is pleasure which is the
highest point of the best way of life, while the virtues which III

are now unseasonably fussed over by these people (for they transfer them from the category of the productive into that of the end) are in no way the end but are productive of the end.

Let us now show that this is true, beginning like this; if some-
IV one were to ask another—it is a silly question really—who it is that these virtues help, it is clear that he will say, 'Mankind'. The virtues are not concerned with how these birds we see flying past will fly well, or with any other animal; they do not so abandon the nature to which they belong and by which they have been brought into being; rather it is for the sake of this nature that the virtues do everything and exist. So each one . . .

PRINCIPAL DOCTRINE 6

To feel secure against the world the possession of power and kingship is a natural good, so long as that end can be achieved by them.

PRINCIPAL DOCTRINE 8

No pleasure in itself is a bad thing, but the means of producing some pleasures bring annoyances many times greater than the pleasures.

FRAGMENT 27

I . . . I wish, therefore, after this to examine the mistake about feeling which prevails among you, and in particular to say something about one doctrine of yours which is untrue. It is this. Not all causes in things are antecedent to their effects, even if the
II majority are; some are antecedent, some simultaneous, and some occur afterwards. The cause is antecedent when, for instance, cautery or surgery brings a cure. Here the pain must be applied first for health and strength to follow afterwards. A simultaneous cause is exemplified by dry and liquid refreshment, and, as well as these, by the pleasures of love. We do not eat bread and *then*
III feel pleasure, we do not drink wine and *then* feel pleasure, nor do we emit semen and *then* feel pleasure; (we enjoy the sensation at once) . . .

For although people feel pleasure *now* because there will be IV
a pleasant memory of them after they are gone, nevertheless the
cause of the pleasure occurs later. You, therefore, being unable
to make these distinctions, and not knowing that the virtues belong to the class of causes which are simultaneous with their
effects (for they go along together . . .)

PRINCIPAL DOCTRINE 10

If those things which produce the pleasures of profligates put
an end to mental fears about celestial phenomena and about
death and pain, and, besides, taught the limits of desire and
pain, we should never be able to criticize such men, as they
would be sated with pleasures from every source, and know
neither mental nor physical pain, which is the evil.

FRAGMENT 28

. . . (a sure hope) based on the selection of (such things) and the II
treatment of erring feelings. So where, I insist, the danger is
great, so also is the fruit. And here we must avoid those sophistic
arguments as treacherous and captious, and devised from a
similarity of words for the confusion of unfortunate mankind . . . III
. . . (since advantage does not always come at once but just as IV
one thing bears its fruit at once and another brings benefits
which appear after some years, so it is with pain also. For after
the sowing of the seed it does not all produce the same benefit
for the sower; some shows germination and growth at once) . . . V
(We, therefore, making this selection of the pleasant and the
troublesome and considering the 'ends', place pleasure once more
on its pedestal.)
. . . folly. But we are now inquiring how life may be made VI
pleasant for us both in mental states and actions. Let us speak
first about mental states, noting indeed that when the emotions
that disturb the soul are removed things that give it pleasure
come in to take their place. Now what are these disturbing
emotions? They are fears, of the gods, of death, and of pain; VII
and, in addition, desire which far exceeds its natural bounds.

These are indeed the root of all evil, and if we cut them off no evil will grow up in their stead to trouble us. Now the fear which we feel about the gods . . .

PRINCIPAL DOCTRINE 3

The limit to the intensity of pleasure is the removal of all pain. Whoever enjoys a feeling of pleasure will, as long as it continues, never be annoyed by pain of body or of mind or of both together.

FRAGMENT 29

II . . . In fact this fear is sometimes explained and sometimes not. It is explained when we flee from something obvious like fire, fearing that we shall meet death through it; it is not explained when the mind being in the presence of another kind of nature which is masked and (being unable to throw light upon it, we shudder) . . .

PRINCIPAL DOCTRINE 13

It does not help to secure protection against men if things on high and things beneath the earth and in fact everything in the boundless universe causes us suspicion and uncertainty.

FRAGMENTS 30 AND 31

So why is the coming to pass of certain predictions stronger proof that prophecy is real than the not coming to pass of others is proof that it is not? I think myself . . .

FRAGMENT 32

I . . . (For if anyone believes that what has already been said is not so, and that it is not possible to escape from necessity, he will never be rid of error. But if he does believe it he will dismiss those ideas also without distinction as doubtful and uncertain. For it is plain that he will find no other reason to believe what is

II said.) So if divination is done away with, how is there any other proof of destiny? If someone makes use of the theory of Democritus, saying that there is no free movement for the atoms because

of their collisions with one another, from which it is clear that all
things are moved by necessity, we shall say to him, 'Do you not
know, whoever you may be, that there *is* a kind of free movement III
in the atoms, which Democritus did not discover but which
Epicurus brought to light, an inherent swerve, as he shows from
the phenomena? The most important point is this: if destiny
is believed in, all admonition and rebuke is done away with, and
not even evil-doers ...

FRAGMENT 33

... perished ... and not only Pythagoras is mad ...

PRINCIPAL DOCTRINE 25

If you do not on every occasion refer each action to the end and
purpose of nature but stop short at some other standard when
deciding to pursue or avoid some object, your actions will not
be consistent with your words.

FRAGMENT 34

... migration. For in the interval during which their migration I
is effected, an interval which breaks the continuity of their
nature as living things, they will be entirely dissipated; but if
somehow or other they have this nature (as they must) when
without a body, why do you give yourself, or rather them, so
much trouble, dragging them about and moving them out of
one living thing and into another? And this ...

... It would be better to make the souls simply indestructible II
in themselves and not involve them in a lengthy journey in
order that your very last statement might be more impressive, lie
that it is; or we shall disbelieve you, Empedocles, and your story
of these migrations ...

(Unknown maxim) ... neither small nor great ...

FRAGMENT 35

.   I
... The Stoics, however, wishing here also to say something
stranger than other people, absolutely deny that souls are II

indestructible, but then go on to say that the souls of the foolish perish immediately after the dissolution of the body whereas those of the virtuous survive, and then they also perish in time.

III See how manifestly unconvincing their doctrine is; they make their assertion as though the wise and the unwise are not subject to the same mortality even if they do differ in intelligence. But I am more surprised at their restraint, why, if once the soul is going to be able to exist apart from the body—even, we might say, for the least moment of time—(they do not allow it to last for ever).

PRINCIPAL DOCTRINE 29

Of desires some are natural and necessary, some are natural but not necessary, and some are neither natural nor necessary but arise from empty opinion.

FRAGMENT 37

I The soul provides nature with the reason for the (presence or) absence of life. For even though it does not possess the same number of atoms as the body, being placed in it with its rational and irrational elements, nevertheless it encompasses the whole body and, being bound to it, binds it in its turn just as the shortest dash of acid juice curdles a vast quantity of milk. The following,

II along with many others, is a sign of the superiority of this cause. Often when the body has been brought to surrender by a long illness, and reduced to such thinness and wasting that the dry skin is almost adhering to the bones whilst the nature of the inward parts seems empty and bloodless, nevertheless the soul stands

III its ground and does not permit the creature to die. And this is not the only indication of supremacy; the severing of hands, and often the removal of whole arms or feet by fire and steel cannot undo the bonds of life. So great is the sway over life held by that part of us which is soul.

But often when the body is intact and has suffered no loss of parts (the power of sense leaves it, for if the atoms of the soul do not stand their ground the wholeness of the body does not

I. Part of the walls of Oenoanda (see p. xvii).

Reference

A Theatre 144 feet diameter.
B Flat area with pedestals.
C Helenic or Roman ruins.
D Flagged platform with pedestals probably the Forum.
E Ruins of a Doric Temple.
F City wall 25 feet high.
G Sarcophagi.
H Mausoleum.

Rock Tombs

OOLOOJAH
the ancient
ŒNOANDA
by
Lieut.ᵗ T. Spratt R.N.

II. Spratt's plan of the city (see p. xxx).

help, whereas so long as we see them holding firm like a framework the man lives. Therefore, if the ultimate cause of life is the soul, according as to whether it is joined to the body or separated from it . . .)

PRINCIPAL DOCTRINE 5

It is not possible to live pleasantly without living sensibly and honourably and justly, nor is it possible to live sensibly and honourably and justly without living pleasantly. Where this is lacking a man cannot live a pleasant life.

FRAGMENT 38

. . . feelings are much bigger than the cause which produced I them. A tiny spark kindles a fire so vast that it burns down ports and cities. But the supremacy of those feelings which afflict the soul is hard for the layman to understand. For since it is not possible to experience both kinds of extreme at one time—I mean II of the different feelings which affect the soul and the body—and so make a comparison, since this happens only on rare occasions and when it does happen life is destroyed, a means of testing these two for supremacy is not found. When a man is afflicted with bodily pains he says that they are worse than those of the soul (and when he experiences those of the soul he says that they are III worse). For what is present is always more convincing than what is absent, and clearly each man is inclined either by necessity or through pleasure to award the palm of supremacy to the feeling which has him in its grip. A wise man, however, deduces this difficulty of understanding felt by the majority from many other sources and . . .

PRINCIPAL DOCTRINE 4

Pain does not last continuously in the flesh; when it is intense it is present for a very short time, if it merely exceeds the bodily sensation of pleasure the attack does not last many days. In long illnesses the feelings of pleasure in the flesh outweigh the pain.

D. *Various Maxims*

FRAGMENT 40

Nothing is so productive of contentment as not being too busy, not undertaking disagreeable tasks, and not pushing ourselves beyond our powers; for all these things cause worry and trouble to our nature.

FRAGMENT 41

The most important source of happiness is our disposition, of which we are masters. Military service is burdensome and under the command of others, the life of the speaker is packed with unhealthy excitement and worry as to whether he can carry conviction. Why then do we pursue an object like this, in which others hold the power?

FRAGMENT 42

Extremes of pain cannot last. They either quickly do away with life and so are done away with themselves, or they develop a lessening of their intensity.

FRAGMENT 43

... which of the desires are natural and which are empty.

It is not nature, which is the same for all, which makes the noble and the mean; it is actions and dispositions.

FRAGMENT 44

(Unnatural wealth is no more benefit to men than is water to a full vessel. We must realize that both run over.

We can look without concern upon the possessions of others and enjoy a purer pleasure than they do; for we are not troubled by these appetites.)

FRAGMENT 45

For one groaning in pain to say 'alas' is forced on us by nature, but to lament because (we do not enjoy the lot of the healthy is contrary to nature).

E. *Various Writings*

FRAGMENT 49

... goodwill towards the strangers who are staying in this district. And knowing well that from the knowledge of the matters which I have set out below, matters concerning both nature and the feelings ...

FRAGMENT 50. *Diogenes' Will*

These are the instructions which I, Diogenes, give to my family, relations, and friends. Being so ill that the crisis is now upon me as to whether I am to go on living or live no more—for a disease of the stomach is exhausting me—if I survive I shall gladly accept the life still offered me, but if I do not ...

FRAGMENT 51. *A Letter to Friends*

... (have prepared a wall in the basilica on which you will have   I
the treatise written and corrected. And I thank the woman who formerly entertained me and those with me, and to whom my friends took me in haste.) I am convinced that I owe my recovery   II
particularly to your recommending me to her, dearest Menneas, because of the kindly disposition and care shown towards me by you and by the excellent Carus and my Dionysius at the time   III
when I stayed with her in Rhodes. Farewell again.

FRAGMENT 52. *A Letter to Mother*

... (to cause the greatest concern about them. For the appearance   I
of those who are absent, independent of sight, instils very great fear, whereas if they are present with us it causes not the least dread. But if you carefully examine their nature the appearances) of the absent are exactly the same as those of the present. For   II
being not tangible but intelligible they have in themselves the same capacity towards those present as when they arose, their subjects being present also. Therefore, Mother, take heart; you   III
must not regard visions of me as evil. Rather consider that I am

daily acquiring useful help towards advancing further towards
IV happiness. Not slight or of no avail are the advantages that
accrue to me, such that they make my condition equal to the
divine and show that not even mortality can make me inferior
to the indestructible and blessed nature. For as long as I live
I rejoice even as do the gods . . .

FRAGMENT 53

I . . . the same, if he suffers diminution; but if he has no sensation,
how is he diminished? Surrounded by such good things, then,
think of me, mother, as rejoicing always and have confidence
in how I am faring. But in heaven's name be sparing with the
II remittances you are constantly sending me. I do not wish you
to be in need so that I may have abundance, I would rather
suffer need so that you should not; and yet I am living in plenty
III in every respect thanks to friends and father continually sending
me money; indeed only recently Cleon sent me nine minae. So
neither one nor other of you should worry about me but enjoy
each other's company . . .

FRAGMENT 54: '(The manual of Diogenes of Oenoanda)'

F. *On Old Age*

FRAGMENT 55

I Often, by Heracles, I have been angry, young men, with those
who, not having yet reached old age . . .

II . . . who have proceeded further with their education so as not
only to praise . . .

FRAGMENT 56

(. . . since many) live to the last day of their lives with their
faculties unimpaired. And I, so that I may abundantly retort to
those who (blame . . .)

FRAGMENT 57

... is put forward by me. And the first thing of all is this. If any- I
one were to call the weakening of the eyes suffered by old men
blindness ...

FRAGMENT 58

... elephant ... slowness of a body ... I
   And then the argument about feelings of sadness, since some II
people bring these forward also, can be put like this. In the first
place it cannot be used against the old. As a general rule, where
there is no longing for a thing there is no feeling of sadness about
it either ...

FRAGMENT 59: (Troubles caused by the cough)

FRAGMENT 60

... something like this: 'He slept gently for a time, for that is the
way of old men.' But I say that when the body has aged, the
mind ...

FRAGMENT 61

(The same Homer shows how the man no longer able to be of II
use with his body gives great help in emergencies with counsel,
and the best counsel too, saying, 'And first he called a council
of the old men, great of heart', and again, 'They had ceased III
from war through old age but were good speakers'. And to
Homer's testimony is added the tragic poet.)

FRAGMENT 62

... (and besides [we hear that] many of those already aged have
by their words taken part in counsel with the greatest vigour;
far from being unable to take thought for the matters I have
mentioned, with their clear minds ...)

FRAGMENT 63

Let us not forget that it is not from old age that derangement
comes but from some other natural cause ...

FRAGMENT 64

II (. . . so that bodily pains often allow periods of relief and are not
by nature . . .)

FRAGMENT 66

. . . and besides this, young men, great indeed is the advantage
. . . poverty . . .

COMMENTARY

Alphabetical List of Abbreviations used in
Introduction and Commentary

B.M.	British Museum
B.C.H.	*Bulletin de Correspondance Hellénique*
C	G. Cousin, *B.C.H.* 16, 1892, 1–70
D	Cousin's copy of the inscription
DK	*Die Fragmente der Vorsokratiker*, ed. H. Diels and W. Kranz, Berlin, 1959
D.L.	Diogenes Laertius
F	Heberdey and Kalinka's drawings of the inscription
G^1	A. Grilli in *Studi di filosofia greca*, Bari, 1950, 345–435
G^2	*Diog. Oen. Fragmenta*, ed. A. Grilli, Milan, 1960
G.M.T.	W. W. Goodwin, *Syntax of Greek Moods and Tenses*, London, 1897
HK	R. Heberdey and E. Kalinka, *B.C.H.* 21, 1897, 346–443
I.G.	*Inscriptiones Graecae*
I.G.R.	*Inscriptiones Graecae ad res Romanas pertinentes*
KR	G. S. Kirk and J. E. Raven, *The Presocratic Philosophers*, Cambridge, 1957
L.S.J.	Liddell–Scott–Jones, *A Greek–English Lexicon*, Oxford, 1940
O.G.I.S.	*Orientis Graeci Inscriptiones Selectae*
P.D.	Principal Doctrines (κύριαι δόξαι) of Epicurus
P.P.	*La Parola del Passato*
Ph	R. Philippson in *R.E.* Supplbd. V, 1931
R.E.	*Real-Encyclopädie der klassischen Altertumswissenschaft*, ed. A. Pauly, G. Wissowa, and W. Kroll
Rh. Mus.	*Rheinisches Museum*
Riv. di fil.	*Rivista di filologia*
Sent. Vat. (S.V.)	Sententiae Vaticanae (= Gnomologium Vaticanum Epicureum)
S.V.F.	*Stoicorum veterum fragmenta*, coll. J. von Armim, Leipzig, 1903
Us	H. Usener (esp. *Rh. Mus.* 47. 1892, 414–56)
fr. . . . Us	Usener, *Epicurea*, Leipzig, 1887
W	*Diog. Oen. fragmenta*, ed. J. William, Leipzig, 1907

Foreword

This consists of two fragments. Fr. 1 apparently opens in the middle of a complaint by the body against the soul that the body's wants are few and easy to satisfy while the soul's inordinate desires are the opposite and cause the body nothing but trouble. So seeing men in this condition (II 4–7) Diogenes has taken pity on them and decided to help as far as he can. The third column is unfortunately badly damaged. Fr. 2 II–V has a similar message; at some length he dwells on his desire to help his fellow men, present and to come, fellow citizens and strangers, and so has decided to use 'this stoa' (V 12) to set out the 'recipe for salvation' (IV 14–V 2).

This is clearly introductory material, and although the stones were found widely scattered (there are three of them) it has been accepted since the time of HK that they are parts of the same whole. The questions to be decided are, first, in what order should they stand and, secondly, to what are they an introduction—to the inscription as a whole, to the Ethics and Physics together, or to the Physics only. Various arguments, from content and physical appearance, can be found to support all three possibilities.

As to appearance, fr. 1 consists of one block (HK 59) with two columns and the remains of a third; it has one curved παραγραφή and is 48 cm. tall. Fr. 2 is a combination of two blocks; one, rather damaged, (HK 57) has one column with παραγραφαί of both kinds and a wide margin to the right; the other (HK 58) has five columns (the first and fifth being rather damaged) all without παραγραφαί. The height of both blocks (46·5 cm. and 47 cm.) is much the same as the first. They were first put together, and in the present order, by Cousin, though found separated, and so they have remained ever since. W numbered them as fr. II I–VI to make one of the longest fragments of the whole inscription. There are oddities about this arrangement—the rather wide margin to the right of col. I and the total absence of παραγραφαί in cols. II–VI—but appearance and content argue in its favour. The stones obviously stood in the same course, and the subject-matter is clearly of a piece. It is just conceivable that HK 57 (col. I) might have come *after* HK 58 (cols. II–VI); this would explain the margin, and a different restoration of col. I might make it fit, but the argument against this suggestion is the convincing link between cols. I and II at present provided by τὴν δευτέραν οὖν ἀποδοὺς αἰ|[τί]αν τοῦ συγγράμ[μ]ατος. In view of this it is better to leave the columns in their traditional order.

But was Us right to place HK 59 before HK 57 and 58? He did it because of the words quoted above. If HK 57–8, the present fr. 2, speak of the 'second reason for the work' it is surely probable that the other introductory passage will refer to the first. W believed also that the ψευδοδοξία of 2 IV 7 is a reference to fr. 1. Philippson accepted this proposal and actually restored fr. 1 III to speak of the πρώτη αἰτία τῆς γραφῆς. There can be no final solution to this problem, but I find these arguments convincing enough in the present state of our text.

What then are the reasons which Diogenes brings forward for his work? The first (fr. 1) must be general sympathy for mankind, who are misled by the inordinate demands of the soul, presumably, that is, by longing for expensive pleasures, political power, etc. The second has already been given by the end of fr. 2 I. We are left to deduce, then, the gist of the material which has been lost between frs. 1 and 2. At least one block, i.e. two columns, must be missing, and of course there may be more. All we can say for certain is that by the middle of 2 I Diogenes is asserting that the 'natural good' (τὸ τῇ φύσει συμφέρον), which is ἀταραξία, is the same for one and all. This being so it is possible that the passage went something like this:

Fr. 1: Men have been led astray by false opinions about what really brings happiness. I want to help. (Col. III) Most men are unnecessarily afraid of death, and it is not a life of ease and indulgence which brings happiness. (The restoration of col. III can only be very tentative but the almost certain βαλανεῖα of l. 11 is strong support for this interpretation.)

Missing portion: It is not a life of ease; it is rather the 'study of nature' (φυσιολογία) which removes misguided fears and by teaching us the truth about desires etc. brings us the blessing of peace of mind (ἀταραξία). The study of nature is therefore very important and those who attack it are misguided (hence the suggested introduction to fr. 2).

Fr. 2: This then is my message, and I insist that this ἀταραξία is the same for everyone, etc.

The final question to be considered is to what this foreword is the introduction. Does it introduce the Physics, as W thought, followed by G in his 1960 edition? Or the work as a whole, as G suggested in his 1950 commentary, or the Physics and Ethics together, which is Philippson's proposal? Any of these views can be supported. It speaks in general terms of Diogenes' benevolent feelings towards mankind; at the same time it seems to have praised the study of nature as the key to true happiness; but the study of nature is only the preliminary to ethics which is the real science of living. Perhaps the

strongest argument for regarding it as a preface to the Physics is the
appearance of the stones. They are 47 cm. or so in height and have
14-line columns in small lettering; they must therefore have stood in
the second course, i.e. in the same course as the Physics. On the other
hand two out of the three stones have παραγραφαί, which do not occur
in the Physics. They cannot of course stand in the bottom row with
the Ethics and Letter to Antipater, which also have παραγραφαί,
because they are considerably less tall. But apart from the presence of
παραγραφαί—which, as we have seen, occur in only two of the seven
columns concerned—I feel that the content is against assigning this
preface to the Physics alone. It is true that the Ethics has a kind of
preface of its own (fr. 24), as does the diatribe on Old Age (fr. 55),
whereas in the Physics nothing comparable has survived (though see
pp. 37–8), but the subject-matter of this Foreword is of too general a
nature to be affixed before any one part of the work. Diogenes is here
speaking about the motives which persuaded him to set about pub-
lishing any inscription at all. I would therefore regard it either as
a general introduction to the work as a whole or, and this is perhaps
more probable, to the Physics and Ethics together. These two treatises
were the all-important section of the inscription and were very likely
inscribed and finished before the material on the higher courses was
added.

FRAGMENT I (height 48 cm., width 80·5 cm., thickness 31 cm.)

W's suggestion for the preceding words is reasonable in view of
col. II 4 τούτους οὖν ὁρῶν . . . διακειμένους οὕτως; they would have
been part of another column on another block. Only the first line of
this column is damaged. The restoration proposed by HK is rather
long, that of Grilli is somewhat short for the gap but it has the virtue
of beginning with a Δ. The first letter of the lacuna is more likely to
have been A or Λ, but it could have been Δ.

3. For the idea that the body is not to blame for human troubles
cf. Democritus B 159 DK εἰ τοῦ σώματος αὐτῇ δίκην λαχόντος, παρὰ
πάντα τὸν βίον ὧν ὠδύνηται ⟨καὶ⟩ κακῶς πέπονθεν, αὐτὸς [i.e. Democri-
tus] γένοιτο τοῦ ἐγκλήματος δι⟨καστής⟩, ἡδέως ἂν καταψηφίσασθαι τῆς
ψυχῆς . . .; and Porphyry, Ad Marcellam 29. 292. 22 N² (fr. 445 Us)
μηδὲ αἰτιώμεθα τὴν σάρκα ὡς τῶν μεγάλων κακῶν αἰτίαν . . .

8. That bodily needs are small is an Epicurean commonplace;
cf. e.g. Sent. Vat. 33 Σαρκὸς φωνὴ τὸ μὴ πεινῆν, τὸ μὴ διψῆν, τὸ μὴ
ῥιγοῦν. ταῦτα γὰρ ἔχων τις καὶ ἐλπίζων ἕξειν κἂν ⟨Διὶ⟩ ὑπὲρ εὐδαιμονίας
μαχέσαιτο.[1] They are also easy to procure (εὐπόριστα). Cf. for instance

---

[1] Many references to this aphorism, from Aelian, Clement of Alexandria,
Julian, and Cicero, are collected by Usener in fr. 602.

Principal Doctrine 15 ὁ τῆς φύσεως πλοῦτος καὶ ὥρισται καὶ εὐπόριστός ἐστιν, ὁ δὲ τῶν κενῶν δοξῶν εἰς ἄπειρον ἐκπίπτει.

The same sentiment is echoed in the Letter to Menoeceus (*Ep.* iii) 130. 9, in fr. 469 Us, and is quoted by Porphyry in his *De abstinentia* i. 49, except that he writes ὁ δὲ τῶν κενῶν δοξῶν (sc. πλοῦτος) ἀόριστός τε ἦν καὶ δυσπόριστος.

On the other hand P.D. 20, which begins 'Η μὲν σὰρξ ἀπέλαβε τὰ πέρατα τῆς ἡδονῆς ἄπειρα, καὶ ἄπειρος αὐτὴν χρόνος παρεσκεύασεν, asserts that the *wants* of the flesh, i.e. body, may well be unlimited but that these are restrained by the διάνοια, τοῦ τῆς σαρκὸς τέλους καὶ πέρατος λαβοῦσα τὸν ἐπιλογισμόν (cf. Bailey, pp. 360–1, Diano, *Ethica*, p. 122, Arrighetti, *Epicuro*, pp. 501–2). If διάνοια there = ψυχή, as Diano (p. 121) maintains, this might seem inconsistent with the view Diogenes expresses here. But Epicurus normally assigns desire, as well as the φρόνησις that censures it, to the soul. Diogenes is not therefore 'unorthodox' in this. (Plato also could assign desire to the bodily factor in the *Phaedo* and to the third 'form' of the soul elsewhere: in the *Philebus* he saw fit to stress that desire arises from ψυχή.)

10. Plutarch, in his book entitled "Οτι οὐδὲ ζῆν ἐστὶν ἡδέως κατ' 'Επίκουρον (or *Non posse suaviter*) 1088 e (fr. 429 Us), says that Epicureans maintained that the soul can find pleasure and calm in nothing but the pleasures of the body, present or expected. Cf. Clement of Alexandria (fr. 451 Us), quoting Antiochus of Ascalon, ὁ δὲ 'Επίκουρος πᾶσαν χαρὰν τῆς ψυχῆς οἴεται ἐπὶ πρωτοπαθούσῃ τῇ σαρκὶ γενέσθαι, and frs. 418 and 425 Us.

II. 1. Cf. fr. 469 Us Χάρις τῇ μακαρίᾳ Φύσει, ὅτι τὰ ἀναγκαῖα ἐποίησεν εὐπόριστα, τὰ δὲ δυσπόριστα οὐκ ἀναγκαῖα. Cf. 8 above.

The greed of the soul is the subject of S.V. 69 τὸ τῆς ψυχῆς ἀχάριστον λίχνον ἐποίησε τὸ ζῷον εἰς ἄπειρον τῶν ἐν διαίτῃ ποικιλμάτων. Cf. Lucr. iii. 1003–10.

3. κίνδυνος is a word not found in Epicurus' extant works. The dangers would seem to be those of ambition and excessive desires, cf. S.V. 81.

κατολοφύρομαι before Dion. Hal. is used only by Euripides in two lyrical passages (*I.T.* 644 and *Or.* 339) and by Xenophon (*Cyr.* 7. 3. 16).

10. Death is final and so those who pursue the wrong things waste their time. Cf. Epictetus, *Diss.* iii. 26. 36 … δύστηνε, οὕτως ἀπώλεσας τὸν μέχρι νῦν χρόνον.

In S.V. 14 we read Γεγόναμεν ἅπαξ, δὶς δὲ οὐκ ἔστι γενέσθαι· … ὁ δὲ βίος μελλησμῷ παραπόλλυται …

13. ἡμεῖν here is clearly used for ἐμοί.

14. εὐσύνκριτος is not found earlier than Diogenes, who uses it here and at 2 III 4–5. Usener (*Rh. Mus.* xlvii. 431), deriving it from κρίνω, took it to mean 'the discriminating who can estimate the worth or worthlessness of the various principles of life'.

William, however, notes that Epicurus calls all bodies compounded of atoms (i.e. everything in this world) συγκρίσεις, and quotes Plutarch "*Ὅτι οὐδὲ . . .* 1100 a–b (fr. 178 Us) . . . *Νεοκλῆς δὲ ὁ ἀδελφὸς εὐθὺς ἐκ παίδων ἀποφαίνοιτο μηδένα σοφώτερον Ἐπικούρου γεγονέναι μηδὲ εἶναι, ἡ δὲ μήτηρ ἀτόμους ἔσχεν ἐν αὐτῇ τοιαύτας οἷαι συνελθοῦσαι σοφὸν ἂν ἐγέννησαν.*

He therefore concludes that the εὐσύγκριτοι are those whose atomic composition has endowed them with good natural parts, or, as L.S.J. puts it, the 'well-compounded'. This passive meaning seems more likely to be correct.

III. This column is unfortunately very mutilated and nothing certain can be said about it. However, it would seem very probable that the writer is concluding the first reason for his project (the second is completed by 2 I 13) and then going on to list the various things that do *not* bring happiness. The text adopted is based on W in the light of G's criticisms; my observations on it are:

1. G seems wrong to go back to HK's restoration; there is only one letter left in l. 1 and the first letter of l. 2 is clearly O.

4. G's rejection of W's γάρ on the ground that a new topic is beginning would appear to be justified. It is reasonable to assume that Diogenes completed his first reason at III 3 and is now opening a discussion of the various hindrances and mistaken helps to happiness— a discussion which would have been continued on the block or blocks missing between frs. 1 and 2. This does, however, leave the sentence without a connecting particle, and this is rare in Diogenes.

5. There is little to choose between W's δείξω and G's φημί but G is probably right when he says that φημί is better for an unproved assertion such as this (cf. 28 II 4). W's restoration of this line would leave it rather short.

10–14. These lines cannot be restored with any certainty but it would appear probable that they contained a list of luxuries which do *not* bring happiness. The gap in l. 10 need not necessarily imply a stop; the same feature can be found in the long list in 2 III 6–8.

ll. 7–14, thus restored, recall Epicurus, *Ep.* iii. 132: *οὐ γὰρ πότοι καὶ κῶμοι συνείροντες οὐδ' ἀπολαύσεις παίδων καὶ γυναικῶν οὐδ' ἰχθύων καὶ τῶν ἄλλων ὅσα φέρει πολυτελὴς τράπεζα τὸν ἡδὺν γεννᾷ βίον . . .*

As to the language of this column, if the restoration is correct εὐθυμία is the most interesting word; it occurs again, used with

ποιητικόν, in fr. 40. 1–2. As a word for 'cheerfulness, contentment' it is used by Pindar, Xenophon, and Menander among others, but philosophically it is a Democritean word not found in Epicurus, e.g. B 4 DK ἀλλὰ καὶ οἱ Ἀβδηρῖται τέλος ὑπάρχειν διδάσκουσιν· Δ. μὲν ἐν τῷ περὶ τέλους τὴν εὐθυμίαν, ἣν καὶ εὐεστὼ προσηγόρευσεν; B 191 DK Δημοκρίτου. ἀνθρώποισι γὰρ εὐθυμίη γίνεται μετριότητι τέρψιος καὶ βίου συμμετρίῃ; Cic. De fin. v. 29. 87 'id enim ille [i.e. Democritus] summum bonum εὐθυμίαν et saepe ἀθαμβίαν appellat, id est animum terrore liberum'.

εὐθυμία, then, is the Democritean antecedent to the Epicurean ἀταραξία and, if fr. 40 is a maxim of Epicurus, was used by him when he was still under the influence of the Democritean Nausiphanes, whose pupil in Teos he may have been at some time between 321 and 311 B.C. On this cf. De Witt, *Epicurus and his Philosophy*, iii, p. 55, and Festugière, *Epicurus and his Gods* (Eng. trans.), p. 19 and note.[1]

χαρά (— joy, delight) is more often found in verse but prose writers evidently used it as a synonym for ἡδονή. Prodicus, according to Aristotle (*Topica B* 166b22) divided pleasure into χαρὰν καὶ τέρψιν καὶ εὐφροσύνην. Plato (*Phil.* 19 c) speaks of ἡδονὴν καὶ τέρψιν καὶ χαράν. Democritus used it in the same way (ἀπορέουσι δὲ οἰκηίης χαρᾶς— B 293 DK). Epicurus, however, applied it and εὐφροσύνη to one kind of pleasure in particular—'active' pleasure, as opposed to the 'static' pleasures of ἀταραξία and ἀπονία; cf. Diogenes Laertius x. 136.

It is probable, then, that the writer is referring to the two kinds of pleasure, both of which Epicurus admitted as pleasure as opposed to the Cyrenaics who would allow the name only to 'active' pleasure (ἡδονὴν ἐν κινήσει), cf. D.L. loc. cit. and Festugière (Eng. trans.), pp. 44–5. And the sense of the passage would be much the same as that of S.V. 81: Οὐ λύει τὴν τῆς ψυχῆς ταραχὴν οὐδὲ τὴν ἀξιόλογον ἀπογεννᾷ χαρὰν οὔτε πλοῦτος ὑπάρχων ὁ μέγιστος οὔθ' ἡ παρὰ τοῖς πολλοῖς τιμὴ καὶ περίβλεψις οὔτ' ἄλλο τι τῶν παρὰ τὰς ἀδιορίστους αἰτίας. It may be added that the Stoics allowed their wise man χαρά but not ἡδονή, cf. D.L. vii. 116.

FRAGMENT 2 (col. I: 46·5 cm., 40·5 cm., 27 cm.; cols. II–VI: 47 cm., 158 cm., 58 cm.)

I. Opinions have differed on the punctuation of this column, mainly as to whether the first sentence should end in line 3 or line 4. I have reverted to the punctuation of Cousin and Usener, i.e. a full stop in line 3, and read ποιῶν, so as to have another participle at the beginning of the sentence to balance οὐ πολιτευόμενος.

---

[1] See now Festugière, 2nd edn. (1968), pp. xvii–xviii.

4–5. It was a basic doctrine that Epicureans should keep out of politics, cf. Diogenes Laertius x. 119 οὐδὲ πολιτεύσεται (ὁ σοφός), Cicero, *Ad Att.* xiv. 20. 5 'Epicuri mentionem facis et audes dicere μὴ πολιτεύεσθαι', and the other references in fr. 8 Us. Grilli considers that there is a close connection between this passage and Philodemus, *Rhet.* ii, p. 154, fr. 13 (Sudhaus), where Philodemus scoffs at the belief that [τοὺς φιλοσοφίαν ἐπιτηδεύ]οντ[ας μη]δὲν περιποιεῖν τ[ῇ π]ατρίδι συμφέρον, but goes on : κἂν οἱ φιλόσοφο[ί γε μ]ὴ πολιτεύωνται, μ[εγ]άλως ταῖς πα[τ]ρίσι βοηθ[ο]ῦσι τοὺς νεάνιας διδά[σκ]οντες αἰεὶ πείθεσθα[ι το]ῖς νόμοις. The connection, however, seems to be mainly verbal.

11. ἀταραξία—the *summum bonum* of Epicurus used first by Democritus, A 167 DK (Stobaeus) τὴν δ' ⟨εὐδαιμονίαν καὶ⟩ εὐθυμίαν καὶ εὐεστὼ καὶ ἁρμονίαν, συμμετρίαν τε καὶ ἀταραξίαν καλεῖ, but taken over and made his own by Epicurus, e.g. *Ep.* i. 82 ἡ δὲ ἀταραξία τὸ [τῷ Us] τούτων πάντων [i.e. fear of gods etc.] ἀπολελύσθαι καὶ συνεχῆ μνήμην ἔχειν τῶν ὅλων καὶ κυριωτάτων, and *Ep.* iii. 128 τούτων γὰρ ἀπλανὴς θεωρία πᾶσαν αἵρεσιν καὶ φυγὴν ἐπανάγειν οἶδεν ἐπὶ τὴν τοῦ σώματος ὑγίειαν καὶ τὴν ⟨τῆς ψυχῆς⟩ ἀταραξίαν, ἐπεὶ τοῦτο τοῦ μακαρίως ζῆν ἐστι τέλος.

We find the same expressions in Philodemus, Περὶ οἰκονομίας, p. 63 J : ὅσα πρὸς τὴν ἐκ [τ]ῶν κ[υ]ριωτάτων ἀταραξία[ν σ]υντείν[ει.]

II. 1. Philippson, in his *R.E.* article, thinks that by σύγγραμμα, used only here and in V 11 of this same fragment, Diogenes means his two treatises on Physics and Ethics, while γράφη refers to the inscription as a whole in 1 III 3, 2 I 6, and, possibly, 24 III 5. The evidence is hardly sufficient to support this distinction and certainly Diogenes Laertius uses the word σύγγραμμα (in x. 138) of his entire work.

3. The end of this line is very frustrating. Cousin read ΓΑΝ, HK record an upright stroke, then what looks like a small erasure, followed by ΛΝ or ΑΝ. Cousin's γ' ἄν is impossible, as the present indicative is never found with ἄν (G.M.T. 195), nor is HK's κ' ἄν-much better, as there is no compound ἀμπροστίθημι or ἐμπροστίθημι. W would supply either νῦν or ἤδη, but νῦν is impossible and ἤδη not supported by the two other supposed examples of confusion between Ν and Η which he quotes (8 I 7 and 2 VI 14). In the former Η is clearly a mistake of the lapicide for Ν, in the latter the Ν is carelessly formed; but the last letter of this line is a clear Ν. If something must be supplied πᾶν is the most likely restoration.

6. The break on the left-hand side of the stone begins here, and the rest of this line was found erased by HK, who doubt whether it ever contained anything after the end of φύ]σιν. So it is difficult to

account for the [ΥѠΝ]ϹΥΝ[Α].. recorded by Cousin. Grilli has a note, 'haud scio an 3 priores litterae nihil aliud sint quam [πα]ρὼν (v. 6–7, columnae I) in rasura', as though presumably the lapicide had crossed from one column to another by mistake, but why should these letters occur in the *middle* of the line, and after a wide margin?

7. The metaphorical use of δυσμαί, usually with τοῦ βίου, is not uncommon and there is little to choose between ἐπὶ δυσμαῖς and ἐν δυσμαῖς. Grilli quotes Plato, *Laws* vi, 770 a, and the unknown philosopher Juncus (whose book περὶ γήρως is partially preserved by Stobaeus iv. 1028. 12 H) for the use of ἐν, and Clem. Alex. *Protrepticus* 108. 3 for ἐπί, to which might be added Dion. Hal. iv. 79. 3 and Herod. iii. 104 (this latter actually referring to the sunset). A point in favour of ἐν is that it is slightly shorter than ἐπί, but the difference between a compressed ΠΙ and a broad Ν can be very small indeed.

9. Grilli prints a comma before διά because of the gap shown by ΙΙΚ. But there is an even bigger gap in line 12 before μετά.

11. ἀναλύειν in the metaphorical sense of 'casting off from life', i.e. dying, is evidently an expression of the Koine, cf. St. Paul, *Epistle to the Philippians* 1. 23: τὴν ἐπιθυμίαν ἔχων εἰς τὸ ἀναλῦσαι καὶ σὺν Χριστῷ εἶναι. Cf. *I.G.* xiv. 1794.

13. This is a restoration by Diels in view of the saying of Metrodorus (S.V. 47) first published by Wotke in 1888, though the emendation of πλείονος to παιῶνος is the work of Usener: ἄπιμεν ἐκ τοῦ ζῆν μετὰ καλοῦ παιῶνος ἐπιφωνοῦντες ὡς ἐν ἡμῖν βεβίωται. Usener suggested that the picture is of the comic chorus marching off at the end of the play singing τήνελλα καλλίνικος, cf. Aristophanes, *Acharnians* 1232, *Birds* 1764.

παιάν is a choral song which can apply to many occasions—as thanksgiving for deliverance from evil (Homer, *Il.* i. 473); as a song of triumph (*Il.* xxii. 391); as a battle song (Aesch. *Persae* 393); as a solemn chant before beginning an enterprise (Thuc. vii. 75). The meaning here is clearly that of a song of triumphant conclusion.

14. W's restoration *exempli gratia* is certainly *non male*, as G says; but the only word which survives looks much more like ΤΗΝ than ΤѠΝ.

III. 1–4. HK (p. 437) make μὴ προλημφθῶμεν . . . εὐσυνκρίτοις dependent on ἠθελήσαμεν but W saw that ἵνα μὴ προλημφθῶμεν is a parenthesis and that ἠθελήσαμεν governs βοηθεῖν directly. Usener referred ἤδη to τοῖς εὐσυνκρίτοις but again W is surely right to attach it to βοηθεῖν.

III. The 'Great Wall' (see p. xxxiii).

```
]ΚΕΦΑΛΑΙΟΝΤΗϹΕΥ[
]ΛΟΝΙΑϹΗΦΙΛΟϹ[
]ϹΙϹΗϹΗΛΛΕΙϹΚΥΡΙΟ[
]ΧΑΛΕΠΟΝϹΤΡΑΤΕΙΑ[
]ΚΑΙΕΤΕΡΩΝΑΡΧΗ[
]ΤΟΡΗΤΟΡΕΥΕΙΝϹΦΥΓΜΟ[
]ΚΑΙΤΑΡΑΧΗϹΙΕΜΟΝ[
]ΕΙΠΕΙϹΑΙΔΥΝΑΤΑΙΤΙϹ[
]ΜΕΤΑΔΙΩΚΟΜΕΝΠΡ[
]ΜΑΤΟΙΟΥΤΟΝΟΥΤΗΝ[
]ΟΥϹΙΑΝΕΧΟΥϹΙΝΑΛΛ[
```

IV. Fragment 41.

1. For other uses of πλήρωμα by Epicureans cf. S.V. 59 τοῦ ⟨τῆς Us⟩ γαστρὸς ἀορίστου πληρώματος; Metrodorus (Pap. Herc. 831. 14) τὸ πλήρωμα τῶν ἀγαθῶν, and Polystratus (Pap. Herc. 346, Vogliano, p. 81) τὸ ὁμοειδὲς τούτω[ν] πλήρωμα, referring to πάντων τῶν καλῶν.

9. ἄνθρωπε commonly has a contemptuous sense in Attic prose, as in Herod. iii. 63, and often in Plato, but here the sense is rather that of 'fellow man', 'brother', as in P. Oxy. 215. 1.

III. 13–IV. 3. HK's restoration of ll. 13–14 is clearly right but their comment on the construction of the sentence cannot be. They say: 'offenbar πάντα ἔπραττον das regierende Satzglied ist, alles Übrige aber zu ἐκκαλούμενος gehört', or, as W explains, read the sentence as though it were κἂν καθ' ἕνα ἐκκαλούμενος παρ' ἐμαυτὸν εἰς συμβουλίαν τὴν ἀρίστην, πάντα ἔπραττον. But, as W points out, πάντα πράττειν εἴς τι is common (there is an example in Epicurus, Ep. iii. 122 πάντα πράττομεν εἰς τὸ ταύτην ἔχειν) and πάντα παρ' ἐμαυτὸν = 'everything in my power'. This use of παρά is a development of the meaning 'owing to' found in Thucydides, e.g. i. 141. 7, and the orators, e.g. Demosthenes, First Phil. 11, Aeschines ii. 80. By a natural transition παρά then acquired the meaning of 'depending on' and in early philosophical use is to be found in Aristotle, Nic. eth. 1114ᵇ17 εἴτε δὴ τὸ τέλος μὴ φύσει ἑκάστῳ φαίνεται οἰονδήποτε, ἀλλά τι καὶ παρ' αὐτόν ἐστιν . . .

Epicurus, for his part, says in Ep. iii. 133 that the wise man considers τὴν τύχην ἄστατον, τὸ δὲ παρ' ὑμᾶς ἀδέσποτον.

Later still, in Plutarch and Epictetus, the phrase acquired the article and was used adverbially as the equivalent of τὸ ἐπ' ἐμοί etc., e.g. Epictetus, Diss. ii. 2. 20 πεῖσαι τό γε παρ' αὐτόν (= σεαυτόν); Plutarch, Nic. et Crassi comp. 566 e δοκῶν . . . τὸ παρ' αὐτὸν ἀποστερεῖν Σικελίας τὴν πόλιν. This is why W suggests reading πάντα [τὰ] παρ' ἐμαυτόν, but there is no room for the extra two letters at the end of III 14.

IV. 3–VI. 2. There seems to be no reason to doubt that W was right to regard this as one long sentence, as opposed to HK who print a full stop at V 2 and others at V 4 and V 8. The only gaps in the transcript occur after κοινῶς, IV 8, and ξένοις, V 8. Diogenes, it would appear, originally meant to write a much shorter sentence, ἐπεὶ δέ, ὡς προεῖπα, οἱ πλεῖστοι . . . νοσοῦσι κοινῶς, ἠθέλησα τῇ στοᾷ ταύτῃ κτλ., i.e. 'But since the disease of false opinion affects most people like a plague, I decided to use this colonnade to make a statement for all to see'. But after writing νοσοῦσι κοινῶς he was led to add other reasons: 'besides, their numbers grow; we ought also to think of future generations; we should surely help foreign visitors too'. At this point, V 8,

Diogenes realizes that he has wandered some distance from his opening words, leaves a gap, and resumes with ἐπειδὴ οὖν . . . συγγράμματος.

7. All editors quote Epicurus, fr. 224 Us (from the Florilegium Monacense) ὁ αὐτὸς ('Επίκουρος) τὴν οἴησιν ἱερὰν νόσον ἔλεγεν, i.e. 'He also called false opinion the sacred disease (epilepsy)', presumably, suggests W, because in sheep the disease is contagious. However, W also notes that the same remark is ascribed by Diogenes Laertius (ix. 7) to Heraclitus. It seems unlikely, then, that it has anything to do with Epicurus; Arrighetti does not accept it in his *Epicuro*.

In spite of L.S.J. Grilli insists that ἱερὰ νόσος in this quotation means *leprosy* 'as in the *excerpta Valesiana*', but gives no ref.

13. Cf. Thucydides, describing the Plague at Athens, ii. 51. 4 ἕτερος ἀφ' ἑτέρου θεραπείας ἀναπιμπλάμενοι ὥσπερ τὰ πρόβατα ἔθνησκον.

IV. 13–V. 4. The statement that future generations are in some way our responsibility seems not to occur in any other Epicurean source. Grilli refers to Cicero, *De finibus* iii. 19. 64 (= *S.V.F.* iii. 341), where Cato, outlining Stoic doctrine, says:

'Quoniamque illa vox inhumana et scelerata ducitur eorum qui negant se recusare quominus ipsis mortuis terrarum omnium deflagratio consequatur (quod vulgari quodam modo versu Graeco pronuntiari solet), certe verum est *etiam iis qui aliquando futuri sint esse propter ipsos consulendum*.

'Ex hac animorum affectione testimenta commendationesque morientium natae sunt.'

It is not an idea that one would expect to find in Epicurus; he constantly insists that a man's concern must be with this life only, since after death he does not exist, cf. *Ep.* iii. 125 ὁ θάνατος οὐθὲν πρὸς ἡμᾶς, ἐπειδήπερ ὅταν μὲν ἡμεῖς ὦμεν, ὁ θάνατος οὐ πάρεστιν· ὅταν δ' ὁ θάνατος παρῇ, τόθ' ἡμεῖς οὐκ ἐσμέν.

His attitude to the future was neutral, cf. *Ep.* iii. 127 μνημονευτέον δὲ ὡς τὸ μέλλον οὔτε ἡμέτερον οὔτε πάντως οὐχ ἡμέτερον, ἵνα μήτε πάντως προσμένωμεν ὡς ἐσόμενον, μήτε ἀπελπίζωμεν ὡς πάντως οὐχ ἐσόμενον, and this refers only to the individual's personal future as long as he lives.

It is true that Epicurus' will, recorded in D.L. x. 16–21, does make fairly elaborate arrangements for the future, including settlements for the son and daughter of Metrodorus, and the son of Polyaenus, but it still seems clear that this thought for future generations as a whole is an example of Stoic influence permeating Epicurean doctrine.

There is an oddity in the text of V 3–4. In spite of some disfigurement it is plain that the words are καὶ εἶναι γεγόνασί πω. εἶναι was

corrected to εἰ μή by Usener and this has been universally accepted. πρός is here used adverbially.

V. 4–8. The thought for strangers occurs again in fr. 49. This cosmopolitanism, originally Stoic, became very much a part of the spirit of the age and is another example of Stoicism invading even Epicurean doctrine. For other instances of it cf. Plutarch, *De Alex. virtute* 329 a ἀλλὰ πάντας ἀνθρώπους ἡγώμεθα δημότας καὶ πολίτας; and Marcus Aurelius vi. 44 πόλις καὶ πατρίς, ὡς μὲν Ἀντωνίνῳ μοι ἡ Ῥώμη, ὡς δὲ ἀνθρώπῳ ὁ κόσμος.

9–10. W's understanding of διαβαίνειν as meaning 'to concern, or affect' (for which he found support in the eighth-century A.D. author Stephanus (in Arist. *Rhet.* ed. Acad. Ber. xxi. 2, p. 281. 5) εἰ γάρ τις ἐπαινεῖ Ἀθηναίους ἐν Ἀθηναίοις εὐπαράδεκτα καὶ καλὰ ἔσονται τὰ λεγόμενα ὡς καὶ εἰς αὐτοὺς τοὺς ἀκροατὰς διαβαίνοντα) has been accepted by L.S.J. He adds that the perfect has a present meaning as in 27 I 14 and 38 III 9–10.

12. This stoa must be Spratt and Forbes's 'flagged platform with pedestals'. When HK visited it, and identified it as Diogenes' stoa, they found walls standing to a height of 1·5 metres as well as the pedestals. The latter are still there but the walls have gone, removed by HK in their efforts to find more of the inscription. Their success was not great but no conclusion can be drawn from this as the inscription would have been carved at eye level and would not have reached below 1·5 metres.

W thought the stoa mentioned by Diogenes might have been the site of his school, Grilli that the author more probably had had a school in Rhodes, then retired to his native town and built this colonnade as his final statement of doctrine and resting place. Philippson's restoration *exempli gratia* of 51 I would imply that the wall on which the inscription was carved was part of a basilica.

Of these suggestions Grilli's tomb of Diogenes is most unlikely, and Philippson's basilica at best tentative. The most probable conclusion is that Diogenes obtained permission to carve his message on the wall of a stoa already standing in the centre of the town, but he may well have presented the stoa to the town (see Introduction, p. xxi).

VI. 1–2. φάρμακα (HK) is more likely to be correct than Usener's τελικά. The remedies will be the study of nature (φυσιολογία) and of ethics (ἠθική). In Epicurus himself the word is only found once, in a fragment of the περὶ φύσεως (14 col. c. 4) quoted by Arrighetti, p. 253, but Philodemus' 'Fourfold Remedy' is well known, preserved in his *Adversus [sophistas]* (P. Herc. 1005 col. IV, ed. Sbordone): καὶ

πανταχῇ παρεπόμενον ἡ τετραφάρμακος· ἄφοβον ὁ θεός, ἀνύποπτον ὁ θάνατος, καὶ τἀγαθὸν μὲν εὔκτητον, τὸ δὲ δεινὸν εὐεκκαρτέρητον.

2–4. The restoration by Gomperz and HK is the most convincing. Sudhaus cannot be right, if only because the fourth letter of line 3 is clearly Γ and not Π. W understood these lines to mean 'of which [i.e. remedies] we would say that all kinds can be included in one term [i.e. the removal of mental disturbance]', but this must be mistaken. Grilli translates, 'Dei quali potrei dire in breve tutte le forme via via apparse', i.e. 'Of which I could say in brief that all the forms have appeared at one time or another'.

6. i.e. fear of the gods, of pain, and of death; cf. frs. 28 VII and 29 II of this work, and Epicurus' Principal Doctrine 10: τοὺς φόβους τῆς διανοίας τούς τε περὶ μετεώρων καὶ θανάτου καὶ ἀλγηδόνων.

7–8. Both Γεs are quite clear in both transcripts, but in view of the unfortunate gap in line 8 it has been usual to alter one or the other. In line 8 HK first attempted to retain both by reading τὰς μέν γ' ἐ[ξῆ]s (i.e. 'some we have cut off one by one'), but later altered this to τὰς μὲν ⟨κ⟩ε[νὰ]s so that it might anticipate the τὰς δὲ φυσικὰς of line 10; this is adopted by Grilli. William would alter the first γε; Usener's proposal is too long. Grilli, accepting HK's restoration enthusiastically, says (p. 372) that from the two kinds of ἐπιθυμίαι, κεναί and φυσικαί (for which cf. in particular Epicurus, Ep. iii. 127 ἀναλογιστέον δὲ ὡς τῶν ἐπιθυμιῶν αἱ μέν εἰσι φυσικαί, αἱ δὲ κεναί κτλ.), spring two kinds of λῦπαι, also κεναί and φυσικαί. Those that are κεναί can be banished completely, the φυσικαί must be borne but may be alleviated, says Diogenes.

This is certainly a reasonable comment on a tempting restoration, and it is supported by the use of the adverb in Ep. iii. 125 ὃ γὰρ παρὸν οὐκ ἐνοχλεῖ προσδοκώμενον κενῶς λυπεῖ.

Epicurus is here referring to the fear of death. It may, then, be only an accident that no actual reference to κεναὶ λῦπαι has survived in Epicurean texts, though there are frequent instances of κεναὶ δόξαι (e.g. Ep. ii. 87) and we find also κενὰ ἀξιώματα (Ep. ii. 86), κεναῖς φωναῖς (P.D. 37), and κενὰς ἀρετάς (Plut. Adv. Col. 1117 a [fr. 116 Us] quoting from a letter of Epicurus to Anaxarchus).

A more serious objection is that it does involve ignoring the clear testimony of both copies of the original. The Γ in line 8 is quite distinct, on the other hand the final letter could be part of an Ο; we might then possibly read τὰς μέν γε [πρ]ο|εξεκόψαμεν . . . προεκκόπτω, i.e. 'cut out, or destroy, first', is used surgically by Galen (2. 682) and figuratively by Libanius (Or. 39. 15).

12. The form ἐλαχιστιαῖος seems to be peculiar to Diogenes; it is restored at 35 III 12–13.

14. H and N often look very much alike and there can be no doubt that HK's restoration is correct. The omission of the iota before ε or η is regular in Attic inscriptions of the classical era (e.g. *I.G.* i². 39. 6; 82. 9; 154. 7) and required by the metre in Sophocles, *Philoc.* 120 (cf. Jebb's note ad loc.), *Trach.* 285, etc. For later times cf. Crönert, *Memoria Hercul.* 116. It does not occur in Epicurus, or the New Testament.

The wise man will inevitably suffer grief (D.L. x. 119 καὶ λυπηθή-σεσθαι δὲ τὸν σοφόν); according to Plutarch (*Non posse suaviter* 1101 a) Epicureans regarded it as unnatural harshness not to grieve at the death of friends. But such grief can be alleviated, partly by grateful recollection of what is past and by accepting the inevitable (cf. S.V. 55; Plut. *Non posse suaviter* 1099 e), partly by recalling the mind to pleasurable thoughts, cf. Cicero, *Tusc.* iii. 15. 33 'levationem autem aegritudinis in duabus rebus ponit, avocatione a cogitanda molestia et revocatione ad contemplandas voluptates'.

A. *The Physical Treatise*

This consists of only twelve fragments (3–14), although originally it must have been much longer. No introduction immediately recognizable as such has survived, but it is highly probable that fr. 3, which refers to critics of the study of nature, formed part of some prefatory matter. Fr. 4 also may belong to the same part of the treatise; it considers and criticizes the belief in the impossibility of knowledge of the world outside us held by Sceptics and the post-Platonic, sceptical, Academy, strangely singling out Aristotle in particular as a holder of such views. Fr. 5 consists mainly of a rapid review of pre-Socratic plus Stoic theories of basic substance, breaking off, apparently, at the beginning of the refutation of Heraclitus. Frs. 6 and 7 seem to be part of the Epicurean doctrine of atoms; fr. 6 is concerned with the essential reality of qualities in bodies; fr. 7, as far as we can tell, criticizes Stoic theories of perception and cognition.

Fr. 8 is all that remains of what must have been an important part of the treatise—the astronomical section; in 9 and 10 we have moved on to the origin of human life and the development of speech and the civilized arts. This fragment, no. 10, is one of the most interesting and important of the whole inscription. Fr. 11 is concerned with religion; it is probably part of a defence of the Epicureans against the charge of atheism but all we have left is a rather involved examination of the agnosticism of Protagoras. Leaving aside the badly damaged 12–13 we end with fr. 14. Its position here is open to discussion, but since the only column which can be read with reasonable certainty is an expression of thanks to Epicurus for banishing the terrors of the next world it seemed reasonable to include it in this part of the work.

When we recall how much store Epicurus set by the 'study of nature' (he is credited with 37 books on the topic), and reflect that in the arrangement of this inscription it is generally held that the Physical Treatise took up the whole of one course of stones, i.e. extended for probably more than 100 columns, it is obvious that these few pages can represent nothing more than a tiny, pathetic fragment of the original whole.

FRAGMENT 3 (31 cm., 48 cm., 26 cm.)

A badly broken block discovered by HK near to the northern side of the great wall. Only a few letters survive from col. I; from col. II we have most of ll. 1–9. This fragment was almost certainly part of the introduction to the Physical Treatise.

2–3. οἱ περὶ Σωκράτην would mean Socrates himself, the Cynics, who were supposed to be descended from Antisthenes, and the Cyrenaics, who were connected with Aristippus. It would certainly not include Plato.

For *Socrates* the references must be Xenophon, *Memor.* i. 1. 11 οὐδὲ γὰρ περὶ τῆς τῶν πάντων φύσεως ἧπερ τῶν ἄλλων οἱ πλεῖστοι διελέγετο σκοπῶν, ὅπως καλούμενος ὑπὸ τῶν σοφιστῶν κόσμος ἔφυ, καὶ τίσιν ἀνάγκαις ἕκαστα γίγνεται τῶν οὐρανίων, ἀλλὰ καὶ τοὺς φροντίζοντας τὰ τοιαῦτα μωραίνοντας ἀπεδείκνυεν; Plato, *Ap. Soc.* 19 c; and the longer passage in the *Phaedo*, 96 a–99 d, where Socrates describes, in apparently autobiographical detail, how he was interested in the 'study of nature' as a young man but grew disillusioned with it later, mainly as a result of his disappointment with the νοῦς of Anaxagoras.

How far these πάθη Σωκράτους can be accepted as genuinely autobiographical has been discussed by many commentators from Cicero onwards. Hackforth (*Plato's Phaedo*, pp. 127 seqq.) says Plato has reached a point where he must give a new account of causation and recalls his own early interests, but with historical accuracy in terms of Socrates' known interest in 'the material or mechanical causation of Ionian science'. This view mediates between literalist acceptance, as by Burnet and Taylor, and views referring the experiences in fact to others, whether Plato (so Archer-Hind) or fifth-century intellectuals in general. R. S. Bluck more decisively (*Commentary*, pp. 105 seqq. and 198) says 'we may accept 96 a seqq. as reflecting, roughly, Socrates' mental history'. See also K. J. Dover (*Clouds*, Introduction, esp. pp. xlix, liv) on the relevance of the 'skit' in Aristophanes' comedy.

The *Cynics* were universally regarded as a Socratic sect because of their supposed foundation by Antisthenes, a belief which had been fostered by the Alexandrian composers of *Successions of the Philosophers*.

The result of their work can be seen in Diogenes Laertius. How unsure this derivation is can be learnt from Dudley's *History of Cynicism*, especially Chapter I. He shows conclusively that Cynicism began with Diogenes of Sinope. That the latter had no time for scientific studies is evident from Diogenes Laertius' account of him; he would wonder, says Diogenes Laertius vi. 28, τοὺς μαθηματικοὺς ἀποβλέπειν μὲν πρὸς τὸν ἥλιον καὶ τὴν σελήνην, τὰ δ' ἐν ποσὶ πράγματα παρορᾶν. When someone had said that there is no such thing as motion (ὅτι κίνησις οὐκ ἔστιν) he got up and walked about, and he asked a man who was talking about τὰ μετεώρα how long it took him to come from the sky (D.L. vi. 39 ποσταῖος, ἔφη, πάρει ἀπὸ τοῦ οὐρανοῦ;).

The actual Antisthenes may have had a little more interest in natural science than Diogenes the Cynic; the seventh volume of his works, listed in Diogenes Laertius vi. 17, includes works 'On Nature', but we do not know what these contained and it is improbable that our Diogenes knew anything of them. For him Antisthenes was the founder of a sect which concentrated exclusively on ethics.

As for the *Cyrenaic* sect of hedonists it is probably no more than an accident of name which allowed them to acquire a Socratic connection, the Aristippus who was their founder being confused with his grandfather who was a companion of Socrates. They too had no interest in natural science. In the summary of their doctrine which Diogenes Laertius includes in his life of Aristippus we read (ii. 92) ἀφίσταντο δὲ καὶ τῶν φυσικῶν διὰ τὴν ἐμφαινομένην ἀκαταληψίαν· τῶν δὲ λογικῶν διὰ τὴν εὐχρηστίαν ἥπτοντο. But Diogenes Laertius goes on to say that Meleager and Clitomachus assert that they regarded both Physics and Dialectic as useless.

The attitude of *Epicurus* was quite different; for him the study of nature, φυσιολογία, was essential for happiness, cf. *Ep.* i. 37 ὅθεν δὴ πᾶσι χρησίμης οὔσης τοῖς ᾠκειωμένοις φυσιολογίᾳ τῆς τοιαύτης ὁδοῦ, παρεγγυῶν τὸ συνεχὲς ἐνέργημα ἐν φυσιολογίᾳ καὶ τοιούτῳ μάλιστα ἐγγαληνίζων τῷ βίῳ ἐποίησά σοι καὶ τοιαύτην τινὰ ἐπιτομὴν καὶ στοιχείωσιν τῶν ὅλων δοξῶν. 'Therefore, since such a method is useful to all who are accustomed to the study of nature, I, who recommend the constant practice of that study and find my greatest peace in such a life, have made for you both such a summary and an outline of the whole doctrine.'

FRAGMENT 4 (48 cm., 85·5 cm., 40 cm.)

It seems certain that only a little is missing between fragments 3 and 4, perhaps no more than two columns; in them Diogenes turns from those who regard natural science as possible but useless (the Socratics) to those who maintain that it is impossible. Hence the various

proposals for the preliminaries to this fragment and for the restoration
of the broken top left-hand corner. They range from Usener's

> ἄλλοι δὲ | [εἰπεῖν μὲν ἄ]ντικρυς οὐ
> [τολμῶσιν μ]ὴ φυσιολογίαν
> [δεῖν πράττει]ν αἰσχυνό-
> [μενοι κτλ. as the text

to Sudhaus's

> οὐ πᾶσαν τοίνυν τὴν τοιαύτην ἐπιμέλειαν τολμῶντες ἀποδοκιμάζειν
> οὔτε τὴν περὶ τὰ μετέωρα ζήτησιν ἐκβάλ-
> [λουσιν ἄ]ντικρυς οὔ-
> [τε τὴν περ]ὶ φυσιολογίαν
> [διατριβὴ]ν κτλ.

which Grilli has adopted, adding Us's ἄλλοι δὲ as a beginning and
reading ἐπιβάλ[λουσιν.

I. 2. φυσιολογία. Cf. *Ep.* i. 37, quoted above, and Principal Doctrine
12 : . . . οὐκ ἦν ἄνευ φυσιολογίας ἀκεραίους τὰς ἡδονὰς ἀπολαμβάνειν.

7. ἀκατάλημπτος with the meaning of 'incomprehensible' is used
once by Philodemus (*Acad. index*, p. 91 M), Marcus Aurelius vii. 54,
and Sextus Empiricus, *Adv. math.* vii (= *Adv. dog.* i). 432. Its opposite
καταληπτός (comprehensible) is almost entirely a Stoic term, though
it occurs in col. II 14 of this fragment.

12. ἃ μήποθ' εὔρῃ. The omission of ἄν 'sermo vulgaris est', according
to William; he quotes Ditt. *O.G.I.S.* ii. 331 ὃς κενὸς εἰσαχθῇ.

I. 13–II. 8. William's comment on this passage is 'imprudens Aris-
toteli attribuit sententiam Heracliti', and he quotes Arist. *Met.* A,
987ᵃ32 . . . ταῖς Ἡρακλειταίαις δόξαις, ὡς ἁπάντων τῶν αἰσθητῶν αἰεὶ
ῥεόντων καὶ ἐπιστήμης περὶ αὐτῶν οὐκ οὔσης.
Sudhaus (*Rh. Mus.* lxv. 312) also thought that Diogenes was the
victim of error but he reverted to an earlier solution. Usener (*Rh. Mus.*
xlvii. 416) had suggested that Diogenes was confusing Aristotle with
a Sceptic and suggested Aenesidemus—a suggestion endorsed by
Crönert (*Kol. u. Mened.*, p. 183. [121–22]); on similar lines Sudhaus
imagined that Diogenes had used a source which referred to Arcesilaus
but gave the name in the abbreviated form APK, which Diogenes mis-
took for APIC, i.e. Aristotle. Apart from the inherent improbability of
this explanation it is to be doubted whether Arcesilaus' scepticism is
the same thing as the extreme Heraclitean denial of the possibility of
knowledge which we find here. Arcesilaus' position was one of ἐποχή,
suspension of judgement, and he would make no positive statement

of any kind (cf. Sext. Emp. *Pyrr. hyp.* i. 232), still less support it with reference to the Heraclitean doctrine of flux.

The same objections can be made against Philippson, who argued in *R.E.* (Suppl. Bd. v. 157–8) that Diogenes' mistake might be due to his following some later Imperial Platonist such as Favorinus, the second-century rhetor and friend of the Emperor Hadrian, who seems to have embraced the Scepticism of the New Academy and the Pyrrhonists and at the same time fervently admired Aristotle (cf. Plut. *Quaest. conv.* 734 f). Such a writer might, says Philippson, have been the innocent cause of Diogenes' ascription of Scepticism to Aristotle. But it may still be asked whether it is merely Scepticism which is being ascribed to Aristotle; in fact closer examination of Diogenes' words shows that, if he has mistaken Aristotle for someone else, that someone else can *only* be Aenesidemus or one of his associates. Sextus Empiricus tells us (*Pyrr. hyp.* i. 210) that οἱ περὶ τὸν Αἰνησίδημον ἔλεγον ὁδὸν εἶναι τὴν σκεπτικὴν ἀγωγὴν ἐπὶ τὴν Ἡρακλείτειον φιλοσοφίαν, but he immediately goes on to say that this understanding of Scepticism is mistaken. We then have to explain how, if Aristotle in the text is a mistake for Aenesidemus, Diogenes could possibly have made it.

There still, however, remains the possibility that there is no mistake, that Diogenes means exactly what he says. This point of view was first put forward in 1933 by Bignone (*Riv. di fil.* lxi. 16–43, 155–76). He maintains that the denial of the possibility of knowledge of the sensible world is a well-attested Platonic doctrine (cf. for instance *Phaedo* 78 d–e, *Tim.* 27 d seqq.) which could be found also in the early exoteric works of Aristotle. Diogenes ascribes the doctrine to Aristotle, says Bignone, because he was using Colotes' book Ὅτι κατὰ τὰ τῶν ἄλλων φιλοσόφων δόγματα οὐδὲ ζῆν ἔστιν, whose contents can be deduced from Plutarch's Πρὸς Κωλώτην (*Adv. Col.*). Colotes evidently said that Plato's doctrines were followed by Aristotle and all the Peripatetics, and in any case Cicero, *Acad.* i. 8. 33, shows that in his time Academics and Peripatetics were regarded as forming a single school.

Five years later Philippson (*Riv. di. fil.* lxvi. 235–52) rejected this view and reverted to Favorinus, suggesting that the latter may have misunderstood *Anal. post. A* c. 2, or even *Nic. eth.* 1140ᵇ33, but in the same year Bignone again demonstrated that a belief in the impossibility of ἐπιστήμη (i.e. scientific knowledge) of this world because of flux is a good Platonic doctrine and perfectly attributable to the young Aristotle. Two years later, in 1940, G. Capone-Braga came to Bignone's aid in *Atene e Roma* (viii [xlii]. 35–47) with evidence that such a doctrine can be found even in the later esoteric works of Aristotle, e.g. *Anal. post. A* 31, 87ᵇ28–39, *Met. Z*, 1036ᵃ8–12 and 1039ᵇ27 seqq.,

and he produced indications to show that Epicureans knew such later writings as well as the earlier. Finally, another Italian scholar, Gaetano Pisano, summed up the controversy in *Atene e Roma*, xliv no. 2 (1942), 67–75, and lent his assistance to Bignone's explanation; he emphasized particularly the evidence of Sextus Empiricus, *Adv. math.* viii (= *Adv. dog.* ii). 6–7 and 56, regarding the former reference as especially significant because of the similarity of language between *Adv. math.* viii. 7 and this passage of Diogenes. Sextus says that οἱ περὶ τὸν Πλάτωνα καὶ Δημόκριτον μόνα τὰ νοητὰ ὑπενόησαν ἀληθῆ εἶναι, ... ὁ Πλάτων διὰ τὸ γίγνεσθαι μὲν ἀεὶ τὰ αἰσθητὰ μηδέποτε δὲ εἶναι, ποταμοῦ δίκην ῥεούσης τῆς οὐσίας, ὥστε ταὐτὸ μὴ δύο τοὺς ἐλαχίστους χρόνους ὑπομένειν ... διὰ τὴν ὀξύτητα τῆς ῥοῆς.

He repeats Bignone's assertion that to Epicureans Platonists and Peripatetics formed one school and indeed believes that the similarity of expression in this passage of Sextus proves that Diogenes and Sextus were using the same source, probably Colotes.

What conclusion are we to draw from all this discussion? In the first place there can be no doubt that Plato was convinced that knowledge (ἐπιστήμη) of sensible particulars is impossible. Quite apart from the statement of Aristotle, *Met.* A, 987ᵃ32, quoted at the beginning of this note (William did not give it in full, but it reads ἐκ νέου τε γὰρ συνήθης γενόμενος [sc. Πλάτων] πρῶτον Κρατύλῳ καὶ ταῖς Ἡρακλειταίαις δόξαις κτλ. . . . ταῦτα μὲν καὶ ὕστερον οὕτως ὑπέλαβεν), there are ample references in Plato himself to prove the point, e.g. *Theaet.* 182 d, where the permanence even of qualities in a flux is denied. The same doctrine would almost certainly have been found in the early dialogues of Aristotle, cf. frag. 2 of the Περὶ ἰδεῶν in Ross's *Fragmenta Selecta*, where it is emphasized that 'particular things all change and never remain the same; universals are unchangeable and eternal' (τὰ μὲν μερικὰ πάντα μεταβάλλουσι καὶ οὐδέποτε ὡσαύτως ἔχουσι, τὰ δὲ καθόλου ἄτρεπτα καὶ ἀΐδιά ἐστιν); and then there is evidence produced by Capone-Braga to show that such an idea, if we bear in mind the proper meaning of ἐπιστητός (i.e. *scientifically* knowable), is not foreign to the later Aristotle. (It may be added that a superficial reading of such a passage as *Metaphysics* Γ 5 (especially 1009ᵇ10 ff.) might well seem to imply that Aristotle discarded sense data as variable and unknowable. He is in fact merely refuting arguments of a Heraclitean and Protagorean type against the law of contradiction at this point.)

The only alternative would be to assume that Diogenes derived his information from some first- or second-century Peripatetic eclectic who combined Aristotelianism *not* with the ordinary Scepticism of the later Academy, but with a very developed Aenesidemean kind of Scepticism indistinguishable from the extreme Heracliteanism of

Cratylus. Such a source may have existed, and Diogenes may have used it, but both chances seem very remote. It would be far simpler to accept that Diogenes has made no mistake but actually means what he says.

II. 2. περίπατον—probably a sneer, as the verb certainly is in the quotation from Epicurus to be found in Plutarch, *Non posse suaviter* 1091 b (fr. 423 Us) ἄν τις ὀρθῶς ἐπιβάλῃ ἔπειτα σταθῇ καὶ μὴ κενῶς περιπατῇ περὶ ἀγαθοῦ θρυλῶν.

6. ῥεῦσις is only used once by Epicurus, at *Ep.* i. 48, where it means the flow of atoms from the surface of bodies which is responsible for sensation.

III. It seems clear from Plut. *Adv. Col.* 1108–9 that Colotes had attacked Democritus for saying that an object is οὐ μᾶλλον τοῖον ἢ τοῖον, since Plutarch replies that the Epicurean doctrine that all sensations are true must turn the accusation back on the Epicureans themselves. For this doctrine cf. Cic. *De fin.* i. 19. 64 and Lucr. iv. 480 seqq.

14. Sudhaus's attempt to read the name of Lacydes in this line stems from his belief, mentioned above, that the name of Aristotle in I 14–II 1 is a mistake for Arcesilaus. Lacydes of Cyrene became head of the Academy in succession to Arcesilaus about 241 B.C., and is said to have been the first to put the sceptical doctrines of the Middle Academy into writing; cf. Cic. *Acad.* ii. 6. 16, Aelian, *V.H.* 2. 41.

FRAGMENT 5 (46 cm., 86 cm., 36 cm.)

A doxographical and polemical passage corresponding to Lucretius i. 635–920, as is noted by Bailey (ii. 708 seqq.), Ernout and Robin (i. 134–6), and Grilli (p. 374). The thinkers mentioned by Diogenes and Lucretius are slightly different, and there are minor variations in the order in which they occur, but there is one striking similarity: both open with Heraclitus and both attack him with particular violence. It is evident that they are following an Epicurean tradition, based according to Robin on the Ἐπιτομὴ πρὸς τοὺς φυσικούς of Epicurus. Heraclitus is singled out for attack as he is regarded as the inspirer of the Stoics, the principal enemies of Epicureanism.

I. 10. For Heraclitus cf. B 30 DK (= Kirk and Raven 220) κόσμον τόνδε [τὸν αὐτὸν ἁπάντων] οὔτε τις θεῶν οὔτε ἀνθρώπων ἐποίησεν, ἀλλ' ἦν ἀεὶ καὶ ἔστιν καὶ ἔσται· πῦρ ἀείζωον, ἁπτόμενον μέτρα καὶ ἀποσβεννύμενον μέτρα. (On the reasons for the colon after ἔσται cf. Kirk, *Heraclitus, The Cosmic Fragments,* pp. 310 seq.)

12. Our knowledge of Thales' doctrines is dependent on Aristotle, *Met. A* 3, 983ᵇ6 (A 12 DK = KR 87) where he says ἀλλὰ Θαλῆς μὲν ὁ τῆς τοιαύτης ἀρχηγὸς φιλοσοφίας [i.e. Monism] ὕδωρ εἶναί φησιν [sc. the first principle].

14. For Diogenes of Apollonia cf. B 5 DK (= KR 606) καί μοι δοκεῖ τὸ τὴν νόησιν ἔχον εἶναι ὁ ἀὴρ καλούμενος ὑπὸ τῶν ἀνθρώπων, καὶ ὑπὸ τούτου πάντας καὶ κυβερνᾶσθαι καὶ πάντων κρατεῖν. αὐτὸ γάρ μοι τοῦτο θεὸς δοκεῖ εἶναι καὶ ἐπὶ πᾶν ἀφῖχθαι καὶ πάντα διατιθέναι καὶ ἐν παντὶ ἐνεῖναι.

II. 1. Aristotle, *Met. A* 3, 984ᵃ5 (A 4 DK = KR 142) is our main authority for Anaximenes also. He there says: Ἀναξιμένης δὲ ἀέρα καὶ Διογένης πρότερον ὕδατος καὶ μάλιστ' ἀρχὴν τιθέασι τῶν ἁπλῶν σωμάτων.

2. Cf. fr. B 6 DK (= KR 417)

τέσσαρα γὰρ πάντων ῥιζώματα πρῶτον ἄκουε·
Ζεὺς ἀργὴς Ἥρη τε φερέσβιος ἠδ' Ἀιδωνεὺς
Νῆστίς θ' ἣ δακρύοις τέγγει κρούνωμα βρότειον.

These mythological characters represent the four elements, and the order is usually taken to be Fire, Air, Earth, and Water.

2–3. No one has satisfactorily explained the odd phrase ὁ Ἀκράγου, which would seem to mean, as William says, that Diogenes called Empedocles 'son of Acragas'. HK simply comment 'Fehler für Ἀκραγαντῖνος'. Grilli suggests that Diogenes has mistaken the form of the genitive of Ἀκράγας, the town, declining it like νεανίας, as the only description applied to the other philosophers in this passage is the name of their town. But this still does not explain why Diogenes does not use the adjective here as he does in every other instance.

6. ὁμοιομέρεια strictly means 'similarity of composition' and is so used by Epicurus in *Περὶ φύσεως* 14. 15 II (Arrighetti, p. 268) τό γε ἤδη τὴν ὁμοιομέρειαν τῷ φαινομενῷ κεκτημένον. But it was particularly applied by later writers to the doctrine of Anaxagoras that there is a portion of everything in everything, cf. B 6 DK (= KR 508) . . . καὶ οὕτως ἂν εἴη ἐν παντὶ πάντα· οὐδὲ χωρὶς ἔστιν εἶναι, ἀλλὰ πάντα παντὸς μοῖραν μετέχει. This is the name of the doctrine in Lucretius i. 830

Nunc et Anaxagorae scrutemur homoeomeriam.

The use of the word in the plural to describe the actual material ἀρχαί in this theory is a much later development, cf. *Placit.* 1. 3. 5 and D.L. ii. 8. Aristotle's term was τὰ ὁμοιομερῆ, e.g. *Met. A* 3, 984ᵃ11, *De caelo* III. 3, 302ᵃ28.

8–9. The same statement of Stoic doctrine occurs in Simplicius *Ad Aristot. physica* 1. 25. 17 Diels (quoted by G) ὡς οἱ Στωικοὶ θεὸν καὶ ὕλην (ἀρχὰς λέγουσιν); and cf. also D.L. vii. 134.

10–11. The simplest statement of Democritus' doctrine is quoted by Sextus Emp. (B 9 DK = KR 589) and Galen (B 125 DK) where we read that colour, taste, and sensation exist by convention, ἐτεῇ δὲ ἄτομα καὶ κενόν; cf. fr. 6. II. 8.

12–13. Cf. Epicurus *Ep.* i. 54–6. As against Democritus, Epicurus maintained:

(*a*) That the atoms possessed weight as well as shape and size.

(*b*) That there were not, however, atoms of *all* sizes.

III. 9–13. Cicero records similar arguments in *D.N.D.* iii. 14. 35–7 against the Stoics, who are regarded as disciples of Heraclitus. The speaker there asserts that fire cannot be indestructible because:

(*a*) If it is the source of feeling it must itself possess sensation, but whatever is liable to pain must also be liable to death.

(*b*) It is agreed that all fire requires fuel; it must therefore perish if it is not fed.

13–14. The point of the final argument is lost. W's proposal for its continuation is reasonably convincing.

FRAGMENT 6 (49 cm., 82 cm., 44 cm.)

A fragment which seems to have been broken in two between being read by Cousin and re-recorded by HK. They found cols. II and III separate from col. I and several letters missing from the beginning of ll. 9–14 of col. II. Fortunately C's copy seems to be reasonably accurate.

Grilli would insert between frs. 5 and 6 my fr. 19 (W XX) believing that as it refers to the unlimited number of the atoms it will be more appropriate here than in the treatise on the Innumerability of the Worlds. I will discuss the point more fully at fr. 19: here I would say merely that while both the Physics and the later treatise are so fragmentary and disjointed that either position could be right, I find Grilli's arguments unconvincing.

I. Unfortunately this is too damaged to admit of any reasonably certain restoration. W considered that the matter under discussion is empty space (τὸ κενόν, l. 6) and restored ll. 6–11 accordingly; the atoms themselves, he says, must have been dealt with in a previous

passage. If he is right, and it seems probable that he is, then the points being made here are those found in Epic. *Ep.* i. 67, τὸ δὲ κενὸν οὔτε ποιῆσαι οὔτε παθεῖν δύναται, ἀλλὰ κίνησιν μόνον δι' ἑαυτοῦ τοῖς σώμασι παρέχεται, and in *Ep.* i. 41, καὶ μὴν καὶ τῷ πλήθει τῶν σωμάτων ἄπειρόν ἐστι τὸ πᾶν καὶ τῷ μεγέθει τοῦ κενοῦ.

In W's restoration the infinity of empty space is being proved by the argument used by Lucretius in i. 968 seqq., οὗτος in l. 13 referring perhaps to some previously mentioned ὀϊστός corresponding to the *volatile telum* of Lucretius. Grilli objects that this is a Roman example, not Greek, because the fetial hurled a lance over the border into enemy territory, but the 'flying arrow' is not unknown to Greek philosophy, since it provided Zeno with one of his paradoxes.

For the whole argument Grilli refers to fr. 297 Us.

II. 1–2. 'Iocosus est scriptor ut Fr. XI et XXV III 2/3' is W's comment.

Diogenes now goes on to criticize Democritus for denying the reality of qualities and asserting that they exist only 'by convention' as opposed to atoms and space which exist in fact. The language of ll. 11–12 suggests that his source is again Colotes' book "Ὅτι κατὰ τὰ τῶν ἄλλων φιλοσόφων δόγματα οὐδὲ ζῆν ἔστιν. Cf. Plut. *Adv. Col.* c. 8 seqq.

Epicurus' doctrine on qualities is that whereas it is true that they cannot exist independently some (τὰ συμβεβηκότα) are nevertheless physical constituents of composite objects, and such objects owe their essential nature as much to the presence of these qualities as to the atoms and space of which they are composed. Cf. *Ep.* i. 68–9, where we read that shape, colour, size, etc.

οὔθ' ὡς καθ' ἑαυτάς εἰσι φύσεις δοξαστέον ... οὔτε ὅλως ὡς οὐκ εἰσίν [as Democritus maintained] οὔθ' ὡς ἔτερ' ἄττα προσυπάρχοντα τούτῳ [i.e. σώματι] ἀσώματα, οὔθ' ὡς μόρια τούτου, ἀλλ' ὡς τὸ ὅλον σῶμα καθόλου μὲν ⟨ἐκ⟩ τούτων πάντων τὴν ἑαυτοῦ φύσιν ἔχον ἀΐδιον ... Cf. Lucr. i. 451–4.

5. Bignone (*L'Ar. perd.* i. 18) would insert ⟨καὶ τὸ κένον⟩ after μόνας. Perhaps strictly speaking Diogenes should have put these words in but he clearly did not. The most likely explanation of the omission is that Diogenes is concentrating rather on the material aspect of reality than the immaterial. Grilli discusses the point at p. 376 of his commentary.

8. Or, as Democritus himself put it (B 9 DK = KR 589), νόμῳ γλυκύ, νόμῳ πικρόν, νόμῳ θερμόν, νόμῳ ψυχρόν, νόμῳ χροιή, ἐτεῇ δὲ ἄτομα καὶ κενόν.

For the word νομιστί Usener quotes Galen, *De elem. sec. Hippocr.*

i. 2 (p. 417 K, 3. 20 H = A 49 DK), Marcus Aurelius vii. 31, and Sextus Emp. *Pyrrh. hyp.* iii. 232.

11. Cf. Plut. *Adv. Col.* 1, 1107 e, and note in Loeb edn., pp. 158–9.

FRAGMENT 7 (46 cm., 86 cm., 28 cm.)

A stone which has unfortunately suffered heavy erasure of the text, especially col. I 1–3 and col. III.

Philippson would reverse the order of frs. 6 and 7 since he thinks that this fragment criticizes Stoic ideas about the elements whereas 6 ends with an attack on those of Democritus; and as the Stoics are mentioned before Democritus in fr. 5, col. II, so we should expect their ideas to be criticized first.

He therefore considers that in fr. 7 Diogenes, in criticizing the doctrine that φάσματα are empty figments of the imagination, deals with one aspect of the Stoic theory of elements; that in fr. 6, col. I, he attacks the belief that the universe is finite, again a Stoic doctrine, and defends its infinite nature (a necessary hypothesis for the innumerability of the atoms); and that then in fr. 6, col. II, he turns to defend the reality of secondary attributes in combinations of atoms as against Democritus.

Such a transposition is not necessary. In fr. 5, cols. I–II, Democritus is not included in the list of earlier thinkers who were completely wrong; he is in fact praised as having been on the right lines and in need of only slight correction. W was right, therefore, to assume that all the discussion about the atoms as elements has been lost between frs. 5 and 6, that 6 I is the end of the section on the void, and that the remainder of fr. 6 and fr. 7 deal with other topics. Grilli (p. 377) agrees with this.

In this passage Diogenes is criticizing an aspect of the Stoic theory of cognition. This, briefly, is as follows. Since Stoic physical doctrine is essentially materialist, and only body can act on body, cognition must ultimately begin with sensation—on the effect produced by external objects on the soul. The Stoics therefore believed that the essential quality of an object is somehow conveyed to the soul where it makes an impression (literally, as in wax, according to Zeno; cf. *S.V.F.* i. 58, ii. 83). This impression was called a φαντασία; φαντασίαι, however, had to be accepted by the reason and only those which were καταληπτικαί (i.e. 'comprehensible', not 'gripping' as the term later came to be understood) were so accepted. A number of καταληπτικαὶ φαντασίαι produced an ἔννοια and knowledge is the result of the systematization of ἔννοιαι (cf. again *S.V.F.* ii. 83).

But, of course, hallucinations, apparent visions of the unreal, can occur. This phenomenon was called a φάντασμα. Cf. *S.V.F.* ii,

p. 22, l. 10, where we read φάντασμα δέ ἐστιν ἐφ' ὃ ἑλκόμεθα κατὰ τὸν φανταστικὸν διάκενον ἑλκυσμόν. ταῦτα δὲ γίνεται ἐπὶ τῶν μελαγχολώντων καὶ μεμηνότων—as happened to Orestes.

Such manifestations could be described as κενά and would be rejected by the healthy mind.

This was unacceptable to Epicurus. According to his materialism nothing which produces an impression on the senses or mind *can* be κενόν, i.e. non-corporeal. And so even the visions of madmen are real; cf. D.L. x. 32 τά τε τῶν μαινομένων φαντάσματα καὶ ⟨τὰ⟩ κατ' ὄναρ ἀληθῆ, κινεῖ γάρ· τὸ δὲ μὴ ὂν οὐ κινεῖ. Cf. also Epic. *Ep.* i. 67. This is the point being made by Diogenes here, though he uses φάσμα instead of the Stoic term φάντασμα.

W, followed by Grilli, saw rather a reference to the Stoic doctrine of a 'third nature' apart from body and empty space, the existence of which is implied in D.L. vii. 61 ἐννόημα δέ ἐστι φάντασμα διανοίας, οὔτε τὶ ὂν οὔτε ποιόν ὡσανεὶ δέ τι ὂν καὶ ὡσανεὶ ποιόν, οἷον γίνεται ἀνατύπωμα ἵππου καὶ μὴ παρόντος.

Such a notion was rejected by Epicureans, e.g. Lucretius i. 445–8:

> ergo praeter inane et corpora tertia per se
> nulla potest rerum in numero natura relinqui,
> nec quae sub sensus cadat ullo tempore nostros
> nec ratione animi quam quisquam possit apisci.

This explanation seems to fit the context less well. For more on the Epicurean doctrine of dreams cf. fr. 52 (the Letter to Mother).

II. The restoration of l. 2 is very difficult and no solution is entirely satisfactory. Some points are clear:

(*a*) Nothing can follow the final Λ, so that HK's λ[ε-] and W's δ[εῖ] are not possible.

(*b*) The final Λ does not stand, as G² says in the app. crit., 'in medio spatio quod cols. II et III dividit', it is directly above the final A in l. 3. On the other hand he is probably right to expel it as redundant exactly as in l. 8 below. (The other redundant Λ, in 11 II 13, is rather different from the two in this column; it is a much clearer letter and stands well away from either column.)

(*c*) It seems impossible that εἰδωλοποϊκά, which I print, and still less Grilli's εἰδωλοποιητικά, could ever have stood in the original. There is not enough room between the surviving certain letters, Δ and K, to admit either restoration (it would seem impossible that more than four or five letters are missing), and the remnants that are preserved do not fit either suggestion. Hence the original restoration of HK εἰδοποιητικά which fits the gap much better; unfortunately where this

word occurs elsewhere it means either 'specific' or 'creating a form or pattern' (L.S.J.) and εἶδος itself never seems to occur in Epicurean sources as the equivalent of εἴδωλον.

8. There is room for no more than four letters between the Γ and Τ so that the proposal of Diels, adopted by W, would be too long, as would HK's preferred reading for this lacuna.

11. G refers to Epicurus' statement in *Ep.* i. 46–7 of the doctrine of εἴδωλα, which being of unsurpassed fineness of texture and speed of movement account for the sensation of sight. Lucretius' version of the doctrine begins at iv. 110,

> nunc age quam tenui natura constet imago
> percipe . . .

It is impossible to make anything of col. III.

FRAGMENT 8 (46 cm., 122 cm., 35 cm.)

A block of nearly four columns complete except for a small piece missing from the top affecting the first lines of cols. I and II. It is all that remains of the astronomical section of the Physics which would presumably have corresponded to Epicurus' Letter to Pythocles (*Ep.* ii) 90–116. Col. I is reminiscent of *Ep.* ii. 112–14, cols. II and III of secs. 90–3.

Various guesses have been made as to what preceded this fragment (cf. the critical apparatus), but it is clear that the subject of φέρουσιν must have been some word meaning 'orbits'.

3. I have preferred G²'s κατ' ἰδί]αν to the ἰδέ]αν of HK and the φορ]άν of Philippson because it gives a better sense and because the erasure is big enough for at least five letters. In support of his reading Grilli refers to Democritus A 39 DK, which is a quotation from [Plutarch], *Strom.* 7 reading κατ' ἰδίαν φέρεσθαι ταῦτα [i.e. heavenly bodies] . . .

5–8. ὀρθὸν perpendicular *to the equator*, as Ph explains; he also correctly interpreted ἕως τινός, which puzzled William, and translated it 'in gewisser Beziehung', i.e. to a fixed relation, or bearing.

9. Cf. Epic. *Ep.* ii. 112 τινὰ ἄστρα στρέφεσθαι αὐτοῦ συμβαίνει . . . (Us). [Bailey reads . . στρέφεται αὐτοῦ ὃ . .]

The MS. reading of this passage is τινὰ ἀναστρέφεται αὐτοῦ ὃ συμβαίνει; it was emended by Usener with reference to Homer, *Il.* xviii. 487, Ἄρκτον . . . ἥ τ' αὐτοῦ στρέφεται.

H. van Herwerden quotes Sophocles, *Trach.* 130–1 in support of C's αὐτοῦ but it is difficult to see why.

II. This column greatly worried William. He took it to refer to the sun's size, and he understood ἀπόφασις in l. 8 to be an unusual equivalent for φάσις or φάσμα in the sense of 'Abglanz', i.e. presumably 'reflection' or 'appearance'. How then, he asks, can any Epicurean say that we see the 'visum solis', not 'ipsum solem'? And as to l. 5, how can the sun, which is, as Epicurus says, only more or less the same size as it appears to us (*Ep.* ii. 91), burn up the earth? He concludes that Diogenes has misunderstood Epicurus' teaching. It is possible, he thinks, that, just as Epicurus said of the sun's *size* (loc. cit.) κατὰ μὲν τὸ πρὸς ἡμᾶς τηλικοῦτόν ἐστιν ἡλίκον φαίνεται, κατὰ δὲ τὸ καθ' αὐτὸ ἤτοι μεῖζον τοῦ ὁρωμένου ἢ μικρῷ ἔλαττον ἢ τηλικοῦτον τυγχάνει, so he also said that its distance from the earth may be greater than it appears to be; and Diogenes on his part added an 'ineptam causam' why it could not be in fact as low as it sometimes appears to be.

Philippson interpreted the passage differently. The subject under discussion, he says, is the sun's *orbit*, not its size, and he translates ἀπόφασις as 'rising' (referring to Philodemus, *Sign.* 10. 2 and 6 where ἔκφασις has the same meaning), i.e. the sun at its rising appears to be low whereas in fact it is not. Grilli accepts this interpretation.

Philippson's first point is obviously right. Diogenes *is* discussing the sun's orbit, saying that it is not as low as it appears to be; if it were the earth would be burnt up. This latter remark seems to be one addition of his own; no other Epicurean writer expresses any fear of the sun burning the earth. However, to revert to W for a moment, Lucretius (v. 592 seq.) makes it plain that the sun, small as it is, can emit so much light and heat

> quod maria ac terras omnis caelumque rigando
> compleat et calido perfundat cuncta vapore.

But in fact the sun is never as low as it sometimes seems to be, says Diogenes; we mistake its ἀπόφασις for the sun itself. This word is certainly a puzzle. In Epicurus himself (cf. Arrighetti) it means 'statement', and the other uses listed by L.S.J. are similar—'denial', 'decision', etc. The meaning here, however, can hardly be other than 'appearance', 'reflection', or 'image'—quite a possible derivation from ἀποφαίνω. Yet the idea is still very strange; how indeed could an Epicurean say that we do not see the sun itself but its image? Professor Skemp suggests that we may here have an echo of some later Epicurean speculation which toyed with Empedocles' theory (cf. A 56 DK and KR p. 334) that we see a reflection of the sun rather than the sun itself. This is possible, but quite unparalleled in any Epicurean source. Or is Diogenes simply using ἀπόφασις as a variation for εἴδωλον? Epicureans were well acquainted with optical illusions, which they explained as being caused by the εἴδωλα of objects being

damaged on their journey to the eye. Perhaps he means only that some people, seeing the sun apparently near the earth (very likely at its rising or setting), mistake the εἴδωλον, the image, for the reality— the sun itself not yet having risen (or having set).

13–14. Cf. Epic. *Ep.* ii. 92.

III. The thought of this column is a basic Epicurean tenet which both Epicurus and Lucretius constantly repeat when treating of astronomical subjects. Cf. e.g. Epic. *Ep.* i. 79–80, *Ep.* ii. 87; Lucr. v. 526–33.

6. W observes that καταποφαίνεσθαι, a more emphatic form of ἀποφαίνεσθαι, occurs nowhere else, and that ὅδε τις in the sense of 'individual' is a term introduced by Aristotle.

7. Cf. Epic. *Ep.* ii. 113 τὸ δὲ μίαν αἰτίαν τούτων ἀποδιδόναι, πλεονα-χῶς τῶν φαινομένων ἐκκαλουμένων, μανικὸν καὶ οὐ καθηκόντως πραττό-μενον ὑπὸ τῶν τὴν ματαίαν ἀστρολογίαν ἐζηλωκότων . . . , where Bailey translates ἀστρολογίαν as 'astrology'.

One wonders whether Diogenes was thinking of this passage but read μαντικόν instead of μανικόν.

14. All editions refer to fr. 343 Us, where it is said that Epicurus compared the sun to pumice-stone.

He may have borrowed this suggestion from Diogenes of Apollonia, who, according to Aëtius ii. 13. 5 (KR 611), considered that the stars were 'pumice-like, and the breathing-holes of the world, penetrated by fire'.

It is curious how in II 11 the H in πλήν is an obvious N whereas in III 9 the N in ἀνδρός is an equally obvious H.

IV. 1–3. W notes here that whereas Epicurus believed that the earth was held up by air it is not elsewhere recorded that he thought the sun was sustained by winds. Philippson has no explanation to offer, but Grilli, comparing the whole passage to Lucr. v. 590 (594) seqq. in particular quotes ll. 597–601 in his commentary (p. 379),

> nam licet hinc mundi patefactum totius unum
> largifluum fontem scatere atque erumpere lumen,
> ex omni mundo quia sic elementa vaporis
> undique conveniunt et sic coniectus eorum
> confluit, ex uno capite hic ut profluat ardor,

and maintains that Diogenes' πνεύματα (l. 3) correspond to the *vapor* of Lucretius and have nothing to do with wind. He therefore translates πνεύματα by 'correnti di calore' and quotes Democritus

B 25 DK τὰς ἀτμίδας αἷς ὁ ἥλιος τρέφεται. Such an interpretation is certainly more suited to the remainder of the column, but there is no evidence to support it; πνεῦμα is always 'wind' in Epicurus.

4–5. For the sun as a fountain of light cf. Lucr. v. 597–8 quoted above.

9–10. W here refers to Lucr. ii. 652 and comments, 'mundum variis rebus mixtum esse admonet ne quis miretur unde elementa vaporis ad solem veniant'. But the Lucretian passage reads

> terra quidem vero caret omni tempore sensu
> et quia multarum potitur primordia rerum
> multa modis multis effert in lumina solis,

which refers to this earth of ours. Diogenes' τὸ σύμπαν here must mean the entire universe, though of course that is equally a mixture of everything.

13–14. W sees here the explanation for the sun's heat to be found in Lucr. v. 604–7,

> est etiam quoque uti non magno solis ab igni
> aera percipiat calidis fervoribus ardor,
> opportunus ita est si forte et idoneus aer
> ut queat accendi parvis ardoribus ictus.

Grilli agrees, but instead of W's εὐεμπρήστου, which is not found elsewhere, proposes εὖ ἐμπύρου, since ἔμπυρος does occur at least twice in similar contexts; but surely this combination of adverb and adjective is very unlikely syntax.

FRAGMENT 9

A fragment recorded only by Cousin and not found again by HK. In Cousin it appears as the bottom half of a column with three letters remaining from l. 7 and all lines defective at the right. Cousin does not transcribe it.

The length of line in D is fifteen letters instead of the normal eighteen in this part of the inscription. Usener's restorations as a rule keep to the shorter line; William assumed a longer one, as did Grilli originally, but in his printed text he has contracted ll. 11 and 12. He deals with this fragment in *P.P.* xv (1960), 150–1.

Diogenes has now moved on from the movements of the heavenly bodies to the origins of human life, as Lucretius does in Book v. This passage corresponds to ll. 805–20 of that book, where Lucretius describes the first humans emerging from wombs fixed to the earth by roots and being fed by milky juices flowing from pores in the earth.

The abundance of heat and moisture at the time gave rise to the process.

Grilli refers also to Diodorus Siculus i. 7. 2 seqq.

7. Philippson thought the passage possibly began, 'Not from the sky, nor from the sea, but from the earth . . .'

FRAGMENT 10 (46 cm., 135 cm., 40 cm.: 46·5 cm., 36 cm., 28 cm.)
This is a combination of two blocks, one containing cols. I–IV and another containing col. V. The first is complete but several lines are partly erased; the second, smaller one has suffered damage as well as erasures.

The origins of human life having been dealt with Diogenes now turns to the development of the arts and crafts of civilization. According to Epicurean doctrine these, language included, were not god-given but arose naturally from the needs and circumstances of life. The fullest description of the process is again to be found in Lucretius v. 925 seqq., the only extant treatment in Epicurus himself is to be found in the Letter to Herodotus (*Ep.* i) 75–6, where it *precedes* the astronomical section of the treatise. William refers to Diodorus i. 8. 6; cf. also the references given in G².

I. 3. ἐπινό[ησιν οἰκ]ημάτων, adopted by HK and W, is certainly too long as G says, but οἰκημάτων seems better than νημάτων, as clothing would appear to be the *next* subject for discussion, and it would be natural to mention the protection of houses also. (Cf. Lucr. v. 1011 'inde casas postquam ac pellis ignemque pararunt'.) If, however, οἰκημάτων is to be read the preceding word must be shortened as the maximum number of letters missing is 7; hence my proposal of ἐπίνοιαν.

11–12. Both στρεπτός and κασωτός raise difficulties as to their exact meaning. στρεπτός is of course the verbal adjective of στρέφω and so should mean 'pliant', 'flexible'; the στρεπτὸς χιτών in Homer (*Il.* v. 113, and xxi. 31) is taken to be a flexible coat of chain mail. What sense Diogenes attached to the word it is impossible to say, except that from the context one would expect some such meaning as 'textile'. William has a long note on κασωτός (p. xxxiv). He considers that the form of the word, which is not uncommon, suggests its derivation from a verb κασόω, but we have no examples of that either. However, there is a word κάσος, or κάσσος, which Hesychius defines as a ἱμάτιον παχὺ καὶ τραχὺ περιβόλαιον. W therefore thinks the meaning must be 'felt', since woven cloth could not be made until the discovery of iron made possible the making of weaving implements. Lucretius makes this point at v. 1350–60.

II. Epicureans always insisted that the gods had nothing to do with man's discovery of the arts of civilization, but they were not the only ones to think so, nor probably were they the first. W quotes Xenophanes B 18 DK (= KR 191) from Stobaeus (*Anth.* 1. 8. 2)

> οὔτοι ἀπ᾽ ἀρχῆς πάντα θεοὶ θνητοῖσ᾽ ὑπέδειξαν,
> ἀλλὰ χρόνῳ ζητοῦντες ἐφευρίσκουσιν ἄμεινον.

11. They particularly stressed that language was not brought down from Heaven by Hermes or any other god, nor was it invented and taught by some human genius, as many philosophers seemed to believe. Such a view is ascribed to Heraclitus, Democritus, and Aristotle but it is urged most fully in Plato's *Cratylus* 389 d seqq. Lucretius devotes more than 60 lines, v. 1028–90, to refuting it. I have discussed this Epicurean doctrine fully in an article entitled 'The Epicurean Theory of the Origin of Language', published in *A.J.P.* lxxxiii. 2 (1962), 159–67.

III. 4. Cf. Diodorus Siculus i. 15–16.

9. Cf. note to II 11 above.

IV. The unfortunate lacuna in l. 11 makes it impossible to be certain of the meaning of this column. Before 1907 it was assumed by all authorities that the πλήθη in l. 9 referred to the multitudes of *people* who had to be collected. HK's restoration of F (D's reading seems hopeless) then makes good sense however dubious the form of the word βασιλέες may be. William, however, convinced himself and all later scholars that the multitudes are of *words*. In view of Lucr. v. 1050–5, esp. 1050–1

> cogere item pluris unus victosque domare
> non poterat rerum ut perdiscere nomina vellent,

this view seems to me most unlikely, and it is certain that none of the restorations proposed by W or his successors agree with the fragments of letters recorded in F. βασιλέες, however, fits them exactly; C and Є are often confused.

V. This is numbered as a separate fragment by W but clearly runs on from the previous column.

1. D here reads .... TⲰTOCAYN. EΓ [Ⴈ]

F has only the faint remains of a few letters; any restoration must be regarded as very uncertain.

6–7. D's OPKEIΔOC is unknown, and F has only an erasure of two or three letters at the end of l. 6. Us proposed δοκίδος, but the iota is short and so could not be spelt ει by Diogenes. Presumably Rhode thought there might have been an alternative spelling with a long iota. My own proposal is not found elsewhere, but it is the singular of a word the plural of which is given by Hesychius as a synonym of ὀρόδαμνοι, κλάδοι, i.e. 'boughs, branches'. Cf. the article in *A.J.P.* mentioned in note on line II. 11.

14. Once again D records a line which apart from the first five letters is meaningless and not very like the few remnants found by HK.

FRAGMENT 11 (48 cm., 71 cm., 31 cm.)

This block, unfortunately broken on both sides with heavy damage to Col. I and rather less to Col. III, was discovered by HK. It is placed here because it deals with religion, a subject which follows the discovery of the civilized arts in Lucretius v (1161 seqq.). It might perhaps be worth mentioning that the lettering in F is quite different from that in which frs. 10 and 13 are written and very like that of fr. 4 (in which Scepticism is attacked), but I have not seen the actual stone and this may mean only a change of transcriber.

I. Ph's proposed introduction (i.e. 'the most pious, like Socrates, who perished at the hands of the Athenians . . .') would accord well with an attack on superstitious heresy-hunters. In spite of the heavy restorations the sense of this column seems reasonably certain. A reference to persecution is strongly suggested by κατατρέ[χουσιν] and ll. 5–7 can hardly fail to be an echo of Epicurus *Ep.* iii. 123 ἀσεβὴς δὲ οὐχ ὁ τοὺς τῶν πολλῶν θεοὺς ἀναιρῶν, ἀλλ' ὁ τὰς τῶν πολλῶν δόξας θεοῖς προσάπτων.

8. Diagoras was introduced by HK in view of Col. II. Grilli refers to Cicero, *D.N.D.* i. 42. 117 where Diagoras (and Theodorus) are mentioned as complete atheists while Protagoras, though professedly an agnostic, is nevertheless classed with them.

10. If the restoration is correct the reference is to Eudemus of Rhodes, the pupil of Aristotle who lived in the second half of the fourth century B.C. and gave his name to the *Eudemian Ethics* of Aristotle. A work of his was entitled Τῶν περὶ τὸ θεῖον ἱστορία. He, like Diogenes himself, may have opened a school in Rhodes. A collection of fragments was published by E. Spengel (1866 and 1870).

II. 8. Protagoras' words, as quoted by Diog. Laert. ix. 51, were περὶ μὲν θεῶν οὐκ ἔχω εἰδέναι, οὔθ' ὡς εἰσὶν οὔθ' ὡς οὐκ εἰσὶν οὔθ' ὁποῖοί τινες ἰδέαν· πολλὰ γὰρ τὰ κωλύοντα εἰδέναι ἥ τ' ἀδηλότης καὶ βραχὺς ὢν ὁ βίος τοῦ ἀνθρώπου.

10–12. I cannot understand why Diogenes should say that a statement of agnosticism about the existence of gods is the same as a denial.

The remainder of this argument, from II 12 to the end of the defective col. III, is far from certain, and my restorations are by no means the first to be attempted. I think that Diogenes is trying to say that although Protagoras did also say that he did not know that gods do *not* exist, this statement of complete scepticism left his position exactly what it would have been had he made only his first statement, i.e. that he did not know whether gods exist. This, as we saw above, was for Diogenes the same as saying that he knew they do not.

I have discussed this question more fully in *Phronesis* (vii, no. 2 (1962), 105–9), but it may be useful to include the gist of that article here.

The two restorations of col. III by HK need not detain us, they have serious defects both in language and, as far as they can be understood, in content. W is much better. He would read

"...[ὅτι μή εἰσιν", [δῆλός ἐστι] | σχεδὸν ἐγχει[ρῶν πρόφα]|σίν τινα πρὸς [τὸ μὴ δο]|κεῖν τελέως [ἀναιρεῖν] | τοὺς θεούς, ε[ἰπὼν καὶ] | εἶναι αὐτοὺς [ἄπορον καὶ] | μὴ εἶναι, τὸ ἀ[ληθὲς δὲ] | ποιῶν ἴσον Δ[ιαγόρα, εἰ] | εἰπὼν τὸ μὴ [εἰδέναι] | ὅτι εἰσὶν αὐ[τοῦ δὴ ἐ]|παύσατο. τ[αὐτὸν οὖν, ὥσ]περ λέγω, ἢ [τὸ ταὐτὸν] δυνάμενο[ν ἐκείνω] ἤνενκε[ν ἐς μέσον],

i.e. '"... that they do not exist", it is obvious that he is more or less trying to make an excuse so as not to seem to be doing away with the gods entirely by saying that it is doubtful whether they exist or not; but he is in truth doing (? would be doing) the same as Diagoras if, having said that he did not know that they exist, he (had) stopped there. The view propounded then is, as I say, the same or has the same force as the former.'

This makes reasonable sense but is not entirely satisfactory, mainly because, as W himself notes, Protagoras did *not* stop after his first remark.

Grilli objected to it on technical and linguistic grounds, and after a preliminary attempt in his 1950 commentary (*Studi di Filosofia Greca*, p. 382) proposed in *La Parola del Passato* (xv (1960), 141–3) the following (which he printed in his 1960 text):

"... ὅτι μή εἰσιν", [δῆλός ἐστι] | σχεδὸν ἐγχει[ρῶν πρόφα]|σίν τινα πρὸς [τὸ μὴ δο]|κεῖν τελέως [ἀναιρεῖσθαι] | τοὺς θεούς. ε[πεὶ δὲ καὶ τὸ] | εἶναι αὐτοὺς [καὶ τὸ δὴ] | μὴ εἶναι τὸ α[ὐτὸ εἶπε] | ποιῶν ἴσον Δ[ιαγόρα,] | εἰπὼν τὸ μὴ [εἰδέναι] | ὅτι εἰσὶν αὐ[τὸς οὐκ ἐ]|παύσατο. τ[οῦτον οὖν, ὅν]|περ λέγω ἢ [τὸν ταὐτὸν] | δυνάμενο[ν τούτω προ]|ήνενκε λ[όγον ...

He translated thus:

'"... that they do not exist", it is clear that he was looking for an excuse so that it should not seem that the gods were being entirely

eliminated; but since he said that it was the same whether they exist or, indeed, do not exist—doing the same as Diagoras—in fact he did not cease to say that he did not know whether they exist. So he put forward the statement I quote or one which means the same.'

There is no great improvement on W here:

(a) The sense is unconvincing—why should a statement of complete scepticism as to the existence of gods in any way affect Protagoras' continuing to assert that he did not know whether they exist?

(b) The introduction of Diagoras in a parenthesis is scarcely effective if Diogenes is trying to establish that Protagoras and he held identical views.

(c) The construction of οὐκ ἐπαύσατο taken with the aorist εἰπών is very doubtful.

As to my own proposed reading, I must add that J. B. Skemp is suspicious of αὐτοῦ at III 10, which he considers stylistically unlikely; he suggests αὐ[τοὶ διε]|παύσατο. Diogenes' only certain use of αὐτοῦ is at 8 I 9, the astronomical fragment, where it does indeed mean 'on the spot'. Such a change would be, as Skemp says, a harmless substitute and could well be right.

Fragments 12 and 13, also discovered by HK, are too heavily damaged for anything definite to be made out. The few words which can be read suggest that the subject is still the gods.

FRAGMENT 12 (46 cm., 80 cm., 30 cm.)

II. 12. Epicurus is fond of the words ὑποψία and ὑποπτεύομαι: cf. P.D. 11 which begins, Εἰ μηθὲν ἡμᾶς αἱ τῶν μετεώρων ὑποψίαι ἠνώχλουν καὶ αἱ περὶ θανάτου . . .

14. Ph considers that there may be a reference here to Plato's Demiurge, as part of an Epicurean demonstration that the world cannot be a divine creation. However, the Stoics also say that God ἀίδιον ὄντα διὰ πάσης αὐτῆς (i.e. ὕλης) δημιουργεῖν ἕκαστα (D.L. vii. 134).

FRAGMENT 13 (46 cm., 133 cm., 34 cm.)

II. 8. There might be another reference here to P.D. 11.

III. 12–14. Ph believes that the few surviving words here may refer to the Epicurean criticism of the slavery of the gods mentioned by Philodemus (Piet. 42 g, cf. Hermes lv, pp. 225 seqq.). Grilli sees rather a reference to Epic. Ep. iii. 124 (men's enslavement to the beliefs of the many). But this, as well as Ep. iii. 134 (their slavery to the 'destiny' of the natural philosophers), is less likely.

FRAGMENT 14

This fragment is recorded only by Cousin and was not found again by HK; we do not know, therefore, either its size or whether it had παραγραφαί. W included it, with some hesitation, in the Letter to Antipater because of the second person singular found in I 2. Ph objected to this arrangement and thought that it, and fr. 17, belonged to a dedicatory letter to the Ethical Treatise, a letter under which no P.D. was written. That he was right to remove it from the Letter to Antipater is certain; it is out of place there and, as G points out, the tone of this fragment is that of an inferior addressing a superior, not Diogenes speaking to Antipater. But it does not seem to belong to the Ethical Treatise and I agree with G who, reverting to HK's original arrangement, places it here, in the section on religion in the Physics, as an expression of thanks to Epicurus for removing the fear of gods and death.

That death is nothing to us, and that therefore there is no need to fear what may come after it, is one of the commonest of Epicurean commonplaces. It is perhaps best summed up in P.D. 2: ὁ θάνατος οὐδὲν πρὸς ἡμᾶς· τὸ γὰρ διαλυθὲν ἀναισθητεῖ· τὸ δ' ἀναισθητοῦν οὐδὲν πρὸς ἡμᾶς.

I. 5. Cf. Lucr. iii. 978 seqq., where he maintains that the torments of these mythical sinners are really to be found in this life.

The curious mistake of repeated TAN and NA at the beginnings of ll. 5 and 6 would be easily overlooked in reading but it is strange that the stone-cutter should make it.

8–9. φρίττω is a favourite word of Philodemus, e.g. *D.* i. 12; i. 19. 7; *Mort.* 4. 39. 6; *Piet.* fr. 101. 6 Phil.

The spelling mistake in l. 9 was first corrected by H. van Herwerden.

10. Epic. *Ep.* i. 65 makes the point that once the soul is lost the body ceases to feel any sensation.

12–13. G's restoration is too far from D to be convincing. Further, in l. 13 there is hardly room for his αὐτῶ τῆς, and his assumption that D's AICAPE should be taken as AIϹAPE = AKAPE, though possible, is unlikely; there is also no room for the final I which has to be supplied. The objections to Ph's restoration are:

(*a*) the οὐκ is oddly misplaced in that it must be taken with δυσαρεστεῖσθαι,

(*b*) Diogenes normally negatives the infinitive with μή,

but his reading fits D well and gives a good sense.

II. G's restoration of ll. 1–10 would mean,

'For it is clear that I am not upset on this account, that I shall be robbed of life and pleasure, but I shall abandon everything which I now enjoy here, suffering no evil after death. And in view of this firm belief . . .'

He refers, for l. 4 to [Plato], *Axiochus* 365 c–d; for ll. 7 seqq. to Lucr. iii. 832 and 838 seqq., and fr. 495 Us; and for l. 10 to frs. 458 and 470 Us. For further details see *P.P.* (1960), 143–4.

He may well be on the right lines, but I am reluctant to include such heavy restoration in the text.

B. *The Letter to Antipater on the Innumerability of the Worlds*

A short treatise (frs. 15–22), first recognized as a separate entity by William, who entitled it *Diogenis de Innumerabilitate Mundorum Epistula ad Antipatrum* (hence the conjectured heading by Grilli). It consists basically of frs. 15 (W XV), 16 (W XVIII), 18 (W XIX), and 20 (W XXI). The height of these blocks places them in the group cm. 56–62 and they all have παραγραφαί. W also included his frs. XVI, XVII, and XX. Of these XVI and XX are recorded only in D and so we possess nothing but the text, and XVII is merely the bottom right-hand corner of a block. The first (XVI) is unlikely to be part of this treatise for the reasons given above, where it is fr. 14; XVII and XX I have retained as frs. 17 and 19, though Ph would expel the former and G the latter for reasons given ad locc. Frs. 21 and 22 contain only a few letters each, but were included in this treatise by G because of the physical appearance of the blocks.

The doctrine of innumerable worlds, existing at the same time, is fundamental for Epicurus, cf. *Ep.* i. 45 ἀλλὰ μὴν καὶ κόσμοι ἄπειροι εἰσὶν οἵ θ' ὅμοιοι τούτῳ καὶ οἱ ἀνόμοιοι. Lucr. ii. 1023–89 repeats the same argument, that innumerable atoms flying about in unlimited space are bound to create more than one world, and adds a further argument that nothing in the totality of things is unique.

FRAGMENT 15 (59 cm., 40·5 cm., thickness omitted by HK)

I. Many attempts have been made to supply the missing left-hand part of this column; certainty is not possible, but some things can be said:

(*a*) The letters begin very large (*c.* 12 per line in ll. 1 and 2) and become smaller until by l. 6 they are back to the usual 17 or 18 per line. Many suggested restorations would give too long a line.

(*b*) There are slight erasures noted by HK at the beginning of some lines but where they record letters the record is distinct except for

l. 13. Therefore, the first extant letter in l. 4 is clearly I, not H, and in l. 11 there is no justification for the readings of W or Wilhelm. In v. 13 HK's reading is almost certain, and there seems to be no good reason to revert to D as Grilli does (cf. *P.P.* xv (1960), 138–40).

II. 3. The original school of Epicurus (the Garden) still existed in Athens and not many years before Diogenes an imperial chair of Epicurean studies had been founded there (together with chairs for the Stoic, Platonist, and Peripatetic systems); cf. Introduction, p. xxv.

9. For another reference to Diogenes' stay in Rhodes cf. fr. 51 III. According to Philodemus there was a flourishing Epicurean school there in the first century B.C.

FRAGMENT 16 (59 cm., 52 cm., 45 cm.: 59 cm., 61 cm., 30 cm.)

The two stones were found together by Cousin. The second is broken on the right so that very little survives of col. IV, the first is undamaged. There are a few erasures where they join in the middle of col. II.

Any of the openings proposed would make reasonable sense.

I. 2–3. In Epic. *Ep.* iii. 133 the prudent man is the one who realizes that τύχη is ἄστατος.

3–4. Diogenes refers to his age in fr. 2 II 9.

II. 2. ἔναρθρος is not found earlier than the second century B.C. (in the Stoic Diogenes of Babylon, *S.V.F.* iii, p. 212. 17), but this is probably an accident. It is connected with ἄρθρον—a joint—used by Aristotle to mean also articulation of speech (*H.A.* 536ᵃ3) and, in a grammatical sense, a connecting word (*Poet.* 1457ᵃ6); this last use was adopted by Stoic grammarians. ἄναρθρος occurs in Plato, *Tim.* 75 a in its original meaning of 'not articulated' (anatomically) but is applied by Theophrastus (*Sens.* 41) to sound. Its opposite (ἔναρθρος) must have been equally common in the metaphorical sense of 'connected' or 'clear'.

III. 2. Usener thought that τῶ was a mistake for σοί, ἴσον being taken with the καί of κἄν in l. 3. Grilli accepts the correctness of this construction, though he retains the τῶ. I am inclined to agree with William, who (p. xlvi) maintains that τῶ, governed by ἴσον, is an article prefixed to the whole clause which in full would be (ἵνα δὴ τὸ ἴσον γένηται) τῷ γενομένῳ ἄν, εἰ παρῆσθα καὶ αὐτὸς ὁμοίως κτλ.

As he points out there is a similar construction at fr. 52 II—a possible reason for ascribing that letter to Diogenes though not a very compelling one.

13. To the passages from Epicurus and Lucretius referred to in the introduction to this part of the inscription (p. 59) can be added the notices from Galen, Aëtius, Cicero, etc. collected by Usener in his fr. 301.

FRAGMENT 17 (25 cm., 25 cm., 13 cm.)

A tiny bottom right-hand corner of a block discovered by HK. W, reading the last word but one as $\pi o \theta \epsilon \hat{\iota} s$, was induced by the 2nd person to assign it to this letter and numbered it XVII. Ph proposed to eject it with XVI (now 14) because he was certain that XVIII (now 16) follows immediately after XV (15). G, in his 1950 commentary (G¹), though he ejected XVI left this fragment with W's text between XV and XVIII. Antipater, he thought, had asked Diogenes for a complete statement of the cosmological doctrine; Diogenes replies by sending him an account of his dialogue with Theodoridas, the account which ends so unfortunately in fr. 16. In his latest text (G²), however, he has abandoned the 2nd person and places this fragment after my 18 and before 20. (My fr. 19 [W XX] he had already put into the previous section, between my frs. 5 and 6.) He also prints some rather bold restorations which do not always accord with F; in particular the I in l. 14 is clearly not T.

It seems better to leave the fragment unfilled and place it here. The lettering, if one may judge from the HK transcript, is very similar to that of frs. 16 and 18.

FRAGMENT 18 (56 cm., 41–5 cm., 34 cm.)

A single block, also found by HK. A large piece of the stone is missing in the left centre and what does survive is heavily disfigured. The $\pi a \rho a \gamma \rho a \phi \dot{\eta}$ above the top line looks a little doubtful—it could be only a scratch on the stone. But W was clearly right to include this fragment in this treatise. The height of the stone shows that it cannot belong to the Physics and the absence of a 15th line excludes it from the Ethics. There are also the practically certain readings $\kappa \acute{o} \sigma \mu o s$ in l. 5 and $\tau \dot{\eta} \nu$ $\gamma \hat{\eta} \nu$ in l. 14. But it is not easy to make out what the point or context of the fragment was. W's restoration of ll. 4–10 is very bold and not always consistent with the letters which can be read.

3. A note in G¹, p. 389, would seem to suggest that the last three letters, which look like TAC, are a mistake for the article $\tau \hat{\omega} \nu$ before the participle $\dot{a} \sigma \kappa \acute{o} \nu \tau \omega \nu$. But they are the first three letters of the participle itself; $\tau \hat{\omega} \nu$ precedes them.

11. Grilli earlier proposed [τοιοῦτον] at the beginning of this line but later dropped it.

13–14. Neither the reading nor the meaning of these lines is at all clear.

FRAGMENT 19 (no measurements)

As this fragment is recorded only by Cousin and was not found again by HK we do not know the size of the stone or lettering, or whether it had παραγραφαί. However, we can be sure from the subject-matter that it belongs to one or other of the physical treatises. W included it in this one because of the phrase οὐδ' ὅδε ὁ κόσμος in col. II 12–13. The argument is, he presumed, as follows: atoms must be unlimited in number because of the infinity of empty space; if they were limited not even this world would have arisen, but as they are innumerable, then so are the worlds.

It is true that this fragment preserves only the first part of the argument—that the number of atoms must be unlimited. This is the point made by Epicurus in *Ep.* i. 41–2, especially καὶ μὴν καὶ τῷ πλήθει τῶν σωμάτων ἄπειρόν ἐστι τὸ πᾶν καὶ τῷ μεγέθει τοῦ κενοῦ. | εἴτε γὰρ ἦν τὸ κενὸν ἄπειρον, τὰ δὲ σώματα ὡρισμένα, οὐδαμοῦ ἂν ἔμενε τὰ σώματα ἀλλ' ἐφέρετο κατὰ τὸ ἄπειρον κένον διεσπαρμένα, οὐκ ἔχοντα τὰ ὑπερείδοντα καὶ στέλλοντα κατὰ τὰς ἀνακοπάς.

The last two lines of this passage correspond exactly to col. II 6–9 when we remember that the sideways motion of atoms is caused by collisions (cf. Epic. *Ep.* i. 61 ἡ εἰς τὸ πλάγιον διὰ τῶν κρούσεων φορά).

The second part of the argument is not here, that innumerable atoms imply innumerable worlds (the gist of Epic. *Ep.* i. 45), and it is to be noted that Lucretius separates the two parts, arguing the first at great length in Book i. 951 seqq. and the second in Book ii. 1023 seqq. Grilli, therefore, in his commentary, noting that in fr. 25 II 8 the words τοῦδε τοῦ κόσμου mean simply 'our world', proposed a reversion to the arrangement of earlier editors (i.e. Us and HK) and placed this fragment in the Physics between frs. 5 and 6; it belongs there, he maintains, as part of the statement of Epicurean doctrine on the atoms; the innumerability of the worlds is not the point. He too quotes Epic. *Ep.* i. 42 and Lucr. i. 1014 seqq.

The attempt to enlist the support of earlier editors is rather misleading. Usener believed the letter to Antipater to be a general introduction to the Physics, HK made part of it (fr. 15) an introduction to the Ethics and placed fr. 16 at the beginning of the Physics; neither knew of a separate treatise on the innumerability of the

worlds. We are therefore left to make our deductions from the text itself and here it must be admitted that either view of this fragment is reasonable. However, I am inclined to agree with W that the word οὐδέ is important, if not decisive—not *even* this world would have arisen (still less all the others). I therefore leave it where W put it.

I. 11. G supports Usener's restoration of πεπερασμέναι by assuming that Cousin misread the stone, as indeed he often does. This can be shown many times over by a comparison of his transcript with that made by HK; there is a good example in the first line of fr. 37 where C's reading ΔΙΠΛΗ turns out to be a very obvious ΑΙΠΑΝ (= αἰτίαν). G thinks the same kind of mistake can be detected in l. 10 of this col.—cf. app. crit.

II. 2. ἀσυνέλευστοι—a word found elsewhere only in the works of Apollonius Dyscolus, the second-century grammarian.

3–9. Van Herwerden was the first to notice that these lines form a parenthesis.

13–14. Or, as Lucretius (ii. 547–50) puts it:

> quippe etenim sumam hoc quoque uti[1] finita per omne
> corpora iactari unius genitalia rei,
> unde ubi qua vi et quo pacto congressa coibunt
> materiae tanto in pelago turbaque aliena?

FRAGMENT 20 (58 cm., 59 cm., 40 cm.)

A stone containing one complete and undamaged column (II), one badly erased (I), and the first two or three letters on the left of the third.

It would seem that the theory of an infinite number of worlds is being defended against those (e.g. the Stoics) who accept an infinite empty space but only one universe and one earth. If they believe this, says Diogenes, do they think, as Xenophanes did, that the earth is limited in the upward direction but extends downwards to infinity? But then sun and stars could not go round the earth, both above and below it, as all lay and expert opinion believes they do.

I. The restorations are many, but in view of col. II seem justified.

9. τρανόω—an uncommon word, used by Philo and found, according to L.S.J., in the *Appendix nova epigrammatum* (*App. Anth.*). It, and the related ἀτράνωτος(?), occurs again in fr. 29.

[1] Munro's text: *sumant oculi* MSS.

10 ff. Xenophanes B 28 DK (KR 183) reads

γαίης μὲν τόδε πεῖρας ἄνω παρὰ ποσσὶν ὁρᾶται
ἠέρι προσπλάζον, τὸ κάτω δ' ἐς ἄπειρον ἱκνεῖται.

12. W considered that the name of Xenophanes occurred at the beginning of this line (cf. app. crit.) but Grilli doubts this since (a) the line would then be too long, and (b) Diogenes attacks the theory of Anaximenes at II 9 without actually naming him. The first argument may have some force since W supplies 13 letters and makes a total of 20 for the line; the normal length is 17–18. But as to the second there is no certainty that Diogenes is referring to Anaximenes at II. 9 seqq.

II. 5–8. This was not necessarily the Epicurean view. No one theory of the movements of the heavenly bodies was adopted to the exclusion of others. Lucretius v. 509–770 offers a variety of explanations for the movements of the stars, the succession of night and day, etc. It did not matter what view the Epicurean took of 'things up above' so long as it fitted the phenomena reasonably well—and did not assume supernatural agencies. Cf. Epic. *Ep.* ii. 95.

8. G thinks that the curved παραγραφή marks the transition from Xenophanes to Anaximenes (the other at III 8–9 would indicate the introduction of another theory). But this interpretation of the use of the curved παραγραφή seems to be quite unwarranted. There are only three instances of it in the whole inscription—here, 26 IV 11–12, and 29 II 1–2. At 26 IV 11–12 certainly, and almost certainly at 29 II 1–2, it marks the end of a participial phrase which has temporarily halted the flow of a fairly long sentence, and the resumption of that sentence. There is no reason to assume anything different here—the parenthesis beginning at l. 3 has ended and the sentence is resumed. This of course means that the people being addressed are still those who hold the theory of Xenophanes about the indefinite extension of the earth downwards in I 14–II 3.

I am now convinced that this is the case, and that the reference to Anaximenes at II 9 is a mistake. In A 7 (6) DK (= 159 KR) Hippolytus records of Anaximenes only that οὐ κινεῖσθαι δὲ ὑπὸ γῆν τὰ ἄστρα λέγει . . . ἀλλὰ περὶ γῆν, ὡσπερεὶ περὶ τὴν ἡμετέραν κεφαλὴν στρέφεται τὸ πιλίον.

Aristotle, *Meteor. B* i, 354ᵃ28 ff. (A 14 DK = 160 KR) ascribes the same belief about the sun to 'many of the old astronomers (ἀρχαίων μετεωρολόγων)'. Who these 'old astronomers' are, apart from Anaximenes, we can only guess, but we can be sure that they conceived of the sun and stars encircling the earth keeping the same, or about the same, distance from it the whole time; this is clear from Anaxi-

menes' simile of the cap going round the head. Diogenes, however, talks of taking the sun out of the universe to the side and bringing it back again. Some such idea *is* found in Xenophanes, as W has pointed out. He quotes A 41a DK (= 182 KR) from Aëtius, ὁ δ' αὐτὸς τὸν ἥλιον εἰς ἄπειρον μὲν προϊέναι, δοκεῖν δὲ κυκλεῖσθαι διὰ τὴν ἀπόστασιν.

It is true that this in its turn is not an exact parallel of Diogenes' statement. Whether we translate εἰς ἄπειρον as 'ad infinitum' with Kirk and Raven, or as 'indefinitely' with Guthrie, there remains the difficulty that Aëtius says nothing of bringing the sun back, that earlier in the same passage he says Xenophanes spoke of many suns and many moons, and that Hippolytus (A 33 (2) DK = 178 KR) says that the sun comes into being each day from little pieces of fire collecting together . . . and there are innumerable suns and moons. But perhaps these difficulties are more apparent than real. The sources are confused and unreliable and it is very probable that, as KR say, 'the plurality of suns and moons is simply due to their being renewed each day'. This would fit Diogenes quite well. The sun goes out to the side and is extinguished at night, is re-kindled and brought back next day.

It might be relevant to recall what W thought the argument behind this fragment might have been. Diogenes, he thinks, is here arguing against those who concede an unlimited number of atoms but not innumerable worlds. They must then, to use up the available atoms, assume an unlimited earth. This was the view of Xenophanes, but it means that the sun (and stars) cannot go round the earth but only past it. Would they perhaps prefer two earths (II 13–III 1)? But not even two earths of limited size would use up all the atoms. There must therefore be no limit to the number of worlds. This, he points out, is the argument more briefly put by Epicurus himself in the Letter to Herodotus (*Ep.* i. 45). Grilli, for his part, would refer the δύ[ο of III 2 to the Pythagorean earth and counter-earth, and assume a *fourth* theory beginning at the παραγραφή at ll. 8–9. As for this, see the beginning of this note (p. 64).

FRAGMENT 21 (12 cm., 19 cm., 14 cm.)

A small fragment found by HK. It is the top left-hand corner of a block with a margin at the top equal in height to two lines. As far as one can tell the lettering is the same as for the other fragments in this section. I follow G in placing it here.

FRAGMENT 22 (not found again by HK)

A fragment similar to the last, i.e. the tops of two columns. Cousin noted that it was 'vide en haut' from which G concluded that it had a wider margin than is found in the Physics.

c. *The Ethical Treatise*

This treatise (frs. 23–39) is the best-preserved part of the whole work, with 43 columns wholly or partly surviving out of a total of about 100. It most probably formed the major part of the lowest of the three great bands of writing (looking like unrolled papyri) which made up the inscription, and below it, as a continuous 15th line, ran a string of aphorisms in a slightly larger lettering. Most of these maxims are taken from the Principal Doctrines of Epicurus, the *Κύριαι Δόξαι*, and this is of the first importance since it enables us to estimate roughly the number of columns lost between fragments. This can be done by counting the number of letters missing from the P.D. (assuming that Diogenes used the text preserved by Diogenes Laertius, even though he did not write them in the same order) and dividing by 16 since that is the average number of letters standing below one column, plus margin.

William in his edition collected the maxims together in a group at the end of the treatise and Grilli follows his example, but it seemed to me preferable to reunite each maxim to the fragment beneath which it stood. They were inscribed on the same block and in some cases it can be argued that there is a sense-connection between column above and P.D. below.

Seventeen fragments in all survive from this treatise. After the title (23) Diogenes begins by insisting on the supreme importance of philosophy for happiness and promises to demonstrate this (24). In fr. 25 he refers to his public spirit in so doing and asks all his readers, native and foreign, to pay careful attention to his exposition. Fr. 26 must have belonged to the beginning of this exposition since it dwells on the doctrine that the *τέλος*, the whole point of life, is pleasure, *ἡδονή*, not virtues as the Stoics, Diogenes' principal opponents, maintain; virtues are only the means to the end, not the end itself. Fr. 27 begins with a reference to a Stoic mistake about feelings (by which, of course, we distinguish between pleasure and pain) but before going on with that Diogenes gives the Stoics a lesson in the *kinds* of causes, showing that a cause may be antecedent, simultaneous, or even posterior.

Fr. 28 seems to refer to the well-known Epicurean rule that not all pleasures are to be chosen nor all pains avoided; some pains are worth enduring for the sake of greater pleasure later. Then, in the middle of this fragment, he turns to the practical question of how to achieve a pleasant life, both in mental states and in activities. The first necessity is to remove the obstacles to happiness (*τὰ ὀχλοῦντα*)—fears (of the gods, of death, and of pain) and excessive desire, beginning with fear of the gods. This, with its attendant superstitions such as belief

in divination and destiny, takes up frs. 29 to 32. The attack on the
fear of death appears to have begun in fr. 33. This fear also has its
sub-divisions which must be combated, so fr. 34 rebuts the doctrine
of the transmigration of souls and frs. 35–7 deal with the more general
belief in the survival of the soul after death. It appears that in fr. 38
Diogenes is dealing with the fear of pain, though this is not certain,
and too little is left of 39 to say what it referred to.

This is all we have of the ethical treatise. The surviving portions
(and there are, of course, gaps between all the fragments) seem all
to belong to its beginning and middle. Nothing about the obstacles
caused by excessive desire, and nothing from the section on activities,
has been discovered.

FRAGMENT 23 (61 cm., 49 cm., 75 cm.)

This, the title to the ethical treatise, must have been inscribed, in
letters twice the normal size, across the centre of two blocks. We
possess only the left-hand block, discovered by HK. How much was
on the companion block is debatable. Grilli assumes that it held
about the same number of letters (7–8) and therefore adopts Diels's
reading for l. 1, William's for l. 2, favours ἐπιθυμιῶν for l. 3, and prints
ἠθική in l. 4. On the other hand, Mr. Woodhead assures me that the
article is not usually found between name and ethnic, and the simple
ἐπιτομή would be a better ending for the whole. It is to be noted that
whereas the first three lines begin the one exactly beneath the other
this fourth line is inset by two letters.

1. This can be restored with confidence to give us the name of
Diogenes' city.

2. Ph says that W's περὶ τέλους is impossible without a following
καί, but the line would then be much longer than all the others.
Diogenes does in fact begin with the τέλος, but he need not have
mentioned it in the title.

W, followed by G, prints Π as the last letter of this line (i.e. π[ερὶ
τέλους]) but although there is an erasure which might well have been
a Π, nothing was read by HK or can be made out now.

3. I have adopted W's reading but Ph's βίων could be right;
ἐπιτομή would then stand squarely under the centre of the line above
it, i.e. inset about two letters from either end.

FRAGMENT 24 (62 cm., 79·5 cm., 58 cm.)

A general introduction to the treatise; the author studies philosophy
not for material gain but to achieve happiness; he will show his

fellow citizens how to win it. The number of letters missing from the beginning of P.D. 1 which stands below shows that about two columns are lost before this fragment begins. They presumably contained some generalizations about philosophy. It is unfortunate that the right-hand half of col. III is also lost.

I. That the philosopher should not seek wealth or fame is an Epicurean commonplace summed up in the later saying λάθε βιώσας. From Epicurus himself we have, on wealth, P.D. 15 ὁ τῆς φύσεως πλοῦτος καὶ ὥρισται καὶ εὐπόριστός ἐστιν, and on fame, the condemnation in P.D. 7 of those who wished to become ἔνδοξοι καὶ περίβλεπτοι. Cf. also, on both, S.V. 81.

It would appear, however, that the Sage did allow for the occasional exception. The rather curious collection of aphorisms brought together by Diog. Laert. and inserted just before the Letter to Menoeceus at x. 121 (usually transposed to 120) contains the statement that the wise man χρηματίσεσθαι, ἀλλ' ἀπὸ μόνης σοφίας, ἀπορήσαντα. καὶ μόναρχον ἐν καιρῷ θεραπεύσειν. (Bailey translated ἀπὸ μόνης σοφίας as 'but only . . . by means of his philosophy'. Schmid (Hermes, 1938, 132) objected that this would reduce the wise man to the level of a sophist and suggested that it means 'but only in accordance with the principles of science', i.e. οἰκονομία, and this has been adopted by Arrighetti.) But this is not to be regarded as normal, and means no more than that the Epicurean, who will normally avoid money-making and fame, may on occasion have to frequent the market-place and the court if ἀταραξία can be found nowhere else. Too much rigidity is a mark of the Cynic, which is perhaps why in the same section (x. 120) we also find εὐδοξίας ἐπὶ τοσοῦτον προνοήσεσθαι ἐφ' ὅσον μὴ καταφρονήσεσθαι.

II. 1. Similar language is found in Polystratus Περὶ ἀλόγου καταφρονήσεως xxiii a 8 (Wilke) . . . διαγνῶναι τί ἡ φύσις ἡμῶν αὐτὴ ζητεῖ τέλος . . .

4–8. On the inability of wealth and political power to bring happiness cf. again S.V. 81, fr. 548 Us, and Horace, Odes ii. 16. 9 seqq.

8–14. Neither can bodily pleasures; the obvious parallel for this is Epic. Ep. iii. 132 οὐ γὰρ πότοι καὶ κῶμοι συννείροντες οὐδ' ἀπολαύσεις παίδων καὶ γυναικῶν οὐδ' ἰχθύων καὶ τῶν ἄλλων ὅσα φέρει πολυτελὴς τράπεζα τὸν ἡδὺν γεννᾷ βίον . . .

III. As W says, we are helped in completing this column by the straight παραγραφαί which indicate that a clause or sentence ends in

the line above, by the spaces after μεν, μεθα, and θα, and by the curved παραγραφή which, as we have seen above (cf. on 20 II), marks the end of a parenthesis.

There are no serious differences of opinion about the restoration of ll. 1–7 but 8–12 have caused considerable disagreement. The text as printed, and translated, is William's but it now seems to me to have several weaknesses. These are the unconvincing nature of l. 12 and the shortness of l. 9 which has only 12 letters as against the usual 15–16. (II 13 has only 12 but there is a gap in the line there.)

Grilli and Barigazzi have also tried their hands at these lines. G's proposal is noted in the critical apparatus and is amplified in *La Parola del Passato* xv (1960), 137–8, but the objections to this are:

(a) The 5th letter in l. 9 is given as O in D and as C (after damage to the edge of the stone) in F; it does not look like Є.

(b) The introduction of two indicative verbs of similar appearance in ll. 8 and 12 is rather awkward; incidentally Grilli translates καταστρεψάμεθα as 'portai a termine'.

Barigazzi's proposal (made in *P.P.* xvi (1961), 216–17) was unfortunately omitted from the app. crit.; it is as follows:

8   κ[ατεσκευασά-]
        μεθα ἐ[ν ἑτοίμω οὗ-]
10   σαν ὑμε[ῖν ἐν τῇ προ-]
        σόδω τρ[ύτου δὴ τοῦ ἔρ-]
        γου κατ' [ὄψιν ἐνταῦ-]
        ‾‾‾‾‾‾
        θα.

He translates 9–13 as follows, 'a vostra disposizione nell'entrata di questo edificio qui sotto gli occhi'. It is possible that this part of the treatise stood at the entrance to the stoa, though it is not very likely, but the phrase κατ' ὄψιν is said by L.S.J. to mean 'in person' in P. Oxy. 1154. 4 and elsewhere, while κατόψιον and κατ' ὄμμα to which Barigazzi refers are entirely poetic.

I would tentatively propose the following to take account of these difficulties:

        κ[ατεσκευασά-]
        μεθα ὅ[πως παροῦ-]
10   σαν ὑμε[ῖν ἐν τῃ προ-]
        σόδω τ' ο[ὗσαν τοῦ λό-]
        γου κατ[αλειπώμε-]
        ‾‾‾‾‾‾
        θα.

9 supplevi   10 suppl. Barigazzi   11 suppl. W   12 supplevi

which I would translate, 'We have prepared (this treatise) . . . that we may leave it ready to your hand, standing at the beginning of the work . . .'

1. G refers to Epic. *Ep.* iii. 122 παρούσης μὲν αὐτῆς [i.e. philosophy] πάντα ἔχομεν, and *Ethica Epicurea* (Pap. Herc. 1251), col. XIII. 6–7 δι' ἧς μόνης [philosophy] ἔστιν ὀρθοπραγεῖν.

13–14. W's restoration looks forward to III 6 of the next fragment.

The amount missing from the end of P.D. 1 and the beginning of P.D. 2 shows that four columns are lost between frags. 24 and 25.

P.D. 1 refers to the nature of the Epicurean gods.

FRAGMENT 25 (65 cm., 79 cm., 50 cm.)

A complete block, with a few erasures: the beginnings of the lines in col. I and the ends in col. III were inscribed on the blocks to left and right.

I. Numerous attempts have been made to restore this column, in particular l. 2; Grilli has considered it in his commentary (p. 401), in *P.P.* xv (1960), 144–5, and in his edition (p. 65). In general his remarks are sound but he makes two strange slips. In *P.P.*, p. 144 n. 27 he gives W's reading as παρα|[στήσο]νται, which he says is clearly a mistake for the πα|ραστήσονται of the stone; but W prints πα|[ραστήσο]νται. Then in the critical apparatus to his edition he records this reading correctly, rightly saying that it is too long, but ascribes it to Philippson who in fact proposed the restoration I have adopted, i.e. πα|[ρήσο]νται.

5. Diogenes refers to his age in 2 II 7 and to the bad state of his health in fr. 50.

10–12. Usener and William attempted to complete these lines but their restorations are very conjectural. In particular the first extant letter of l. 11 is much more likely to be Τ than Π.

II. 3–11. The common citizenship of mankind is a Stoic commonplace which had evidently been adopted by Epicureans before the time of Diogenes. Cf. Musonius p. 42. 1 ed. Hense τί δ' οὐχὶ κοινὴ πατρὶς ἀνθρώπων ἁπάντων ὁ κόσμος ἐστὶν ὥσπερ ἠξίου Σωκράτης; where the editor cites Cic. *Tusc.* v. 37. 108; Plutarch, *De exil.* 600; Epictetus, *Diss.* i. 9. 1, and Seneca, *Dial.* vii. 20. 5, ix. 4. 4 and *Ep.* 28. 4. W adds Cic. *De divinatione* i. 57. 131 'cum domus sit omnium una eaque communis'. There is also Zeno, *S.V.F.* i. 262 (= Plut. *De Alexandri virtute* 1. 6. 329 a), and Marcus Aurelius vi. 44 πόλις καὶ πατρίς, ὡς μὲν Ἀντονίνῳ μοι ἡ Ῥώμη, ὡς δὲ ἀνθρώπῳ ὁ κόσμος.

The sophist Hippias seems to have taught something very similar in the 5th century B.C. Cf. Plato, *Protagoras* 337 c–d μετὰ δὲ τὸν Πρόδικον Ἱππίας ὁ σοφὸς εἶπεν, Ὦ ἄνδρες, ἔφη, οἱ παρόντες, ἡγοῦμαι ἐγὼ ὑμᾶς συγγενεῖς τε καὶ οἰκείους καὶ πολίτας ἅπαντας εἶναι φύσει, οὐ νόμῳ.

It is true that there is nothing in the Epicurean doctrine to contradict this belief, but no Epicurean is known to have stated it explicitly before Diogenes.

12. W quotes two scholiasts on Aristotle for συναρπάζω (with ἀκροατής) in the sense of 'captivate', 'win over'. L.S.J. mentions also Euripides, *I.A.*, Callimachus, Longinus, and Galen.

III. About four letters are missing from the end of each line; there are also erasures of about three letters in ll. 1–5. As a rule all restorations have tended to be too long.

G has a long note on this column also in *P.P.*, loc. cit.; he may be right when he maintains that the absence of a παραγραφή is against W's parenthesis in ll. 2–3, but his own restoration is not very convincing either. I doubt the parenthesis myself but print W's text for want of a better. The meaning of the column is fairly clear; Diogenes is asking his readers to read the inscription carefully and in proper order, not carelessly and in a hurry.

1. W cannot believe that λέγουσιν is right since, he says, Diogenes is concerned with the truth of what he himself says, not others. But the remains of the letters strongly suggest λέγουσιν and it is easy to suppose, with G, that *they* are the Epicureans.

4–5. The reading adopted means much the same as W's but is a little shorter; it is unlikely that more than eight letters are missing.

10. This line is curious. Not only are the Κ and C recut (cf. critical note) but the letters are as widely spaced as in I 1, so that whereas l. 9 contains eleven letters, and l. 11 thirteen, this one has only eight. We should not therefore supply more than five letters and even this may be too many.

10–11. Grilli objects to ἐφιστάναι+dat. in the sense of 'pay attention to' for two reasons; this use of the verb, he says (*P.P.*, p. 147), is only to be found in the aorist ἐπιστῆσαι, and secondly he considers it a contradiction in terms to speak of 'paying attention like a passer-by (who clearly pays none)'.

His second objection may be a perfectly logical one, but Diogenes is writing as an average man, not a logician, and his turn of phrase is surely entirely natural. As to the actual language, it is true that the present ἐφιστάναι is not actually found elsewhere, but it gives the

meaning we want and it seems not unreasonable to regard this as another of Diogenes' *hapax legomena*.

Grilli considers HK's ἐφεστάναι better, but the objection here is that especially in compounds Diogenes always uses the full form ἑστηκέναι for the perfect; and ἐφεστάναι+dat. in this sense is equally unknown; in the end he feels he can justify the use of ἑστάναι so long as it is part of a set phrase, such as ἑστάναι+adverb, commonly found in Polybius and Plutarch. This means, of course, that he must take ἑστάναι and ποικίλως together and place a comma after the adverb, which, he says, has the sense of *inconstanter* (e.g. Polybius iv. 30. 7).

I do not know whether he still holds to this opinion (his edition has the same text as the *P.P.* article but without any commas in l. 12), but it can only be described as rather perverse; one is reminded of Socrates' 'sophistic' interpretation of the ode of Simonides in Plato's *Protagoras*.

P.D. 2 is inscribed beneath this fragment; it would seem likely that it began exactly level with col. I.

FRAGMENT 26 (61 cm., 43 cm., 23 cm.+60 cm., 87 cm., 50 cm.)

This fragment is inscribed on two blocks found a long way apart and reunited by Cousin. The first (HK 66) contains col. I and the first 3–4 letters of col. II, the other (HK 67) the remainder of col. II with cols. III and IV. There is damage to both blocks affecting col. II.

The five or six columns lost before this fragment begins seem to have contained an attack on the Stoics for ill-natured and stupid criticism of the Epicurean doctrine on pleasure—possibly, thinks Philippson, that pleasure-seeking is a mark of animals and fools. Diogenes re-asserts that pleasure *is* the end, and virtue only a means to it.

I. 6. He addresses his readers, especially his fellow citizens.

7. τούτων—the Stoics.

11. The Stoic doctrine was that virtues are both means and ends; they are means in so far as they bring happiness, ends in so far as they complete it and form part of it. Cf. D.L. vii. 97 ποιητικὰ δὲ καὶ τελικὰ εἶναι ἀγαθὰ ⟨τὰς ἀρετάς⟩.

II. 9. Cf. Epic. *Ep.* iii. 128 τὴν ἡδονὴν ἀρχὴν καὶ τέλος λέγομεν εἶναι τοῦ μακαρίως ζῆν. Cicero puts the doctrine into Latin in *De fin.* i. 9. 29 and ii. 15. 49.

13. Fr. 200 Us reads ἀφυσιολόγητον μηδὲν ἡγοῦ βοώσης τῆς σαρκὸς βοᾶν τὴν ψυχήν; cf. also fr. 67 Us Ἐπίκουρος λέγει . . . μεγάλῃ τῇ φωνῇ. Cicero *De fin.* i. 18. 57 also has 'clamat Epicurus . . .'.

II. 14–III. 1. Diano, in a long note in *Epicuri Ethica*, p. 110, points out that in the phrase used by Epicurus in *Ep.* iii. 128 quoted above the word τέλος cannot mean 'end' or 'purpose' because τὸ μακαρίως ζῆν is the purpose; τέλος therefore must mean 'extreme point', or 'fullest realization'. (Bailey, who translated it as 'end', explained that it is the end [of the blessed life] because its attainment is the completion of action.) Arrighetti accepts Diano's interpretation, translating τέλος as *termine extremo*, and Grilli considers that the phrase here τῆς ἀρίστης διαγωγῆς τέλος is of the same kind, with τέλος bearing the same meaning (*fine supremo*). One can admit the truth of these observations without feeling that they are particularly surprising, or that they differ very much from Bailey. All that they would seem to amount to is that in these cases the word τέλος is not used in the rather special philosophic sense of the 'end of action' (Aristotle's final cause), but in its more normal sense of 'completion' or 'consummation', a use which goes back to Homer, where τέλος θανάτου, for instance, and τέλος γάμοιο are little more than periphrases for θάνατος and γάμος.

III. 6. Fr. 504 Us = D.L. x. 138, where we read διὰ δὲ τὴν ἡδονὴν καὶ τὰς ἀρετὰς αἱρεῖσθαι, οὐ δι' αὐτάς.

IV. No other Epicurean text explicitly states that the virtues help only man. The passages quoted by W (P.D. 31–3, 36 and Hermarchus *ap.* Porphyry, *De abstinentia* i. 10. 12) are all concerned with justice, which, they say, cannot arise among beasts because they are unable to enter into a social contract. What can be said of one virtue, says W, can be said of all.

G quotes a Stoic source (*S.V.F.* iii. 372): τῶν ὄντων τὰ μὲν οὔτε ἀρετῆς οὔτε κακίας μετέχει, ὥσπερ φυτὰ καὶ ζῷα ἄλογα . . .

But the idea, like many Epicurean ideas, is to be found in the *Ethics* of Aristotle.

10. i.e. the nature of man.

12. ταύτης = again, the nature of man.

William considers that the argument went on thus: it has been shown that the virtues are of use only to men. This must be because they guarantee the observance of a social contract by which men achieve security. But security is only a condition, although an important one, for the attainment of the supreme good.

G's proposed continuation is based on fr. 504 Us, quoted above at III 6.

The middle portion of the 15th line below this fr. is missing but it is clear that P.D. 6 ends and P.D. 8 begins in it. P.D. 7 is therefore

omitted and P.D. 3, 4, and 5 come later. Diogenes is using a different arrangement from that found in D.L.

A great deal is missing before the next fragment (27) begins. Assuming, as we must, that Diogenes used more or less the same text for the Principal Doctrines as his namesake and contemporary we have lost 80 letters from P.D. 8, which breaks off beneath the middle of 26 IV. If fr. 27 is correctly placed next, then P.D. 10 follows, as part of it is inscribed below that fragment. This part begins at]θεν ἐκπληρ[ο]υμέν[οι]ς. In fact not all the earlier part of P.D. 10 is lost, as can be seen from the text, but the words from τῶ]ν ἀλγηδόνων to εἴχομεν were recorded by Cousin as the sole surviving text on a stone from which all trace of the three columns above had been erased. As regards the ethical treatise, then, we can deduce that at least 16 columns are missing between frs. 26 and 27—ample room in which to develop the proof that virtues are not the τέλος but only productive of it. Philippson suggests that the writer may also have touched on Stoic ἀφροσύνη, as he promised to do in 26 I 3, possibly in connection with a discussion of the other indispensable aid to happiness, φρόνησις.

FRAGMENT 27 (58 cm., 48 cm., (no depth): 61 cm., 80 cm., 30 cm.)

This fragment, like the previous one, is made up of two stones (HK nos. 69 and 70). The former, which was discovered by HK, contains the last 12 letters of each line of col. I and 12 letters or less from the lines of col. II, but there are breaks and erasures, especially in col. II. HK 70 has the heavily damaged remainder of col. II, col. III (also damaged), and col. IV almost complete.

We cannot identify the mistake about feeling of which Diogenes accuses his opponents—no doubt the Stoics—in col. I. But the remainder of the passage is aimed at the Stoic doctrine that virtue itself is happiness. A virtuous condition may indeed coincide with happiness —indeed it does, as Epicurus himself asserts in Ep. iii. 132 συμπεφύκασι γὰρ αἱ ἀρεταὶ τῷ ζῆν ἡδέως καὶ τὸ ζῆν ἡδέως τούτων ἐστὶν ἀχώριστον . . . —but this means only that virtue is a simultaneous cause of happiness, not that it is happiness.

The division of causes into three classes, anterior, simultaneous, and posterior, is not found in Epicurus but had been developed by the first century B.C. According to Philippson Epicureans of the school of Zeno of Sidon, whom Cicero heard lecture in Athens in 79–78, distinguished three corresponding kinds of σημεῖα, i.e. 'signs' from which causes can be inferred. Zeno is very probably the source for such references as Philodemus Περὶ σημείων 36. 18 τῶν τ[ε] προηγου[μέν]ων σημείω[ν, τ]ῶν τ᾽ ἀ[κολου]θικῶν, κ[αὶ] τῶν[ν ὁ]μειδῶν[ν] (on which cf. Ph's article in Rh. Mus. lxiv (1909), 36).

Sextus Empiricus argues against this doctrine of cause in *Pyrr. hyp.*
iii. 13–29, and *Adv. dog.* iii (= Against the Physicists i). 232–6. In
both he attacks the three kinds of cause, and in *Pyrr. hyp.* iii. 26 may
be using the arguments of another first-century B.C. philosopher,
Aenesidemus. This passage begins: ὅθεν κἀκεῖνο λέγουσί τινες. τὸ
αἴτιον ἤτοι συνυφίστασθαι δεῖ τῷ ἀποτελέσματι ἢ προϋφίστασθαι τούτου
ἢ μετ᾽ αὐτὸ γίγνεσθαι. The people referred to are no doubt Epicureans.

Ph points out that only Diogenes uses the distinction in an ethical
context.

I. This block begins at about the 5th letter of the line; in addition
there is a portion missing which is at its widest at l. 10. However,
most restorations are fairly certain.

5. HK's ταῦτα is preferable to μεικρὸν and πολλῶν as being shorter;
there is also part of A, or Λ, visible before **AYTOY**.

8. G's ἀντιλέγειν is much too long.

II. It would seem that there were 11–12 letters of each line of this
column on HK 69, 4 on HK 70, and therefore 2 in between. Unfortunately most of the letters on HK 70 are erased and where they are
not the transcripts of Cousin and HK often conflict. Restoration is
therefore difficult and uncertain.

5–6. Grilli devotes part of his article in *P.P.* xv (1960), 148–50, to this
passage. He objects to HK's στενάζειν, which W accepted, and argues
that the example is medical. Referring to Hipp. *Art.* 62 and Plato,
Protag. 354 a he shows that cautery and surgery are stock instances
of pain which is worth while because it brings health later. This must
be correct. σ[ώζεσθαι] is a little long but there could be room for it.
The **ONC** which Cousin recorded for the last three letters of this line
are completely baffling, but many of his readings in the next col.
also are impossible, as we shall see.

10. HK did not pretend to read anything for certain after the **THN**,
but there is a faint **IC**. They themselves proposed **φω**, i.e. φω[νῆν],
G favours **Pω**, i.e. ῥώμην, but it seems to me that ἰσχύν, in the sense of
'bodily strength', is nearer to the original.

12. G's insertion of the article will make the line too long.

II. 14–III. 1. G²'s restoration is possible for II 14 but too long
for III 1; not more than six letters can be missing, including the
letter before **OY**. So little of this is left that it is impossible to be sure
that it is **I**.

III. This column is very badly damaged. The note in G's edition reads, 'v. 2, 4, 5 quae e D erui possunt supplementa ab Austriacis prolata confirmunt. Paragraphos sub. v. 1 et 3 posui, quod earum vestigia in D inspexi.' The actual reading of D, i.e. Cousin, for the first six lines of this column is

ΓΟΥΟΝΕϹΘΙΟ
ΤΑΙϹΥΔΤΟΝΕΑΙΤΕΘΗ
ΑΕΓΑΟΝϹΥΛΕΠΙΤΙΕΜΕΝ
ΤΟΥϹΝΗΑΓΑΘΗΔΟΜΑ
5   ΑΡΝΗΘΕϹΟΥΑΙΝΟΜΕΝ
ΟΔΗΤΟΙΤΟΝΚΑΙΓΑΘΟ

It is difficult indeed to dig very much out of that; Cousin himself does not attempt to transcribe it. But G's reference to *paragraphos* is puzzling. They are never recorded by Cousin (and HK have no signs of any here). It may be that G is referring to the tops of the Ts in ll. 2 and 4.

IV. 4. W finds similar language in Plutarch, *De curiositate* 520 e ἐμνήσθη ὁ δεῖνα τοῦ δεῖνος ἐπ᾽ ἀγαθῷ, and Polybius ii. 61. 6 τὸ δ᾽ ἀκόλουθον καὶ τὸ τῆς ἱστορίας ἴδιον ἀφεῖλεν τὸν ἔπαινον καὶ τὴν ἐπ᾽ ἀγαθῷ μνήμην τῶν ἀξιολόγων προαιρέσεων.

That a good reputation after death is a good thing is an idea common in Greek literature from the time of Homer, but not one that features much in philosophic writings. Aristotle *might* have included it among the 'external goods' necessary for happiness (*Nic. eth.* 1099ᵃ51 seqq.) but did not, although he considers that the happiness of the dead can be affected by the misfortune and misdeeds of the living (*Nic. eth.* 1101ᵃ22 seqq.).

Grilli has found two references to the subject—Seneca, *Ep.* 102. 3 'Probare conabar id quod nostris placet, claritatem quae post mortem contingit, bonum esse'; and Sextus Empiricus, *Adv. dog.* v (= Against the Ethicists). 107 καὶ γὰρ εἰ τελευτῶσι (i.e. those who die for their country) καὶ τοῦ ζῆν μεθίστανται, ἀλλά τοί γε ὅτε ζῶσιν ἥδονται καὶ γήθονται πρὸς τοὺς ἐπαίνους.

This may be another case of Stoic influence or, more likely, merely an obvious example of what Diogenes regards as a posterior cause, but surely it is the present anticipation of future good reputation which causes pleasure, not the good reputation which ensues later.

9–14. Cf. Epic. *Ep.* iii. 132—quoted above. Similarly S.V. 27 ἐπὶ δὲ φιλοσοφίας συντρέχει τῇ γνώσει τὸ τερπνόν.

P.D. 10. I cannot understand G's note to l. 6. He objects to W's restoration of these lines between τῶ[ν ἡδονῶν and τὸ ἀλγο[ῦν as being

too short to occupy the width of 1⅔ columns, but his own suggestion for the gap [καὶ οὐδαμόθεν οὔτε] is actually shorter—16 letters as against 23 (which is about right).

FRAGMENT 28

This fragment consists of what is left of three blocks: HK 62 (59 cm., 49 cm., 75 cm.), HK 82 (62 cm., 55 cm., 60 cm.), and HK 63 (62 cm., 58 cm., 34 cm.). The last of these is itself in two parts. There can be no real doubt that these do in fact form one whole. The 15th line below HK 62, which contains cols. I, II, and III, belongs to P.D. 3; the last few words of the same maxim appear below HK 63, i.e. cols. VI and VII. There are 47 letters missing from the centre, which is the equivalent of 3 columns. One of these must be the rest of col. III of which only the first two or three letters were engraved on HK 62. The other two are almost certainly those found on HK 82, first inserted here by W to make cols. IV and V. This block is badly damaged and the 15th line is completely missing, but it can be confidently placed here from considerations of context. Cols. I and II are concerned with the great advantage of having a rational understanding of the principles of choice and avoidance of pleasures and pains. In the centre section col. IV refers to the advantages, sometimes delayed, of τὸ πονεῖν. This stage of the discussion ends at V 9 with, most probably, a reassertion of the doctrine that pleasure is the 'summum bonum'. The last two columns proceed to discuss the application of this principle—how, in fact, if this is so, are we actually to achieve a life of happiness.

I. 14–II. 1. Fr. 68 Us (= Plutarch, *Non posse suaviter* 1089 d) asserts the value of πιστὸν ἔλπισμα to the wise. Cf. also S.V. 33 Σαρκὸς φωνὴ τὸ μὴ πεινῆν, τὸ μὴ διψῆν, τὸ μὴ ῥιγοῦν. ταῦτα γὰρ ἔχων τις καὶ ἐλπίζων ἕξειν, κἂν ⟨Διὶ⟩ ὑπὲρ εὐδαιμονίας μαχέσαιτο.

ἐκλογή is not found in Epicurus, but fr. 515 Us has the sentence (ἡ ἀρετὴ) περὶ τὴν ἐκλογήν ἐστι τῶν ἡδέων κατ᾿ Ἐπίκουρον.

4. HK would prefer to omit the commas in this line (cf. app. crit.) so as to account better for the position of οὖν; the sense is not greatly affected.

6 seqq. This charge of distortion is almost certainly, as usual, aimed at the Stoics, cf. Galen, *Hipp. et Plat.*, p. 273 K, 237. 3 Müller, which reads τῶν σοφιστικῶν ⟨λημμάτων⟩, ἅπερ ἐν ὁμωνυμίαις τέ τισι καὶ τοῖς τῆς λέξεως σχήμασι μάλιστα συνίσταται.

Diogenes may be attacking the Stoic use of such arguments, thinks W, either to prove that virtue is the *summum bonum* or, more likely,

to show that Epicurus maintained that the pleasures of the profligate are the *summum bonum*. This is a much more convincing explanation. Epicurus rejects the suggestion at *Ep.* iii. 131 : ὅταν οὖν λέγωμεν ἡδονὴν τέλος ὑπάρχειν, οὐ τὰς τῶν ἀσώτων ἡδονὰς καὶ τὰς ἐν ἀπολαύσει κειμένας λέγομεν, as certain people who misunderstand or disagree maintain. But it is clear that this charge was commonly used as a stick with which to beat the Epicureans.

10. προπηλακιστής is not found elsewhere.

IV. If this column is correctly restored it is making a similar point to Epic. *Ep.* iii. 129: sometimes we pass over a pleasure because it brings greater pain, sometimes we choose pain because after we have endured it for a long time we get greater pleasure. The same idea is to be found in fr. 442 Us (Arrighetti 166). Diogenes introduces a slight variation; pain suffered does not bring pleasure always at the same time, sometimes the result is sooner, sometimes later.

6. The last letter looks more like N than Π, and there is no sign of, or room for, I.

7. Both the restoration adopted and W's are rather long; only about seven letters are missing at the beginning of the line. It is true that the addition to l. 8 is equally long but one more letter is missing there. I would like to read ἐν|[φανείσας], but it seems impossible grammatically.

14. W's restoration, adopted by G, is again too long. The first surviving letter could be Γ; hence my proposal.

V. Little enough is left of this column but many attempts have been made to fill the gaps. W began with ll. 4–6, Grilli attempted to complete 1–7 *exempli gratia*, l. 8, l. 11, and part of l. 12. Barigazzi also, in *P.P. xvi* (1961), 217–19, made an attempt which should be added to the critical apparatus.

His proposal is:

$$[\tau\grave{\eta}\nu \ o\mathring{\upsilon}\nu]$$
$$\dot{\epsilon}\gamma[\lambda o\gamma\grave{\eta}\nu \ \tau a\acute{\upsilon}\tau\eta\nu \ \tau\tilde{\omega}\nu]$$
5 $$\ \dot{\eta}\delta\acute{\epsilon}\omega\nu \ \kappa a\grave{\iota} \ \delta[\upsilon\sigma\chi\epsilon\text{-}]$$
$$\rho\tilde{\omega}\nu \ [\pi]o[\iota o\acute{\upsilon}\mu\epsilon]\nu o\iota \ [\epsilon\mathring{\upsilon}\text{-}]$$
$$\tau\epsilon\lambda\tilde{\eta} \ [\pi\acute{a}\nu\upsilon \ \kappa a\grave{\iota}] \ o\mathring{\iota}\kappa[\epsilon\acute{\iota}a\nu]$$
$$\dot{a}\nu\theta\rho\acute{\omega}\pi\omega \ [\gamma\epsilon]\nu[\nu\tilde{\omega}\mu\epsilon\nu \ \dot{\eta}\delta o\text{-}]$$
$$\nu\acute{\eta}\nu.$$
10 $$\ \kappa a\grave{\iota} \ \tau\grave{a} \ \mu\grave{\epsilon}\nu \ o\mathring{\upsilon}\nu \ \pi[\epsilon\rho\grave{\iota}]$$

[τῆς ἀφροσύνης]
ἐρῶ· ἐν [μ]ὲν γὰ[ρ ἔσ-]
τι ν[ῦν] εἰδέν[αι σαφῶς]

As for the first paragraph of this column, G's Δ in l. 5 is invisible to me, and the line will be very short if only four letters are to be supplied. In l. 6 ποιησάμενοι is too long; there is space for five letters at most. Barigazzi has come to the same conclusion, i.e. the present participle, as myself. In l. 8 the first letters look much more like ΑΝΟΡΘ than ΑΝΘΡω, and I can see no sign of the Πω which G adds.

The rest of the column would seem to be a transitional passage until a new topic begins at VI 2. Barigazzi, on the other hand, thinks that Diogenes now turns to the promised discussion of ἀφροσύνη, and that this is developed in the remainder of the fragment. He translates this last part of col. V as follows:

'Dirò dunque anche della stoltezza, perché ora una sola cosa è possibile sapere sicuramente, che la stoltezza (τὸ ἄφρον—VI 1) è l'unico impedimento alla felicità . . .'

Unfortunately there is so little to support any restoration that this must remain a guess. But it would certainly appear that a new topic begins at VI 2.

10. The final Π claimed by G is invisible to me.

VI. 4–5. The use of καταστήματα here has caused difficulty because of Epicurus' division of pleasures into ἡδοναὶ καταστηματικαί and those κατὰ κίνησιν (cf. frs. 1 and 2 Us). This led W (pp. 91–2) to think that Diogenes has misunderstood the meaning of ἡδονὴ καταστηματική. But it seems clear that he is merely using the word κατάστημα in a non-technical sense, meaning settled condition or state (here of the mind) as opposed to activity of the body (πράξις). κατάστημα can be applied to body also if needed, as in fr. 68 Us τὸ γὰρ εὐσταθὲς σαρκὸς κατάστημα. A pleasant life can be obtained mentally by banishing fear and in action by following the rules of virtue and restraint. G takes the word in a similar sense but reads rather too much into it by his translation 'nelle condizioni di stabile tranquillità'.

9–13. The standard Epicurean doctrine that the absence of pain and worry is itself a pleasurable condition. Cf. Cic. De fin. i. 11. 37 'In omni re doloris amotio successionem efficit voluptatis', and 38 'Omnis enim privatione doloris putat Epicurus terminari summam voluptatem, ut postea variari voluptas distinguique possit, augeri amplificarique non possit'. P.D. 3 below has the same message.

12. ἥδοντα—a use of the active instead of the deponent found in Hellenistic and later Greek.

13. In the sense 'enter in place of' this verb is found nowhere else.

VII. What is left of this column (the last 4–5 letters of each line are missing) is inscribed on two pieces of stone which were first correctly fitted together by HK.

That the main obstacle to tranquillity of mind is fear of the gods, of death, and of pain is another basic Epicurean doctrine. Against it they devised the 'fourfold remedy' found in Philodemus, Πρὸς τοὺς [σοφιστάς] (Pap. Herc. 1005, col. IV 10, p. 87 Shordone) ἄφοβον ὁ θεός, ἀνύποπτον ὁ θάνατος, καὶ τἀγαθὸν μὲν εὔκτητον, τὸ δὲ δεινὸν εὐεκκαρτέρητον.

These fears, plus immoderate desire, must be removed by the study of nature, as witness P.D. 10, 11, and 12. A similar enumeration of impediments to happiness is found in Cicero, De fin. i. 18. 59. They are reduced to two in Porphyry, Ad Marcellam 29. 293. 4 N² (fr. 485 Us) ἢ γὰρ διὰ φόβον τις κακοδαιμονεῖ ἢ δι' ἀόριστον καὶ κενὴν ἐπιθυμίαν.

5. The plural ἐπιθυμίαι read by HK and G, but not W, would perhaps be a more normal Epicurean use but the text does not support it. First, it is true that IT can sometimes look very like Π, but this is a very clear Π. It is also possible that at the end of the line is a faint I after the O. Secondly, in l. 7 the join in the stones comes after XOYCA with room for only one letter before AI, but the mark in F can only be part of K, not I. In fact fr. 485 Us quoted above uses the singular.

11–12. ὑπεκφύσεται, HK and G, is attractive but is not supported elsewhere.

12. The first harmful emotion to be dealt with is fear of the gods. It is therefore the subject of the first Principal Doctrine, and the first topic of the Epistle to Menoeceus (Ep. iii. 123). Cf. also Lucr. i. 62 seqq.

The text of P.D. 3 below this fragment is more than usually different from the version given in D.L.—hence Usener's conjecture for the second sentence.

FRAGMENT 29 (61 cm., 32 cm., 56 cm.)

This fragment consists of a narrow block containing 2–3 letters from the right of col. I and 12–13 from the left of col. II. Below, in the 15th line, are a few letters from the beginning of P.D. 13.

W placed it where he did mainly from considering this 15th line (cf. his p. xiv); he thought that another block of about the same width was missing before this, a block containing the rest of 28 VII

V. The 'flagged area' (see p. xxxiv).

VI. A pedestal on the site; for the text see Dittenberger, *O.G.I.S.* ii, no. 565 (see p. xxxiv).

and col. I of this fragment with, below, the end of P.D. 3, a small gap, and then the beginning of P.D. 13.

G¹ disagrees with this arrangement and places this fragment after fr. 32 on the ground that the distinction of two kinds of fear applies to fear of death, not of gods; he claims (p. 408) that ll. 8–10 prove this. But these lines only cite an example of a fear which is understood; ll. 11–13 can equally well refer to gods. He further says that though Ph kept W's order he referred all frs. 29–35 to fear of death. If G means Ph's article in *R.E.*, as is usual, I cannot understand him; there Ph says that this fragment seems to explain that the fear of gods belongs to the class of fears which arise from an unclear understanding, and frs. 30–2 are linked to false belief about the gods.

If, then, there is nothing decisive in the text the question of the 15th line becomes important. Now P.D. 3 has almost ended with fr. 28; 30 and 31 are too damaged to have anything of a 15th line left; under 32 I begins a new, previously unknown, maxim. If, therefore, 29 follows 32 we must assume *either* (*a*) that 30–1, which may well form only one column as G² thinks, *and nothing else* stood between 28 and 32; below them stood the last 10 letters of P.D. 3, perhaps a small gap, and then the beginning of the new maxim. In this case the fear of gods itself would never be discussed, merely the superstitions derived from it; *or* (*b*) that there were enough columns on either side of 30–1 to accommodate the end of P.D. 3 and another complete maxim which is entirely lost. This is in fact G's assumption. The objection to this is that it implies a gap of indeterminate and probably considerable length.

But if we leave 29 where W put it we can assume that P.D. 3 ended and P.D. 13 began under col. I, and that after col. II we have lost about 6 columns which once stood over the rest of P.D. 13. One of these columns might well be 30–1. The discussion of fear of the gods would have come here, and it is noticeable that P.D. 13 refers to the feeling of uncertainty about unknown powers above and beneath the earth. I therefore retain W's order.

II. 3. τρανόω (make clear, distinct) is used, according to W, by Philo, Nicomachus, Origen, Gregory Nazianzen, and Eustathius.

10. Epicurus makes the point, in *Ep.* i. 81, that two principal causes of unhappiness are (*a*) the belief that the heavenly bodies are divine and (*b*) the belief or suspicion that some everlasting misery will befall. Lucretius deals with the fear inspired by natural phenomena at i. 151 seqq. and with other kinds of baseless fear at ii. 55 seqq.

13. ὑποφωτίζειν, if correct (it is accepted by L.S.J.), is another of Diogenes' *hapax legomena*.

FRAGMENTS 30 (32 cm., 21 cm., 2 cm.) and 31 (not found by HK)

These two fragments were found together by Cousin; his comments are: 30—'complet en haut et à gauche, vide à droite, fin d'une colonne'; 31—'complet en haut; vide à droite; fin d'une colonne'.

Usener thought they belonged to the *left*-hand edge of a column or columns (though this raised difficulties in connection with the unusual division of words) but HK's re-examination of 30 showed that it was in fact the *right*-hand portion. G thinks that they are both part of the same column, and that 31 is what is left of ll. 1–3 of 30. But without a drawing of the stone (HK did not find 31) no certainty is possible.

We may take it that Diogenes has already dealt with fear of the gods in itself and is now considering related topics. Now a superstitious belief in the gods usually implies a belief in fate and its adjunct, divination. This was widespread in his time and actively supported by the Stoics; the Epicureans were renowned for their opposition to it. Any discussion of the fear of the gods would naturally include this subject.

Divination was attacked by Epicurus, as is recorded by D.L. at x. 135: μαντικὴν δ' ἅπασαν ἐν ἄλλοις ἀναιρεῖ, ὡς καὶ ἐν τῇ μικρᾷ ἐπιτομῇ; and the numerous references, from Aëtius, Cicero, Origen, Plutarch, and others, collected by Us (fr. 395) all make the same point. Grilli, in his commentary (p. 407), has collected other Epicurean witnesses, including a long passage in Diogenianus Epicureus (pp. 753–5 Gercke) devoted to proving that οὐδὲν ὄφελος ἡμῖν τῆς μαντικῆς.

The Stoic point of view is to be found in D.L. vii. 149: everything happens by fate, an endless chain of causation which governs the universe. Moreover, divination exists in all its forms (μαντικὴν ὑφεστάναι πᾶσάν φασιν) if providence exists (as of course Stoics believed it did); they ranked it as a science. So Zeno, Chrysippus, Athenodorus, and Posidonius. Only Panaetius seems to have questioned it; cf. Cicero, *De divinatione* i. iii. 6.

5–6. G writes ὑφε[σ|τηκέναι], no doubt to find the 8 letters which are missing at the beginning of all lines; but this makes l. 5 too short by about 2 letters. I divide the word as W did and add δή to l. 6.

FRAGMENT 32 (62 cm., 34 cm., 73 cm.: 62 cm., 14 cm., 68 cm.)

This fragment again is made up of two blocks fitting closely together (HK 80 and 81). HK 80 has the last 6 to 8 letters from all the lines of col. I, and the first 8 to 10 of col. II, except for a piece missing from the bottom right-hand corner affecting ll. 11–14. HK 81 has the rest of col. II and col. III. The maxim below, otherwise unknown and

minus its middle section, begins under the third letter from the end of col. I.

W was the first to attempt a complete restoration of col. I. The thought of the fragment seems to be this: the rejection of divination is essential for the removal of error; this rejection also does away with Fate as divination is its only proof. If anyone turns to Democritus for support, saying that his atomic theory involves necessity, we shall remind him of Epicurus' modification of that theory; and then, if we believe in destiny how can we punish wrong-doers?

I. 2. In his apparatus criticus G criticizes Us for dividing προ|ρρηθέν thus, but Us did not do so; he proposed προρ|ρηθέν, which is Diogenes' normal practice, and the mistake arose in W's app. crit. However, there is no sign of a P after the O at the end of this line.

4. εἴποι is very attractive, but it involves departing from HK's transcript which shows a clear T, as does Cousin, and introducing the unusual construction of εἰ+optative followed by future in the apodosis—a construction which has to be repeated in ll. 8–9.

6–7. G rejects W's restorations partly for reasons of rhythm, partly because of vocabulary, cf. P.P. xv (1960), 132. He considers παρεῖναι and ἐκκρινεῖ as more suited to the context, referring to 27 I 6, where [διακρ]εῖναι πλάνον occurs. This would make ἐκκρεινεῖ necessary here as Diogenes always spells ἰ as ει, and G's suggestion already involves 12 letters as against the normal 10. As for rhythm he objects to οὔποτε παύσει as an epic clausula which D. never uses; in fact W prints λύσει, not παύσει, but it must be admitted that the same objection could be made to that. It may well be a valid one, but G's remedy is not convincing.

11. The difference in reading between D and F is hard to account for; neither is marked as doubtful.

14. There appears to be a small / just before NHCOYN; it could have been part of an A.

II. This column, as mentioned above, is inscribed on two blocks but they fit closely together.

3 seqq. There are many references to Democritus' views on the movement of the atoms. For instance: Aëtius I. 12. 6 (A 47 DK = KR 574) Δημόκριτος τὰ πρῶτά φησι σώματα (ταῦτα δ᾽ ἦν τὰ ναστά) βάρος μὲν οὐκ ἔχειν, κινεῖσθαι δὲ κατ᾽ ἀλληλοτυπίαν ἐν τῷ ἀπείρῳ; Alexander of Aphrodisias in Met. 36. 21 (KR 579) οὗτοι γὰρ [i.e. Leucippus and Democritus] λέγουσιν ἀλληλοτυπούσας καὶ κρουομένας πρὸς ἀλλήλας

κινεῖσθαι τὰς ἀτόμους; Cicero, *De fin.* i. 6. 17 (A 56 DK) says that these collisions result in cohesions which produce the visible universe.

10. Quite apart from the objection that HK's ἔνερθεν would, as W points out (p. 93), give a false picture of Democritus' doctrine (his atoms do not move upwards) the word is much too long. There is room for only one letter between ΕΝΕ and Ν, but what this letter was defies discovery. ἐνεάν would fit but would also give a wrong sense. No alternative to W's reading seems possible.

If the movement of the atoms is the result of chance collisions then they will not have freedom of movement, and everything will be moved by necessity, the necessity of going where they are pushed. This is a kind of fate, or destiny, and is the meaning of the only extant fragment of Leucippus: οὐδὲν χρῆμα μάτην γίνεται, ἀλλὰ πάντα ἐκ λόγου τε καὶ ὑπ' ἀνάγκης (B 2 DK = KR 568). This does not, of course, amount to Stoic Providence (πρόνοια).

III. There is no reference to the 'swerve' of the atoms in any extant writing of Epicurus, but it is clear from later references that it was a fundamental part of his physical theory. He introduced it partly to explain how this or any world ever arose (for otherwise his atoms, having weight, would have fallen for ever in the void without touching one another) but mainly to escape from Democritean 'necessity', and to permit free will in man. Many references were collected by Usener in frs. 280 and 281; two only need be quoted:

Cic. *D.N.D.* i. 25. 69: 'Epicurus cum videret, si atomi ferrentur in locum inferiorem suopte pondere, nihil fore in nostra potestate, quod esset earum motus certus et necessarius, invenit quo modo necessitatem effugeret, quod videlicet Democritum fugerat: ait atomum, cum pondere et gravitate derecto deorsus feratur, declinare paullulum.'

Lucretius ii, the last five lines of the passage 251–93,

> sed ne mens ipsa necessum
> intestinum habeat cunctis in rebus agendis
> et devicta quasi [hoc] cogatur ferre patique,
> id facit exiguum clinamen principiorum
> nec regione loci certa nec tempore certo.

As to *how* this free will is achieved by the swerve, cf. now D. J. Furley, *Two Studies in the Greek Atomists* (Princeton U.P., 1967), Study II.

3. The last letter is Η and no other line goes beyond the edge of the stone; however, the Ν seems to be needed.

10 seqq. Cf. Epic. *Ep.* iii. 133 . . . τὴν δὲ τύχην ἄστατον . . . τὸ δὲ παρ᾽ ἡμᾶς ἀδέσποτον, ᾧ καὶ τὸ μεμπτὸν καὶ τὸ ἐναντίον παρακολουθεῖν πέφυκεν. Plutarch, *De Stoic. repugn.* 34, 1050 c (fr. 378 Us) says much the same.

It is impossible to be certain of either the length or the content of the unknown maxim which stood below this fragment. The efforts made by Ph and G to complete it are not convincing. The former has to assume an omission of ΕΙ at the beginning, and ἔχοις does not fit F; G's restoration is a little long for the gap, which probably held 9–10 letters including the Π of ἄπειρον.

The only virtue I would claim for my suggestion, which is very tentative, is that it is the right length and fits the remains of the letters preserved in F. It might have run, 'If it were possible for those who wish to enjoy unlimited pleasure to live an unlimited time they would still find that the amount of pleasure was the same as in a limited time'—the point made in P.D. 19.

FRAGMENT 33 (18·5 cm., 17 cm., 15 cm.)

A small piece, the right-hand corner of a block. HK noted that the last two lines above the 15th line were in smaller lettering and so close together that they take up little more space than one ordinary line. They therefore regarded them as a correction or postscript.

The 15th line contains nine letters which apparently belong to P.D. 25.

It would seem that Diogenes has now moved on to discuss the second fear, that of death, or rather of survival after death, and is attacking the belief in transmigration of souls associated with Pythagoras, and possibly Empedocles.

FRAGMENT 34 (I recorded by Cousin only, not found again by HK: II 61 cm., 36 cm., 77 cm.)

The understanding of this difficult fragment is made more difficult by the unfortunate circumstance that for col. I we have to rely on the often faulty transcript made by Cousin. However, the general gist of the passage seems to be fairly clear. Diogenes is arguing against Empedocles' doctrine of metempsychosis by saying that if souls only have life when they are joined to bodies then in the changeover from body to body they must perish; if they can live apart from bodies then why bother to switch them about from body to body at all; why not simply say that souls are indestructible?

I. The text is very dubious. C noted that the block was broken on the right and thought that 5–6 letters were missing from each line.

It seems more likely to be 3–4. I have adopted W's restoration as a rule with some slight modifications after G.

It is very likely that the end of the previous fragment was something similar to G's proposal, i.e. 'If souls have a living nature only when joined to bodies, migration is impossible'. This column would then continue as translated. See now Appendix, p. 128.

2. The changes are serious but necessary.

4. G is right to reject W's παρέχοντι on the ground that the division would have been πα|ρέχοντι (cf. 37 I 1); the alternative διέχοντι must then be taken with χρόνω in spite of the awkwardness of the intervening relative, and μή also excluded. W had referred μὴ παρέχοντι to Empedocles, it would seem, i.e. 'If you do not give them a living nature in the interval, etc. . . .' This is certainly easier.

5. G no doubt gave up his first idea as too long; he now suggests that C's ΓΕΧ[Ε] is a misreading of ΓCVC. But γε seems out of place here and it is possible to make sense of C's transcript.

6. This is the main change introduced by G. He thinks that here the writer is giving the alternative to the position suggested in his preamble, and I presume he would translate, 'But if they do not have it—i.e. a living nature only when joined to bodies . . .' This is the same, I suppose, as saying 'But if they have a living nature independently . . .' The parenthesis in 7–8 will then mean, 'as indeed they must have since (while?) they are without body . . .' His 1950 translation and commentary is not a certain guide to this passage since he retains W's punctuation in it, i.e. he reads εἰ δ' αὐτὴν οὐκ ἔχουσιν—δεῖ γάρ—ἄνευ σώματος κτλ. His translation of this is, 'Se invece, essendo senza corpo, non hanno tale natura ed è infatti necessità' etc.—which suggests that 'while they are without body' is more likely to be the meaning. Such a translation is possible even when ἄνευ σώματος is included in the parenthesis, but the expression is rather unusual and would not appear to be immediately obvious to the reader.

W's solution for all practical purposes makes the same point and is much simpler; besides, αὐτήν is not very like the AMH recorded by Cousin.

7. NΔ might have been misread as M but hardly Δ alone; on the other hand it is difficult to account for I being mistaken for N.

8. ἑαυτῷ = σεαυτῷ as often in the New Testament and elsewhere, cf. L.S.J. s.v. ἑαυτοῦ II.

14. The gap after ON must indicate a stop.

Empedocles' views on transmigration are well summed up in B 117 DK (KR 476):

> ἤδη γάρ ποτ' ἐγὼ γενόμην κοῦρός τε κόρη τε
> θάμνος τ' οἰωνός τε καὶ ἔξαλος ἔλλοπος ἰχθύς.

II. Nothing can be made of the first three lines. W's restoration *exempli gratia* is certainly *audacius* (G).

3–4. [ἄμεινον γ]άρ has been generally accepted; the missing word might have been κρεῖττον but it is rather long; only 6 letters are lost.

5. One would like to supply ἂν ἦν—Usener, followed by W, read χρῆν—but the gap cannot be longer than 2, at most 3, letters. The omission of ἄν can be matched by Epic. *Ep.* iii. 134 κρεῖττον ἦν τῷ περὶ θεῶν μύθῳ κατακολουθεῖν ἢ τῇ τῶν φυσικῶν εἱμαρμένῃ δουλεύειν. There is the same kind of omission of ἄν with ἐχρῆν, ἔδει, etc., cf. Goodwin, *M.T.* Appendix V.

9–12. Here lies the main difficulty of this column. The τό in l. 11 is quite clear in both transcripts, but its exclusion by Diels was accepted by W, who translates the clause 'ut postremum mendacium tuum honestius esset', by which he understands the doctrine of Empedocles that souls rise through the different grades of creation until finally they reach the gods. Diogenes, says W, is here making fun of Empedocles by saying that his noble lie would be even nobler if he simply made all souls immortal. W also considers the possibility of reading ὑπήρχετο and translating 'ut mendacium tuum postremum honestius initium habiturus esset'. But the passive of ὑπάρχω seems only to occur in the perfect participle or the pluperfect (e.g. Ar. *Nic. eth.* 1163ᵇ21 ἄξιον τῶν ὑπηργμένων, Thuc. i. 93. 3 ὑπῆρκτο δ' αὐτοῦ [sc. τοῦ Πειραιῶς] πρότερον).

We cannot, I think, accept this; nor can we exclude the clear τό. G suggests taking τὸ πανέσχατον as adverbial on the lines of 26 II 7–8 (... οὗ κατὰ τὸ ἔσχατον ἡ φύσις ἡμῶν ὀρέγεται) and translates, 'affinchè alla fin fine la tua menzogna fosse più degna di rispetto', i.e. 'so that at the very last your falsehood might be the more impressive'. But the parallel between this passage and 26 II is not close, and G's interpretation lacks conviction.

We should after all return to the punctuation adopted by HK, i.e. a comma after ὑπῆρχε, take τὸ πανέσχατον as the subject, and regard τὸ ψεῦσμα as in apposition to it; (cf. HK p. 437 τὸ ψεῦσμα 'in einem Gefüge mit rein problematischem Inhalt').

The 15th line below this fragment does not belong to any known maxim. W thinks it may refer to pain (ἀλγηδών) and refers to P.D.

4, S.V. 4, and fr. 446 Us, but the likelihood of this is lessened when we notice tha ɪP.D. 4 is in fact quoted below fr. 38. It would be unusual to find the same sentiment expressed twice at such a short interval. But so little is left of this maxim that it is profitless to guess what it was.

FRAGMENT 35 (cols. I and II 57 cm., 41 cm., 30 cm.: 20 cm., 14 cm., 15 cm.; col. III 56 cm., 32 cm., 72 cm.)

This fragment is made up of three blocks, two found by HK and one by Cousin. HK 73 is a large block containing the last 4–6 letters of the lines of col. I, and col. II with the exception of the top right-hand corner; this corner is supplied by HK 74, a small nearly square stone found in the same area. Col. III is on a block found by Cousin; it has lost a large piece from the left-hand lower corner, and a smaller piece from the bottom right-hand corner.

Part of P.D. 29 forms the 15th line but 65 letters are missing at the beginning of it so that at least 4 columns are lost before this fragment begins. Even so G considers that col. I may still refer to Empedocles' ideas on metempsychosis before Diogenes turns to attack the Stoics in l. 13. W simply says that apparently it is being shown that the soul cannot survive by itself (μονουμένη) without the body, cf. Epic. *Ep.* i. 65 and the passages cited from Lucretius. But too little of the text remains to justify even the partial restorations of this column which have been attempted.

II. Stoic doctrine did not allow immortality to any human soul. Cleanthes said that all lasted until the 'conflagration', but Chrysippus restricted this measure of survival to the souls of the wise, cf. D.L. vii. 157, Κλεάνθης μὲν οὖν πάσας ἐπιδιαμένειν μέχρι τῆς ἐκπυρώσεως, Χρύσιππος δὲ τὰς τῶν σοφῶν μόνον, and *S.V.F.* ii. 809. Diogenes is attacking the latter doctrine.

5. Ph's restoration is preferable as being shorter.

13. ἐξόφθαλμος has this meaning only here and in Polyb. i. 10. 3.

III. 5. W's note on this line reads: '*κἂν τῷ λογισμῷ διαφέρωσι*, scilicet οἱ μὴ σοφοί. neque tum, si prudentia excellunt, eandem mortalitatem habent.' But Nestle was clearly right to point out (*Berl. Phil. Woch.* 1917, 1093–4) that the subject is both the wise and the unwise, and the verb means 'to differ'.

7–14. The meaning of this half-column is uncertain because of the damage to the stone. A full discussion of it, and of fr. 34, will be

found at pp. 271–8 of the *Actes du VIIIe Congrès* of the Association
Guillaume Budé which met in Paris in 1968 and was devoted to the
study of Epicureanism. Briefly, two interpretations have been put
upon it. The Us/HK/Gomp restoration must mean that the writer is
amazed at Stoic rashness ([τὸ προπε]τές) and wonders how, if the
soul becomes free, it will be able to exist even for a moment apart
from the body.

W objected that this is an argument against *any* belief in survival
of the soul after death, not the Stoic doctrine, and has most likely
been used already in col I. He proposed a different restoration, in
particular inserting a negative in l. 10 and πᾶν τὸ [μέλ]|λον in ll. 12–13,
and understood the writer to be wondering how, if souls are not to
exist for all future time, we are to speak of any time when they can.
But G quite rightly found this restoration impossible to reconcile
with the transcripts and for his part considered that the older interpretation did imply a doctrine, such as the Stoic, which did not
concede immortality to the soul; he therefore returned to it with a
modification in l. 10.

I would agree with him that W's restoration (admittedly *exempli
gratia*) cannot be accepted and that we must return to something like
the HK text, but I find it difficult to believe that the [τὸ προπε]τές
in l. 9 accepted by all other editors is correct. With W's restoration
it is clearly inappropriate and I am doubtful about its suitability in
HK and G. Hence my suggestion of [τὸ ἐνκρα]τές; I imagine that
Diogenes is being sarcastic, which is quite in his manner, and asking
the Stoics why, if they are prepared to allow a limited survival to
souls, they do not go further and grant them full immortality.

10. There does appear to be an erasure of one letter after ΔΥΝΑ
but it cannot be more than one; a Τ at the end of the line would
offend against the rules governing the division of words. Cousin
records an Ι.

FRAGMENT 36 (58 cm., 67 cm., 32 cm.)

A large block with unfortunately very little on it that can be read.
We can only assume that the discussion of the soul's mortality was
continued.

The four dubious letters which are all we have of the 15th line are
equally unhelpful. W thought of a sentence from the middle of P.D. 20
but, as G pointed out, if this was quoted in full a great deal is lost
between frs. 35 and 36, perhaps as many as 8 columns. And yet it
appears that fr. 36 is still discussing the mortality of the soul, a subject
which was moving to its end in fr. 35 (Stoic doctrine on any topic is
always criticized last). Hence G's suggestion of S.V. 24. The objection

to this is that three or four letters are erased between the extant pairs, not two, and besides, the third letter is not really like M.

The order of the next two fragments (37 and 38) is reversed in W. They are both concerned with the superiority of soul to body; fr. 37 maintains that it is the dominant partner in the soul–body combination and in fact holds the key to life, fr. 38 asserts the greater intensity and importance of the emotions of the soul. We have, therefore, says W, finished with the section on removing fears and desires and are now in the middle of a kind of general summary. Ph would not go quite so far; he considers we have reached, in these two fragments, the section on desires. It will be noticed that in W's arrangement these fragments do stand closely together with an interval of at most two columns between them.

G objected to this in his 1950 commentary and proposed their transposition. His arguments are:

(a) The gist of fr. 37 is that soul is the key to life and death; body dies only when soul abandons it. But the arguments used by Diogenes to prove this point are similar to those found in Lucr. iii, where the writer is showing that soul is as mortal as body and, therefore, that death is merely dissolution. This fragment, then, is the end of the discussion of the fear of death before Diogenes goes on to the fear of pain and the effect of desires (cf. 28 VII).

(b) In W's arrangement between his XXXVII (fr. 36)—the last fragment dealing, presumably, with the fear of death—and his XXXVIII (fr. 38), which is already a general conclusion to the discussion of emotions ($\pi\acute{\alpha}\theta\eta$), there is space for only 11 columns. This, says G, is insufficient for the treatment of the fear of pain and the effect of desires. On the other hand, if XXXVIII (38) is placed after XXXIX (37) there will be room for a minimum of 14 columns, perhaps as many as 19, which would give ample room for the completion of the programme outlined in 28 VII.

I am inclined on balance to accept this transposition, although I do not find the second argument particularly convincing. Fr. 38 could form part of the discussion of desires; it could even be part of the section on the fear of pain (cf. II 10–III 3, and P.D. 4 below—though the 15th line only rarely deals with the same subject as the column above it). If this were so 11 columns would not be too small a gap between the two fragments. But the parallels between fr. 37 and Lucr. iii are striking and the conclusions G draws from them seem justified. It is true that in W's order P.D. 5 follows P.D. 4 and transposition will reverse this, but this is not a strong argument against change. Diogenes' ordering of the P.D.s is, as has been seen, quite different from that of Diogenes Laertius.

FRAGMENT 37 (59·5 cm., 117·5 cm., 61 cm.)

A large block which was found by Cousin almost complete except for a piece missing from the bottom right-hand corner. Before HK saw it three pieces, containing col. IV, had been broken off, but they were recovered and fitted together again.

I. 1. αἰτίαν—a good example of how mistakes in D (which baffled Us) were corrected by HK. The ΤΙ is very like a Π but the other letters are quite clear.

3–5. The Atomist theory, shared by both Democritus and Epicurus, was that soul-atoms were mingled with body-atoms in the living creature so as to account for sensation and movement. There is no contemporary account of Democritus' theory, but later writers ascribe to him a doctrine that soul and body atoms were arranged in pairs and alternately throughout the body. This is the gist of Lucr. iii. 370–3

> illud in his rebus nequaquam sumere possis,
> Democriti quod sancta viri sententia ponit,
> corporis atque animi primordia singula privis
> adposita alternis variare, ac nectere membra.

It is supported by the Aristotelian commentator, Alexander of Aphrodisias [*Mixt.* 2 (DK A 64)] : Δημόκριτος μὲν οὖν ἡγούμενος τὴν λεγομένην κρᾶσιν γενέσθαι κατὰ παράθεσιν σωμάτων, διαιρουμένων τῶν κιρναμένων εἰς μικρὰ καὶ τῇ παρ' ἄλληλα θέσει τὴν μῖξιν ποιουμένων . . . This would imply that the numbers of soul and body atoms were equal, and in view of what Diogenes says here this may have been the original form of Democritus' theory, the arrangement in pairs being a later elaboration.

The passage of Lucretius quoted above goes on to reject this arrangement in pairs ; he maintains (iii. 374–7) that as soul-atoms are much smaller than body-atoms they are also fewer, and dispersed at long intervals throughout the limbs (*rara per artus dissita*). This, he says, is shown by the fact that we do not feel specks of dust or feathers settling on the flesh. Bailey asserts in his commentary (p. 1056) that Lucretius has 'hinted at' this point earlier, where he says (iii. 276–8)

> quod genus in nostris membris et corpore toto
> mixta latens animi vis est animaeque potestas
> corporibus quia de parvis *paucisque* creatast,

and claims that Diogenes 'vouches for' it.

Diogenes' answer to Democritus is, however, rather different from that of Lucretius. Though the latter's soul-atoms may be few and widely dispersed there are still enough of them to respond to stimuli at

any point of the body. Diogenes concentrates on their small number, as can be seen from his comparing the soul in its entirety, irrational and rational parts (I 5–7), with ὁ βραχύτατος τῶν ὀπῶν. The irrational soul particles (*anima* in Lucretian terms) must be dispersed to a certain extent to allow for sensation and perception but the implication is that they will still be very few. It may be that Diogenes is thinking more of the rational part (*animus*) throughout this fragment. Cf. below, the note to I 13–IV 9.

5–7. The scholiast to Epic. *Ep.* i. 66–7 describes how with soulatoms the irrational element is distributed through the rest of the body while the rational element is in the chest—as is clear from the emotions of fear and joy. Arrighetti refers to fr. 312 Us. Cf. also Lucr. iii. 136 seqq. for the same statement and evidence.

8 seqq. Or, as Lucretius puts it (iii. 323–4):

> haec igitur natura [sc. anima] tenetur corpore ab omni
> ipsaque corporis est custos et causa salutis.

The passage from Epicurus *Ep.* i. 64, οὐ μὴν εἰλήφει ἂν ταύτην [sc. τὴν αἴσθησιν] εἰ μὴ ὑπὸ τοῦ λοιποῦ ἀθροίσματος ἐστεγάζετό πως, refers to only one side of the coin.

The verbs διέζωσεν, ἀντέδησε are gnomic aorists.

10–12. It has been said that the only two chemical processes known to the Greeks were cooking and curdling milk. G refers to Homer *Il.* v. 902 and Empedocles B 33 DK ὡς δ' ὅτ' ὀπὸς γάλα λευκὸν ἐγόμφωσεν καὶ ἔδησε . . .

I. 13–IV. 9. Both W and G have commented at some length on this passage, referring particularly to Epic. *Ep.* i. 65 and Lucretius iii. 119–20 and 396–416. W is very harsh in his judgement; he considers that Diogenes has stupidly mutilated Epicurus' argument and is saying no more than that as long as life remains in a man he lives. G thinks that the misunderstanding is partial, helped by Diogenes' failure to distinguish between the *anima* (the vital powers in general, but sensation in particular) and the *animus* (the thinking, intelligent part of the soul). He also considers that Diogenes probably did not have the Letter to Herodotus (*Ep.* i) before him but something more like Lucr. iii. 119–20, i.e.

> principio fit uti detracto corpore multo
> saepe tamen nobis in membris vita moretur.

If, however, we examine the passages from Epicurus and Lucretius, especially iii. 396–416, and compare these lines with them we may

feel that Diogenes is saying something slightly different, something which makes reasonable sense.

(*a*) The point made by Epicurus is that soul is the key to sensation; even if some parts of the body are lost—and with them some of the soul-atoms which are scattered throughout it—if the soul exists at all sensation remains. But if a complete body loses its stock of soul-atoms sensation (i.e. life) ceases, though it is equally true that if the composite being is itself dissolved soul by itself cannot feel either.

(*b*) In the Lucretius passage beginning at iii. 396 the poet makes the important distinction within the soul itself between *anima* and *animus*, and is concerned to demonstrate that the *animus* is more important for the preservation of life than the *anima*. A man may be a mutilated trunk yet he lives if mind and *animus* remain.

What Diogenes is saying is a combination of both. He does not trouble to distinguish between *animus* and *anima*, in spite of the mention of τὸ λογικόν and τὸ ἀλόγον in I 5–7, but it will be a convenience to use these terms. Col. I 13–III 2 asserts the superiority of soul in general to body as the key to life. Even if body is reduced to a state bordering on death, soul (i.e. *anima* to a certain extent, but *animus* in particular) will often refuse to give in. In col. III 2–10 his point is that sometimes the *anima* suffers actual loss when limbs, with the soul-atoms they contain, are cut off; but if some of the *anima* (and the *animus*) remains, life persists. On the other hand (col. III 11 seqq.) if *all* soul-atoms leave even a perfect body sensation ceases and death follows.

II. 8. ΔΕω is clear in both transcripts but the infinitive is essential. H. van Herwerden proposed it first, referring to Aristotle *Ath. pol.* 41. 7 and 57. 10. The references are presumably to 19. 39 and 27. 7 (Sandys), where the MS. δεῖ has to be altered to δεῖν in the phrases ἑνὸς δεῖν πεντήκοντα and ἑνὸς δεῖν πεντηκοστῷ.

III. 9–10. G refers to Lucr. iii. 138–9 and 396–7. The former is more apt than the latter. In it Lucretius, after saying that *animus* and *anima* form one whole, continues

> sed caput esse [sc. dico] quasi et dominari in corpore toto
> consilium quod nos animum mentemque vocamus.

Or, in other words, τὸ λογικόν is the dominant element in the body. Diogenes merely says that soul as a whole is dominant, no doubt meaning τὸ λογικόν in particular but speaking of the composite soul without differentiation.

The second reference would hardly seem to apply at all. It is

et magis est animus vitai claustra coercens
et domitantior ad vitam quam vis animai.

Diogenes nowhere opposes the two aspects of soul to one another in this way.

IV. This column is incomplete, less than half the lines are extant, but the sense is reasonably certain.

5–6. ἀκηρασία is doubted by W as it occurs nowhere else with this sense (L.S.J. list it as 'purity' in Hesychius). But it is a reasonable formation from ἀκήρατος 'untouched, unhurt', and all editors read it.

8. G's σύνδεσμα is preferable to W's πῆγμα (which he doubted) as being longer but the last readable letter is almost certainly Γ and not Π.

9. G preferred ἔστιν to W's ζῇ for reasons of rhythm, and also to permit him to remove the μέν which he regarded as unnecessary (cf. *P.P.* 1960, 131). But ζῇ is more to the point than ἔστιν and if ll. 9–13 are only the beginning of a sentence, as they may well be, μέν is not out of place. However, I incline to think that the writer is now starting to sum up this part of his argument—hence the restoration proposed.

11. G² is too short and W unconvincing.

13. Very little indeed remains of this line but the second letter is far more likely to have been I or H than Π. Cousin read nothing.

The text of P.D. 5 has caused editors a great deal of trouble and whereas the discovery of this inscription helped in one difficulty, it does not help in another. It proved that Gassendi was right to insert οὐδὲ φρονίμως καὶ καλῶς καὶ δικαίως in l. 2, but as it breaks off at δικαίως we cannot tell whether Diogenes included the words which in D.L. come between ὑπάρχει and οὐκ ἔστι (i.e. οὐ ζῇ φρονίμως καὶ καλῶς καὶ δικαίως ὑπάρχει). These words are not present in the version of this maxim in the *Sententiae Vaticanae* and von der Muehll is almost certainly right to exclude them. Cf. Bailey, *Epicurus*, pp. 351–2. ὅπου (l. 4) is the reading of V, a 14th-century Vatican codex.

FRAGMENT 38 (61 cm., 88 cm., 31 cm.)

A block with a large piece missing from the top right-hand corner, affecting col. III, and a little missing from the bottom corner on the same side. This fragment is illustrated at Pl. VIII.

Fifty-six letters are lost from P.D. 5 and 164 from P.D. 4, a total of 220. This space, plus the small break that occurs between maxims, is enough to accommodate roughly 14 columns.

Diogenes here discusses the relative intensities of bodily and mental pain.

We have a diatribe by Plutarch, Πότερον τὰ τῆς ψυχῆς ἢ τὰ τοῦ σώματος πάθη χείρονα (Animine an corporis affectiones sint peiores), an essay by Maximus of Tyre (7 Hobein), Πότερα χαλεπώτερα νοσήματα τὰ τοῦ σώματος ἢ τὰ τῆς ψυχῆς, and references to the question by Cicero in *Tusculan Disputations* iii, c. 3 and iv, c. 10. 24—where in fact he complains that the Stoics, especially Chrysippus, devote too much time to comparing the diseases of the body and the soul ('hoc loco nimium operae consumitur a Stoicis, maxime a Chrysippo, dum morbis corporum comparatur morborum animi similitudo').

We may therefore conclude that the theme was a common one in popular philosophy, though the usual comparison seems to be between *affections* (or *afflictions*) of the soul and the body, between the vices which affect the soul, avarice, lust, ambition, etc., and the diseases of the body. It is obvious from col. II 10 seqq. that Diogenes is thinking more of actual pain.

I. The first 3–4 letters are missing from all lines.

1–3. W compares Philodemus, *De ira* xiv. 19 W, where he says, speaking of anger, καταρχόμενον ἀπ' ἐλαχίστου μέχρι καὶ τῶν ἐσχάτων ἐξοκέλλειν ποιεῖ.

3–7. For small sparks causing big fires G compares ps.-Phocylides, *Sent.* 144 Diehl–Young ἐξ ὀλίγου σπινθῆρος ἀθέσφατος αἴθεται ὕλη, Curtius Rufus 6. 3. 11 'parva saepe scintilla contempta magnum excitavit incendium', and other parallel passages.

That it was a common figure of speech is shown by Aristophanes, *Peace* 609 ἐμβαλὼν σπινθῆρα Μεγαρικοῦ ψηφίσματος ἐξεφύσησεν πόλεμον and Polybius xxviii. 39. 2.

9–11. The Cyrenaic view was that bodily pains are worse than mental ones, cf. fr. 452 Us (D.L. x. 137 etc.).

12–13. H. van Herwerden proposed ἀντιπα[ραθέ]σεως, which is attractive in that it does occur in Josephus, Apollonius Dyscolus, and elsewhere, whereas ἀντιπαράκρισις, if it is correct, is a *hapax legomenon* doubted by L.S.J. Unfortunately the I before the C is distinct.

II. 2. Us considered καθώς so misplaced as to require emendation, but both transcripts are clear and such a word-order is not unlike Diogenes' manner.

6. Cf. fr. 448 Us (Plut. *Non posse suaviter* 1103 d) ὁ γὰρ πόνος ὁ ὑπερβάλλων συνάψει θανάτῳ. S.V. 4 also tells with ingenious word-play

(if Usener's emendation is right) that intense pain lasts only a short time: ἡ γὰρ [sc. ἀλγηδὼν] σύντονον [MS. σύντομον] ἔχουσα τὸ πονοῦν σύντομον ἔχει τὸν χρόνον . . . Usener's reading of this line of Diogenes can hardly be wrong, although the letter after συνβῆ looks very like Π and between O and H there is a larger gap than normal for one letter.

III. In spite of l. 7 the subject would still seem to be the greater intensity of mental pain. The references, however—Us fr. 452 (mainly D.L. x. 137) and Cic. *De finibus* i. 17. 55-7—refer to both pain and pleasure. They both make the point that the body feels only present emotion, the soul is affected also by past and future pains or pleasures.

3. W's restoration is too long, and the letter after ταύτας must be Ι or Τ, not Ε.

FRAGMENT 39 (33 cm., 15·5 cm., 10 cm.)

A tiny fragment from the left-hand corner of a block. Only l. 14 is of any interest. G would see in ἀνύπο[πτον] a reference to the fourfold remedy—ἀνύποπτον ὁ θάνατος—and so to the fear of death. ἀνυπό[-στατον] might refer to a false idea about the τέλος as opposed to the ὑφεστηκὸς τέλος of P.D. 22.

Nothing can be made of the few letters which constitute the 15th line.

This is all that we have of the ethical treatise. It relates only to the emotional states (καταστήματα) and, as far as we can see, nothing has survived from the section on actions (πράξεις). In other words, all the extant fragments come from the first half to two-thirds of the inscription and the last, or right-hand, portion is entirely missing. If this is so, we should expect that anything which stood to the right of the ethical treatise itself would also be missing. This applies to the six blocks of maxims on William's plan (his frs. LVI–LXI, frs. 40–5 in this edition), and rather suggests that if these blocks stood in the same course as the ethical treatise, they must have stood on the left—where William has already placed the Letter to Antipater. But on this whole question of the arrangement of the inscription see the Introduction.

D. *Various Maxims*

The maxims in this section (frs. 40–5) are usually regarded as a kind of continuation of the 15th line which has run below the ethical treatise. Their content is obviously similar and in the two cases where the stones are undamaged (frs. 41 and 42) they are of the same height as those of the previous section. Of course, they contain much less

VII. Fragment 25.

VIII. Fragment 38.

text—either one or two maxims, inscribed in larger letters than the treatise and taking up at most ten lines. As to the position they occupied in the inscription as a whole, cf. the end of the last section and the Introduction.

It is uncertain whether these maxims are to be attributed to Epicurus himself or not. Most editors have felt that their content and style are so like the Master's that they must be his; certainly William, Diano, and Grilli accept this. Arrighetti is not so sure; he quotes them in the commentary to his *Epicuro* but does not include them in the text—as he does the Letter to Mother (frs. 52 and 53). Philippson, on the other hand, thought that the language, and the frequent parallels with Democritus, prove that they are part of an Epicurean work on εὐθυμία, based on Democritus and using Democritean terms, such as εὐθυμία itself, which were avoided by Epicurus. This work might, he thinks, have been produced in the school of Zeno of Sidon as a counterblast to the εὐθυμία writings of Panaetius, which in their turn led to the *De tranquillitate animi* of Seneca and the work of the same name by Plutarch.

Bignone has discussed these maxims in *L'Aristotele perduto* ii. 216 seqq., and considers that the Ionicisms are no argument against Epicurus' authorship. In fact he suggests that frs. 42, 45, 41, and 40, in that order, and possibly 47 and 44 as well, formed part of the letter 'To the Philosophers in Mytilene' which, he says, Epicurus wrote in the early part of his career when he was still using Ionic words and spellings. This letter has not survived; all we have of it are two mentions in Diogenes Laertius x and two short quotations (frs. 113 and 114 Us), one from D.L. and the other from Sextus Empiricus, in both of which Epicurus is concerned with abusing Nausiphanes, under whom he had studied between the ages of 14 and 17 and by whom he was no doubt introduced to the doctrines of Democritus.

Festugière, in his *Épicure et ses dieux* (Eng. trans., p. 44 n. 31), finds this theory of Bignone unconvincing, but ascribes fr. 40 at least to Epicurus, accepting a theory of Usener (*Rh. Mus.* xlvii (1892), 425) that it belongs to a time when he was still under the influence of Democritus (through Nausiphanes) and probably still living in Asia Minor. Presumably Festugière would assign all the other maxims in this group to the same period.

My own impression is that these maxims, though fully worthy of the Master himself, were probably not written by him but by a very competent Ionian disciple. His three most intimate associates, Metrodorus, Polyaenus, and Colotes, all came from Lampsacus, a Phocaean colony, and all wrote works which were included in the Epicurean 'canon'. Any one of these might have been the author of these maxims.

FRAGMENT 40

As this was not found again by HK we have no measurements of it.

The language of Democritus is very similar in B 3 DK: τὸν εὐθυμεῖσθαι μέλλοντα χρὴ μὴ πολλὰ πρήσσειν, μήτε ἰδίηι μήτε ξυνῆι, μηδὲ ἄσσ᾽ ἂν πράσσηι, ὑπέρ τε δύναμιν αἱρεῖσθαι τὴν ἑωυτοῦ καὶ φύσιν. Cf. Seneca, De ira iii. 6. 4 'proderit nobis illud Democriti salutare praeceptum quo monstratur tranquillitas, si neque privatim neque publice multa aut maiora viribus nostris egerimus'. G refers also to Seneca, Tranq. an. 13. 1 and Plutarch, Tranq. an. 2, 465 c (which quotes Democ. B 3 above).

3. πράσσειν—'non Attice dictum' says W, who adduces three other instances of Ionic spelling from Epicurus—πυρέσσοντες (fr. 471 K = 189 Arrighetti), συνουσίη (fr. 62 Us), and κυθριδίον (fr. 152 Us = 114 Arrighetti).

7. For βιάζεσθαι see Epic. Ep. ii. 86 μήτε τὸ ἀδύνατον καὶ παραβιάζεσθαι and, perhaps more to the point here, S.V. 21 οὐ βιαστέον τὴν φύσιν ἀλλὰ πειστέον. It should, however, be noted that the connection between these passages and Diogenes' maxim is little more than verbal. The message in S.V. 21 is that we must not do violence to Nature (in its widest sense) but obey her. Diogenes makes it clear that he is thinking only of the individual's personal powers and nature. Ep. ii. 86 is concerned with forcing an impossible explanation of natural phenomena.

FRAGMENT 41 (58 cm., 53 cm., thickness not recorded)

This block, thanks to Professor G. E. Bean, is illustrated at PLATE IV.

2–3. διάθεσις, this is another word which is not found in any work which is certainly by Epicurus. But it occurs four times in a Herculanean papyrus which Arrighetti accepts as one of the books of his Περὶ φύσεως, and four times in this inscription, twice in the section of 'various maxims', frs. 41. 2 and 43. 11, and twice in the Letter to Mother; of these the former might be by Epicurus, though they probably are not, the latter most probably is by him.

Plutarch uses the word (fr. 548 Us = De audiendis poetis 37 a), τὸ εὔδαιμον καὶ μακάριον οὐ χρημάτων πλῆθος οὐδὲ ... ἀλλ᾽ ἀλυπία καὶ πραότης παθῶν καὶ διάθεσις ψυχῆς τὸ κατὰ φύσιν ὁρίζουσα, and D.L. x. 117 says that in the view of Epicurus and his school τὸν ἅπαξ γενόμενον σοφὸν μηκέτι τὴν ἐναντίαν λαμβάνειν διάθεσιν—a Stoic-sounding sentiment expressed in Epicurean language (cf. fr. 42. 7–8 n.).

4. G notes the verbal similarity with Democritus B 49 DK χαλεπὸν ἄρχεσθαι ὑπὸ χερείονος.

5. This line can be taken in two ways depending on the accentuation we supply (cf. app. crit.). Wilhelm's reading would mean 'even if you are in command of others', and this would seem to suit better the remark from Plutarch, *An recte dictum* iii, 1128 f quoted by W Ἐπαμεινώνδα λέγεις "μὴ στρατήγει". (In fact this reference, although it is the only one comparable with this passage in Epicurean literature and is quoted by all editors, is not very relevant. Plutarch is merely saying 'Yet if you give this advice to seek obscurity to the noble, you are saying to Epaminondas, don't be a general'—καὶ μὴν εἴ γε τοῖς χρηστοῖς λανθάνειν καὶ ἀγνοεῖσθαι παραινεῖς κτλ. The point of this is that generalship happened to be Epaminondas' forte. It is not general advice for one and all.)

The argument against Wilhelm's proposal is surely that no Epicurean would normally accept commissioned rank, still less a command. But even in the obscurity of the ranks the ordinary soldier has lost his freedom of choice; important decisions are under another's control.

6. Cf. D.L. x. 118 (fr. 565 Us) οὐδὲ ῥητορεῦσαι (MS. ῥητορεύσειν) καλῶς (τὸν σοφόν οὐ δοκεῖ αὐτοῖς, i.e. Epicureans). σφυγμός is mainly a medical term for pulsation or throbbing.

7. ὁ δίκαιος ἀταρακτότατος, ὁ δ' ἄδικος πλείστης ταραχῆς γέμων, P.D. 17.

11. Philod. Περὶ Ἐπικούρου β fr. 6 II (Vogliano) reads (of Epicurus) οὔτε γὰρ ὑπ' ἐξουσίας ὄχλων ἢ μοναρχοῦντος ἢ γυμνασιαρχοῦντος ἀνδρὸς ...

As to the punctuation of this fragment G says, 'v. 3, 5, 7 vacant in fine, his spatiis nisus interpunxi'. This is true of ll. 3 and 5 but l. 7 does not end noticeably sooner than e.g. l. 9 or 10 and a colon at the end of it will be very awkward.

The last sentence, according to W, applies to both military service and rhetoric; HK, from their punctuation, seem to restrict it to the latter. It could certainly apply equally well to both—see the note to l. 5.

FRAGMENT 42 (57 cm., 33 cm., 76 cm.)

A tall block containing only nine short lines in larger lettering than normal.

The sentiment is an Epicurean commonplace, for which many parallels can be quoted. E.g. P.D. 4 οὐ χρονίζει τὸ ἀλγοῦν συνεχῶς ἐν τῇ σαρκί, ἀλλὰ τὸ μὲν ἄκρον τὸν ἐλάχιστον χρόνον πάρεστι κτλ. Epic. Ep. iii. 133 τὸ δὲ τῶν κακῶν (sc. πέρας) ὡς ἢ χρόνους ἢ πόνους ἔχει βραχεῖς ... S.V. 4 has already been referred to above, p. 95.

There are also all the quotations and notices from Cicero, Seneca, Plutarch, and others collected by Usener in frs. 446–8, and to these could be added Seneca, *De providentia* 6. 6 'contemnite dolorem: aut solvetur aut solvet', and *Ep.* 78. 7 and 17. Cf. also fr. 44.

7–8. W notices Epicurus' fondness for expressions using λαμβάνειν, e.g. λύσιν λαμβάνειν, ταραχὴν λ., σύγχυσιν λ., κινήσεις λ., and many others.

FRAGMENT 43 (39 cm., 19 cm., 32 cm.)

A fragment discovered by HK. The top is broken off, and how many lines are lost is uncertain. HK assumed two, to give two maxims of five lines each. If this is correct the complete stone would not have been more than 50 cm. in height, 7 or 8 cm. less than frs. 41 and 42. If this stone belongs to the same group we must assume a loss of at least three lines.

There are two maxims here. The first one dealt with the classification of desires found in Epic. *Ep.* iii. 127: Ἀναλογιστέον δὲ ὡς τῶν ἐπιθυμιῶν αἳ μέν εἰσι φυσικαί, αἳ δὲ κεναί, καί τῶν φυσικῶν αἱ μὲν ἀναγκαῖαι, αἱ δὲ φυσικαὶ μόνον. The same point is made in P.D. 29, though there the division is into the natural and necessary, the natural and not necessary, and those that arise from empty imagination (κενὴν δόξαν). This was inscribed below fr. 35.

3–4. W thought that δεῖ κατανοῆ|[σ]αι might be possible, but this is unlikely in view of the remains of the letters in l. 3. Bignone takes account of them but his proposal is too long; there cannot be more than seven letters missing after the fragmentary three. Besides, the first letter of l. 4 can hardly be C, Ⲋ is much more likely. The faint O before τῶν in l. 4 is hard to explain.

7 seqq. That we are all born of the same stock is another common-place of late antiquity. It was popularized by the Stoics but has pre-Socratic antecedents. Ph quotes the fifth-century sophist Antiphon (B 44 fr. B col. 2 DK): φύσει πάντα πάντες ὁμοίως πεφύκαμεν καὶ βάρβαροι καὶ Ἕλληνες εἶναι.

A belief that we all have the same (divine) ancestor points to the same conclusion. This is found in Aratus, *Phenomena* 5 τοῦ γὰρ καὶ γένος εἰμέν (quoted in *Acts of the Apostles* 17. 28); it is repeated in the Stoic Cleanthes' *Hymn to Zeus* (*S.V.F.* i. 537) 4 ἐκ σοῦ γὰρ γένος εἴσ' . . . (MS. ἐσμέν), and by Epictetus, *Diss.* i. 13. 3.

The other idea in this maxim, that true nobility is not a matter of birth or wealth but of personal character, is also of pre-Socratic origin. Ph. refers to Democritus B 57 DK κτηνέων μὲν εὐγένεια ἡ τοῦ σκήνεος [MSS. σώματος] εὐσθένεια, ἀνθρώπων δὲ ἡ τοῦ ἤθεος εὐτροπίη.

Epicurus, so far as we know, did not trouble himself about εὐγένεια; it is nowhere mentioned in the extant works.

10. ἐποίησε is another gnomic aorist.

10–11. For πράξεις cf. 28 VI 6 and for διάθεσις 41. 2–3 and note.

FRAGMENT 44 (32 cm., 42 cm., 22 cm.)

A fragment broken on all sides except the left, where there is a wide margin. From the drawing by HK the lettering would appear to be very different from both fr. 43 and fr. 45.

We again have two separate maxims. The restoration of the first must be regarded as tentative; wealth, most probably 'unnatural wealth', seems to be the subject; there is a reference to a full vessel, and overflowing is the verb. The advice given must be something similar to Epicurus' views on 'natural wealth' in P.D. 15 ὁ τῆς φύσεως πλοῦτος καὶ ὥρισται καὶ εὐπόριστός ἐστιν. ὁ δὲ τῶν κενῶν δοξῶν εἰς ἄπειρον ἐκπίπτει.

Epicurus himself does not, however, refer to ἀγγεῖα except in the Letter to Pythocles (Ep. ii) 100, where he says that thunder may be produced by the rushing of wind in the hollows of clouds καθάπερ ἐν τοῖς ἡμετέροις ἀγγείοις. Nor are Lucretius' three references to vas much more helpful; these are iii. 936 and 1009 and vi. 17. With him the vessel is always broken and leaking; the first is a simile for lost happiness, the second a reference to the Danaids, and in the third the vessel represents the soul of man which both taints everything it gets and also, being cracked, can never be satisfied.

We are left, therefore, with very little to guide us and all that can be said is that W's restoration reads better, and seems more complete, than that of HK.

4. ἀμφότερα, both the water and unnatural wealth (W).

5. Diano's ἀποληπτέον gives slightly better sense, though it is found only once elsewhere, in Sext. Emp. Adv. math. 7. 388, where L.S.J. doubt it.

7–11. The second maxim reminded Ph of Democritus again, B 191 DK 9 seqq. ἐπὶ τοῖς δυνατοῖς οὖν δεῖ ἔχειν τὴν γνώμην καὶ τοῖς παρεοῦσιν ἀρκέεσθαι τῶν μὲν ζηλουμένων καὶ θαυμαζομένων ὀλίγην μνήμην ἔχοντα . . . as well as Seneca, Tranq. an. 10. 5 'nec invideamus altius stantibus', and Plutarch, Tranq. an 10. 470 b καίτοι καὶ τοῦτο μέγα πρὸς εὐθυμίαν ἐστί, τὸ μάλιστα μὲν αὐτὸν ἐπισκοπεῖν καὶ τὰ καθ' αὑτόν, εἰ δὲ μή, τοὺς ὑποδεεστέρους ἀποθεωρεῖν καὶ μή, καθάπερ οἱ πολλοί, πρὸς τοὺς ὑπερέχοντας ἀντιπαρεξάγειν.

9–10. ἥδεσθαι καθαρώτερον, W refers to Us fr. 416 (p. 356. 25) as evidence for ἡδονὴ ἀκάθαρτος, but this is not quite what the fragment says; it is a scholion to Gregory Nazianzen which states that Epicurus made pleasure the τέλος of every good, and continues: καὶ οἱ μὲν νῦν ἐξηγηταὶ λέγουσι τίθεσθαι τὴν ἡδονὴν οὐ τὴν ἀκάθαρτον ἀλλὰ τὴν φυσικωτάτην κατάστασιν, i.e. ἀκάθαρτον goes with κατάστασιν; nevertheless the link with ἡδονή is there.

He also quotes Cic. De fin. i. 18. 58 'liquidae voluptatis et liberae', and Lucr. iii. 40 'voluptatem liquidam puramque', where liquidus, of course, has the meaning of 'pure' or 'clear'. G adds P.D. 12 οὐκ ἦν ἄνευ φυσιολογίας ἀκεραίους τὰς ἡδονὰς ἀπολαμβάνειν. But for both language and thought W sees the closest parallel in Vol. Herc. Ser. i, vol. iii, col. XV. 37 seqq. (a fragment of Philodemus Περὶ κακιῶν καὶ ἀρετῶν θ) : το[ῦ]το γὰρ δε[ῖτ]α[ι] ποιεῖν τὴν χρείαν ἄλυ[π]ον, καὶ τὸ διὰ ταύτης τέρπον ἀκέραιον, τὸ μὴ προσεῖναι τῇ πλούτου κτήσει τοῖς σοφοῖς φρυντίδα βα[ρε]ίαν, πῶς δυνήσεται σώζ[ε]σθαι.

10. The last extant letter certainly seems to be O and the evidence points to ταῖς rather than τῆς. Hence my preference for G here; he supports it with a reference to fr. 207 Us : κρεῖττον δέ σοι θαρρεῖν ἐπὶ στιβάδος κατακειμένῳ ἢ ταράττεσθαι χρυσῆν ἔχοντι κλίνην καὶ πολυτελῆ τράπεζαν.

This makes good sense and is of about the right length.

FRAGMENT 45 (37 cm., 28 cm., 40 cm.)

The top part of a narrow block allowing only 11–14 letters per line and no margins at the side. There is a broad space at the top as on fr. 42 but the lettering is smaller than in frs. 42, 43, and 44 and the lines are closer together. If only one line missing—and the average for these maxims is ten lines—then this block cannot have been much more than 40–45 cm. tall. If it was originally as tall as the others in this group then as many as four lines may be lost. This would seem to be unlikely; possibly there was a very wide margin at the bottom.

The loss of the end of this maxim has made its meaning obscure. HK, who read the same text as the present except that they supplied ἤδη in l. 8 instead of οὐ, were, according to W, contrasting those who groan in the middle of pain with those who complain and lament after the pain has gone. W thinks such an interpretation possible but goes on: 'Tamen probabilius esse mihi videtur, gemitui (v. 2) hic opponi luctum et lamentationem quae in ipso dolore fiunt. Quae etiam apud Ciceronem Tusc. ii. 23. 55 gemitui opposita esse videmus: ingemescere nonnunquam viro concessum est, idque raro, eiulatus ne mulieri quidem (cf. 57).'

I must confess that I cannot see how this note squares with the text he prints, nor the relevance of the quotation from Cicero; the latter is a Stoic sentiment which seems to have no connection with this present fragment. And yet W's restoration does have a clear meaning, essentially the same as that of the present text which G made out of HK by altering one word. Epicurus was not opposed, as the Stoics were, to the natural expression of grief, in pain or at the death of friends—cf. fr. 120 Us (Plut. *Non posse suaviter* 1101 a), but this maxim warns against lamentation which is the expression of mere petulance and envy.

FRAGMENT 46 (20 cm., 19 cm., 12 cm.)

FRAGMENT 47 (17 cm., 13 cm., 15 cm.)

FRAGMENT 48 (no measurements recorded)

Three small pieces of which little or nothing can be made. HK put them here because of their appearance in the case of 46 and 47, and for reasons of provenance in that of 48. Fr. 46 has a wide margin on the right similar to that on the left of 44; 47 has a space above rather like 45, and the lettering of both is like that of 44. Fr. 48 was not found by HK but they included it here because Cousin said that it appeared to him to belong to the same part of the inscription as 44, 46, and 47.

No one had attempted to do anything with the few letters that survive until Grilli in *P.P.* 1960, 150 was tempted to try by the first line of 47. He considers that it might be part of an edited version of Epic. *Ep.* iii. 132—οὐ γὰρ πότοι καὶ κῶμοι συνείροντες οὐδ᾽ ἀπο-λαύσεις . . . τῶν ἄλλων ὅσα φέρει πολυτελὴς τράπεζα τὸν ἡδὺν γεννᾷ βίον κτλ.—which may be the source of fr. 476a Us (Ambrose, *Epist.* Classis I 63. 19, vol. xvi, p. 1246 Migne) 'Non immoderatae epulae, non potationes voluptatis suavitatem generant, sed continens vita'.

E. *Various Writings*

Four documents are collected here, a part of Diogenes' will, two fragments concerning his plans for setting up the inscription, and the controversial Letter to Mother. The blocks are not of the same height—they range from 38·5 cm. (fr. 49) to 49 cm. (fr. 51); even so, the size of lettering suggests that they stood in the same course (cf. Introduction, pp. xxxix–xl). We can also feel reasonably certain that with the possible exception of fr. 51 (q.v.) they did not belong to any other recognizable section of the work. It therefore seemed best to put them together in a group of their own.

FRAGMENT 49 (38·5 cm., 44 cm., 28 cm.)

This is a complete block, rather wider than it is tall, containing nine lines with a margin on the left and also along the top; this suggests that whatever went before was inscribed on a block standing to the left. Its size, shape, and content show that it stood above the Physics and Ethics at least. It seems to be part of an introduction of some kind. W thought that it was inscribed after the Physics and Ethics were finished to serve as a preface to the rest of the inscription. Ph considered that it was intended to introduce the entire work and would have referred to all its different sections. G accepts this view and entitles it *Praefatio omnibus scriptis praeposita*.

So little is left that lack of evidence prevents any kind of certainty. If frs. 1 and 2 form the preface to the whole work, as they apparently do, there would not seem to be any need for another general introduction. On the other hand the wording suggests some sort of general survey and this fragment obviously stood in a higher course, above the lower ones which contained the physical and ethical treatises. W may be right, or it may have been part of an introduction only to the treatise on Old Age. The height is the same as that of many of the blocks of that section of the work, and the lettering very similar in appearance.

W suggested that the words immediately preceding might have been πρὸς τοὺς φρονίμους τῶν εἰς τόπους τούτους κτλ.

2–3. φιλάνθρωπον—the same as in 2 V 5. G refers to Epicurus' φιλανθρωπία πρὸς πάντας mentioned in D.L. x. 10, and to *Ethica Epicurea* (Pap. Herc. 1251) XIV (Schmid). The author of the latter, apparently capping P.D. 5 (cf. fr. 37), writes: ἄ]νε[υ τοῦ φρονίμ]ως καὶ καλ]ῶς [καὶ δικαί]ως, ἔτι δ' ἀνδ[ρ]είως [κ]α[ὶ ἐγ]κρατῶς καὶ μεγαλ[ο-ψύ]χ[ω]ς καὶ φιλοπο̣ητικῶς κα[ὶ φιλανθρ]ώπως καὶ καθόλ[ου δ' ἐκ τῶν ἄλλων ἀρετῶν ὑπα[ρ]χουσῶν . . .

FRAGMENT 50 (47 cm., 40 cm., 38 cm.)

The beginning of Diogenes' will. It has 11 lines with no margin at the top, a narrow one on the left, and a broader one at the bottom. The most noticeable feature of this block is that it is much taller than the last and so could have stood in a lower course, most probably in that of the Physics; for this reason Ph considered that it was part of a foreword to the Physics and Ethics. It may have been part of a preface to the Physics alone, but it seems more likely to have been one of a number of documents, such as fr. 51 and possibly also fr. 49, which record Diogenes' arrangements or instructions for the erection of the inscription; cf. again Introduction, p. xl.

7–8. διαφορεῖ: G translates 'tormenta', but 'exhausts' or 'weakens' accords better with the medical use of this verb and its noun διαφόρησις.

καρδιακὸν πάθος is 'stomach trouble' rather than 'heart disease', as is clear from Alexander's commentary on Aristotle, *De anima* (98. 23 ed. Bruns) ἡ γὰρ λεγομένη καρδιακὴ νόσος, ἣν νόσον σώζεταί τινα νοσήσαντα, οὐ καρδίας ἀλλὰ στομάχου πάθος ἐστίν, and Cicero, *De divin.* i. 38. 81 'Aristoteles quidem eos etiam qui valetudinis vitio furerent et melancholia dicerentur, censebat habere aliquid in animis praesagiens atque divinum. Ego autem haud scio an nec cardiacis hoc tribuendum sit nec phreneticis; animi enim integri non vitiosi est corporis divinatio.' In this connection καρδία means the cardiac orifice of the stomach (cf. L.S.J.).

11. For the delayed δέ W compares 53 I 4 ἂν μὴ αἰσθάνηται δέ . . .; there is also 10 II 11–12 καὶ τῶν φθόνγων δὲ ἕνεκεν, and many others.

FRAGMENT 51 (49 cm., 76 cm., 46 cm.)

A block found by HK nearly complete containing the right-hand half of one column, a second with ten lines of the usual length, and a third with eight lines of half the normal length. There is a fairly wide margin at the bottom. Clearly it is the end of a 'letter to friends', as W entitled it, 8 cm. taller than the Letter to Mother; however, there is not much difference in the area actually inscribed. Ph considered it to be a letter of dedication meant to precede the Physics as the Letter to Antipater precedes the treatise on Innumerable Worlds. He was the first to attempt a restoration of col. I, assuming some such subject as 'The officials concerned in Oenoanda . . .' The basilica referred to would be that containing the stoa of 2 V 12 and the treatise mentioned in l. 4 would be the Physics. The last words of col. III suggested to him that this fragment might be only a postscript, the letter proper, in which he dedicated the treatise to Menneas, having been lost.

G accepts Ph's restoration, himself filling up l. 5 which Ph had left incomplete, but not his ascription of the fragment to the Physics; he thinks the treatise more likely to be the work on Old Age. HK, without restoring col. I of course, ascribed the letter to 'an Epicurean' and De Witt (*Epicurus and his Philosophy*, p. 59) considers it was written by Epicurus himself.

The latter view is most unlikely. This must be part of another document concerning Diogenes' plans to put up the inscription. Ph's restoration makes good sense, tentative though it is, but it is pointless to discuss the possible contents of the βιβλίον (l. 4) when the word itself is not certain.

The rather mannered word-order, and the spaces between some of the phrases, make translation of the text that is preserved, cols. II and III, not entirely certain. G would appear to take it to mean:

'I have been persuaded to have myself taken there because I was recommended to her by you as a result of your disposition and constancy towards me, dearest Menneas, and that of the admirable Carus and of our Dionysius at the time when we held our discussions at her house in Rhodes. Farewell again.'

To take points of vocabulary:

It seems to me more likely that ἀνενεγκεῖν is intransitive, and means 'to recover', especially in view of the adverb μᾶλλον; the plural ἡμᾶς etc. I take to mean 'me' in the singular—this is in keeping with Diogenes' usual way of speaking and, incidentally, throws some doubt on the μέ of I 7; a similar mixture of first person singular verbs with plural pronouns is to be found in frs. 1 and 2. In col. III διατριβὰς ποιεῖσθαι can be taken either way, but the whole phrase, ll. 3–6, suggests that 'stayed with her' is more likely.

At one time I thought that the gap in II 7, which is slightly wider than those in ll. 4 and 9, indicated a pause in the sentence at σοῦ, and that καὶ ἐπιστατείαν was the beginning of the second part of it, the καί answering the τε in l. 3 and διὰ τὴν being understood after it from l. 5. II 5 seqq. would then have meant: 'because of your disposition towards me, and of the care taken of me by the excellent Carus and my Dionysius at the time when . . .' But I am now convinced that it is far more natural to take διάθεσίν σου καὶ ἐπιστατείαν together; as to the gap in the line there is an even odder one in l. 10 in the middle of ἡμετέρου.

II. 8–9. HK were convinced that the Κάρος here was in fact T. Lucretius Carus; they accounted for the 250 years difference in dates between him and the erection of this inscription by asserting that this letter was by an older Epicurean who was a contemporary of Lucretius, and even suggest that Lucretius was in Rhodes at the same time as Cicero. Körte in his *Rh. Mus.* article, which appeared in the year following HK's edition, proved conclusively that this identification, attractive as it might be, is impossible. This letter is clearly by Diogenes himself. He must have visited Rhodes frequently, and wrote the Letter to Antipater from there, cf. 15 II 9–11.

FRAGMENTS 52 and 53

A Letter to Mother

This is another of the disputed passages in Diogenes' inscription. The original editor, Cousin (p. 69), believed that it was from the hand of Epicurus himself or a contemporary; the style, he said, is simpler and clearer than the rest of the inscription, and the form ὑφειστήκεσαν

(52 II 9–10) belongs to a much earlier epoch than Diogenes; the name Cleon (53 III 5) occurs at the beginning of Epicurus' second letter, and the material preoccupations of the writer suggest Epicurus. Cousin even thought it possible that these are fragments of the same letter as fr. 184 Us, where Epicurus is asking for 120 drachmae παρ' ἑκατέρου (cf. 53 III 8). Usener also ascribed it to Epicurus, considering that it was written in his youth; the reason he gave for this was the use of the word εὐθυμία, which Epicurus (he says) gave up as he grew older so that it is not found in the later, extant, works. In fact, Usener was under a misapprehension when he argued thus; he believed that fr. 40, where εὐθυμία occurs, was a part of this letter; HK proved that it is not. Even so they themselves accepted the ascription to Epicurus without comment or question.

William entirely disagreed. In a long note in his preface (pp. xx–xxx) he rejected C's arguments from style, showed that both long and short forms of the perfect and pluperfect of ἵστημι can be found in all periods, pointed out Usener's mistake about fr. 40, showed that Cleon was a common name, and considered that there could be no connection, in tone or personalities, between this letter and fr. 184 Us. He then listed a number of expressions which are not found till long after Epicurus' time, even though the Master did often go to the κοινή for his language. His final point was that Epicurus' parents were not wealthy enough to send money to their son συνεχῶς (53 II 3). So why should not the letter be Diogenes' own?

These arguments, exhaustive as they are, have not carried conviction. Philippson dealt with them in detail in *R.E.* (loc. cit. 165–6). As far as language goes W is refuted out of his own mouth since he admits that Epicurus did often use expressions from the κοινή; the fact that they occur only late in literary sources is no proof that he did not use them in his letters. And on the subject of language Ph points out that the writer speaks of μναῖ (53 III 6) whereas inscriptions from the Oenoanda of imperial times refer to δηνάρια. But it is from the subject-matter of the letter that Ph derives his conviction that it was indeed written by Epicurus; the writer is supported by contributions (as Epicurus was); both his parents have sent him sums of money (we know that after their expulsion from Samos in 322 Epicurus' parents both worked in Colophon), yet it is clear that they are not well-off; the recipient is obviously of a superstitious nature (D.L. x. 4 repeats a story that Epicurus' mother used to go round reading καθαρμούς in strangers' houses). All this agrees very well with what we know of Epicurus' circumstances; it does not suit the wealthy and probably aristocratic Diogenes.

Neither Diano, Grilli, nor Arrighetti dissents from this conclusion, though the latter two differ as to date. Grilli thinks that the evidence

of comparative wealth in Epicurus' family points to a time before their expulsion from Samos in 322, but Arrighetti believes that Epicurus could not have written a letter so full of his most refined and finished doctrine at such an early date; he would place it somewhere around 322.

There is little that can be added to these arguments. The whole tone and content of the letter is quite incompatible with the wealthy, aristocratic, and not very philosophic Diogenes, but accords perfectly with our knowledge of Epicurus. Its date is impossible to fix but it was most probably written at some time between 322 and 306, when he left to found his school in Athens. We know that the Master's letters were collected and cherished by his followers (cf. Plut. *Non posse suaviter* 1101 b and *Lettere di Epicuro e dei suoi*, ed. Diano [Florence, 1946]), and it would be as natural for Diogenes to quote one in his inscription as it was for him to include a selection of the Principal Doctrines.

FRAGMENT 52 (41 cm., 71 cm., 49 cm.: 41 cm., 59 cm., 29 cm.)

A fragment inscribed on two blocks, put together by Cousin. We have two columns practically complete and two defective.

His mother seems to have written to Epicurus telling him that he has appeared to her, in dreams perhaps, and this has frightened her. He replies that there is no real difference in the perception of the present and the absent; both are caused by images (εἴδωλα), in the former case striking the eye of the recipient, in the latter the imagination (διάνοια). She should not therefore worry about him; he is making great progress along the road to supreme happiness.

The Epicurean theory of perception is explained in the Letter to Herodotus (Epic. *Ep.* i) 49–51 and Lucr. iv. 26 seqq. It accounts for sight and thought in the same way; external objects continually give off images or models of themselves, similar to themselves in colour and shape, and these enter into the sight *or the mind*. This latter point is made at length by Lucretius at iv. 722 seqq. Some images are so thin that they bypass the organs of sense and impinge directly on the mind (hence our knowledge of the gods). Moreover, these images persist so that it is possible to 'see' or dream about the dead. Perhaps it is this aspect of the doctrine which caused Epicurus' mother concern. His reply is that such an effect can be produced equally well by the living; it is not in itself any indication of harm.

I. This column is heavily restored, mainly by W, but probably conveys the gist of the original reasonably well.

3. An infinitive is better than W's repetition of φαντασίαι. Either
Ph's προσφέρεσθαι or Diano's παρασκευάσαι will do. Ph also proposed
a possible opening for the sentence (cf. app. crit.). G's idea is a little
different; he suggests that Epicurus has told his mother that if she
thinks about him often it is quite possible that she will see him in her
dreams, but these φαντασίαι τῶν ἀπόντων κτλ.

4. φαντασίαι is the correct word for psychic images, both in sleep
and awake, whether true or false. It is difficult to see what can be
added to the very full notice in L.S.J. ad loc.

II. This, the best-preserved column, has caused the most disagreement as to its interpretation. Authorities are divided into those who
think it necessary to introduce a negative into l. 7 and those who do
not. HK proposed a third course, placing a negative in l. 8, but this
has found no supporters and need not detain us.

Those who would alter l. 7 consider that such a step, bold as it is,
is essential for the sense. They take the subject of the sentence to be
φαντασίαι, or some such word, and the meaning to be that such 'appearances, being intelligible . . . have the same capacity for affecting
the *absent* as they had when they arose in their presence', i.e. in the
latter case the effect is felt in the eye of the percipient, in the former
in his mind.

W, however, was sure that the text as it stands makes perfectly
good sense once it is noticed that the subject is not φαντασίαι in general
but only the φαντασίαι τῶν ἀπόντων (I 4–5); the παρόντας of l. 7, he
says, can be none but the recipients of the φαντασίαι, called 'present'
prolepsi quadam to distinguish them from the absent 'senders' of the
appearances. He therefore translates, 'The appearances of the absent
have the same effect on those present as at the time when, they also
being present, they arose in their minds' ('notiones absentium eandem
vim habent in praesentes, atque tum, cum illis quoque [καὶ] praesen-
tibus animo eorum substiterunt').

Diano rejected this argument, preferring Usener's negative in l. 7;
G accepts W's text but thinks the explanation is simpler. πρὸς τοὺς
παρόντας, he says, is merely a condensed way of saying πρὸς τὰς τῶν
παρόντων φαντασίας, and the sentence means that the appearances
of the absent have the same effect *in comparison with* appearances of
those present, as when they arose with the 'senders' themselves
present.

My own feeling is that where the text can be understood as it
stands it should not be altered. There are very few mistakes in this
inscription, and none so serious as the omission of a negative. If we

accept W's point, that the subject is αἱ φαντασίαι τῶν ἀπόντων—and it is a convincing one—then his explanation and translation make good sense. There is, perhaps, one observation to be made. It does not seem quite correct to translate I 10–II 3 as '. . . they are exactly the same both of the absent as of the present' (e.g. G 'sono tali quelle degli assenti, quali quelle dei presenti'). This would surely require τῶν μὴ παρόντων οἷαι καὶ τῶν παρόντων; in the absence of the article the meaning is rather '(The appearances of the absent) . . . are exactly the same both when they are not present and when they are'.

4. G maintains that διανοηταί should be active in meaning; the passive form would be διανοητικαί, which Diano proposed. But διανοητός is translated 'thinkable' by L.S.J. for Plut. *Commun. notit.* 1081 a.

5–6. *In themselves* all perceptible images are the same, i.e. compounds of atoms; the interpretation which the recipient puts upon them is something different.

III. The first 6–7 letters of each line survive on one block but only a few from the ends of the lines on the other.

2. The 7th letter is clearly Λ and it seems needless to alter it to Δ.

IV. 1–2. The last four letters of l. 1 are doubtful and this affects the reading of the beginning of l. 2, but W's solution, which he put forward only tentatively, makes good sense.

3. Epicurus did not hesitate to claim that man could rival the gods in happiness. The last words of the Epistle to Menoeceus (*Ep.* iii. 135) are οὐθὲν γὰρ ἔοικε θνητῷ ζῴῳ ζῶν ἄνθρωπος ἐν ἀθανάτοις ἀγαθοῖς. Not much was needed for him to do so, cf. fr. 602 Us ὁ αὐτὸς ἔλεγεν ἑτοίμως ἔχειν καὶ τῷ Διὶ ὑπὲρ εὐδαιμονίας διαγωνίζεσθαι μᾶζαν ἔχων καὶ ὕδωρ.

4. Nor did mortality detract from this happiness, cf. P.D. 19 and 20 and Cic. *De fin.* ii. 27. 87 'negat Epicurus ne diuturnitatem quidem temporis ad beate vivendum aliquid afferre, nec minorem voluptatem percipi in brevitate temporis quam si illa sit sempiterna'.

FRAGMENT 53 (41 cm., 70 cm., 43 cm.,: 38 cm., 52·5 cm., 41·5 cm.)

This fragment is also a combination of two blocks; one contains cols. I and II with only a narrow space between them and no margin on either side; the other has col. III with wide margins to right and left.

W and Ph differ in their understanding of the connection between this fragment and the last, though both apparently assume that only a little is lost between them. According to W the writer, having said in fr. 52 that while he is alive he is as happy as the gods, went on to say that death does not rob a man of happiness; as he feels nothing he has no sense of loss. He quotes the pseudo-Platonic *Axiochus* 370 a λυπεῖ γὰρ τὸν στερόμενον τῶν ἀγαθῶν ἡ ἀντιπάθεια τῶν κακῶν, ὁ δ' οὐκ ὢν οὐδὲ τῆς στερήσεως ἀντιλαμβάνεται.

Ph's view is that the mother had said that dependence on others is humiliating, and the son replies that this is not so if the recipient makes an adequate return for the money. G, Diano, and Arrighetti accept this explanation of the sense of the passage, the two latter also proposing restorations. Diano's cannot be right for two reasons:

(a) ἀντιποιήσων would be divided ἀντιποι|ήσων (cf. 5 II 11), but in l. 1 there is a letter missing before HC.

(b) His l. 2 apparently begins with ἀντιλάβηται, but there must again be one letter before that.

Arrighetti begins l. 1 with [ἀντιποι]ήσ[ων] but does not indicate whether or how the word is divided.

If only a little is lost between these two fragments W's point of view is rather more convincing. Some kind of discussion about the difference between life and death began at 52 IV 8; the opening words of fr. 53 could well be the conclusion of this discussion. There are also verbal parallels between this passage and the quotation from the *Axiochus*, for instance the absolute use of αἰσθάνηται in l. 4 which corresponds to ὁ δ' οὐκ ὤν, to suggest that the subjects are the same. τοιούτων ἀγαθῶν of 53 I 6-7 would then refer to Epicurus' state of happiness which even death will not take away. This seems better than to assume the introduction of a totally different topic.

I. 3. ἐλάττωσις occurs once in a quotation from Epicurus in Porphyry *De abst.* i. 53 συμβάλλεται δὲ ὡς ἐπὶ πλεῖστον καὶ ἡ τῆς τροφῆς ἐλάττωσις, the object being bodily health. Otherwise the only other use by an Epicurean is in a fragment of Philodemus *Π. πλούτου* (cf. Arrighetti, p. 416), where the meaning would appear to be 'humiliation'; but this instance is heavily restored and could be wrong.

9. It has been pointed out that this is a metaphorical use of the formula, ἔπαιρε σεαυτήν, found in drama with the literal meaning of 'get up, arise', as in the line from Eurip. *Andromache* 1076-7

Χο. ἆ ἆ τι δράσεις, ὦ γεραιέ; μὴ πέσῃς·
ἔπαιρε σαυτόν. Πη. οὐδέν εἰμ'· ἀπωλόμην.

The verb itself is not uncommon in drama in the sense of 'stir up, excite', as for instance in Eurip. *I.A.* 125 (ἐπ. θυμόν τινι) and *Heracl.* 173 (ἐπ. ψυχήν).

II. 1. The only Epicurean use of χορηγία is found in a letter of Epicurus quoted by Philodemus (fr. 197 Us, 84 Arrighetti); it is included by Diano in his edition of letters of Epicurus and his circle (*Lettere d'Epicuro e dei suoi*), p. 7. Arrighetti's text reads:

$$Τιμ[ο-]$$

κρά[τ]ει [δ'· ἰδὼν ὡς] ἡμεῖς [πά]ντα
ταῦτα κ[ατὰ τ]ρόπον [διωρθ]ώ[με-]
θα, συλλάμβανε καὶ αὐτοῖς, οὐ μόνον διὰ τὴν οἰκειότητά [σου ἀλλὰ]
καὶ διὰ τὸ ἦθος αὐτῶν, ὅπ[ως τῆς]
πάσης χορηγίας τυγχάνωσ[ιν]
[τῆς ε]ἰς τὸ [μηθὲν ἐλλείπειν] ἁρ-
μοττούσης καὶ . . .

But it is well attested that Epicurus was helped by friends in Ionia to found the Garden in the first place and received subsidies from friends and disciples all his life. Plutarch, *Non posse suaviter* 1097 c quotes from one letter of thanks: δαΐως [Us δαιμονίως] τε καὶ μεγαλο-πρεπῶς ἐπεμελήθητε ἡμῶν τὰ περὶ τὴν τοῦ σίτου κομιδήν, καὶ οὐρανομήκη σημεῖα ἐδεδείχθε τῆς πρὸς ἐμὲ εὐνοίας (fr. 183 Us = 91 Arrighetti).

III. 1–7. *Variae structurae mire componuntur*, says W, who would rather have liked to write ἀπεσταλκότα in l. 7 to agree with πατέρα (l. 3). But such alteration is unnecessary.

5. From the opening of the Letter to Pythocles (*Ep.* ii. 84) we learn that a Cleon brought a letter to Epicurus from Pythocles. Bailey suspects that he was imaginary.

9. W maintained that βαρεῖσθαι in the sense of 'to be depressed' could only be found in Biblical Greek (**LXX** *Exod.* 7. 14; 2 *Cor.* 1. 8 and 5. 4). Elsewhere the depressing emotion is given, e.g. πένθει βεβαρημένος. He added that βαρεῖν is poetic. Papyrus discoveries have disproved both these statements. Instances of the active in prose are quoted in L.S.J., and the absolute use of the passive is not unknown; it seems to go back to Sappho.

10. G writes τ[ὴ]ν |[ἑτέραν] because 'inter **T** et **N** spatium maius est quam pro litterae **O** exiguitate'. But in this fragment the **O**s are fatter and rounder than usual.

FRAGMENT 54 (35 cm., 58·5 cm., 29 cm.)

A block with part of Diogenes' name carved on its lower right-hand portion in letters at least twice the size of those used in the next section, the treatise on Old Age, and half as big again as those in the only other comparable title in the inscription (fr. 23). Before W it was accepted as part of the title to the entire work and Ph, in view of the size of the letters, was inclined to support this view; he thought it may have stood in the centre of the highest band of the inscription with the various writings in this part of the work on either side.

But W observed that the columns of the treatise on Old Age were, as far as we can tell, divided between an upper and a lower block, just as this title is, and the height of such upper blocks (35 cm.) is the same as the height of this block. He had also noticed the tops of letters showing along its bottom edge. He therefore concluded that the title to which it belongs was the title to this treatise only and suggested that the remnants along the edge could be read as in the app. crit. G agrees with him.

It is certainly a substantial title, extending over at least four blocks, and the early editors may be right. On the other hand, the size of the lettering is not conclusive; it is to be noted that in fr. 23, which is the title to the ethical treatise, the lettering there is twice the size of that used in the treatise. The lettering in this fragment is in the same proportion to the text on Old Age.

F. *On Old Age*

This final section is the least well preserved part of the inscription. Inscribed on wide but not very tall blocks, and in larger lettering than the Physics and Ethics, it must have stood above them in the highest range of the wall. Unfortunately so little survives that it is impossible to say with certainty in what order the fragments stood, or what the complete treatise contained. The arrangement of the fragments is discussed in the Introduction, but as to content we can be fairly sure that we have here the remains of a work, in diatribe form, refuting attempts to disparage old age and speaking in its defence.

Such a theme was evidently common in post-Aristotelian philosophy. Diogenes Laertius records that Theophrastus wrote on it, as did Demetrius of Phalerum; the one perfectly preserved treatment we have is of course Cicero's *De senectute*, but four long fragments of a treatise by a certain Juncus are to be found in Stobaeus' Anthology (cf. fr. 56). Plato touches on the subject at the beginning of his *Republic*, where Socrates finds the old Cephalus at home, but he almost at once moves on to his real interest, the discussion of the nature of Justice.

The philosophic students of Hellenistic and later times were not interested in such large and fundamental topics; in their vastly increased numbers they looked to philosophy to provide moral guidance, and practical rules for living. It was to satisfy this demand that treatises and diatribes such as this were written.

As Ph remarks, the subject would be dear to the old man's heart and this may well be one of the most original parts of the work; certainly we do not know of any other treatment of this theme by an Epicurean. The Master himself seems never to have concerned himself with it at length though his views are clear from no. 17 of the *Sententiae Vaticanae*:* 'It is not the young man who should be thought happy, but an old man who has lived a good life. For the young man at the height of his powers is unstable and is carried this way and that by fortune, like a headlong stream. But the old man has come to anchor in old age as though in port, and the good things for which before he hardly hoped he has brought into safe harbourage in his grateful recollections' (Bailey trans.). Diogenes may well have had this section engraved after the main body of the work was finished.

* Οὐ νέος μακαριστὸς ἀλλὰ γέρων βεβιωκὼς καλῶς· ὁ γὰρ νέος ⟨ἐν⟩[1] ἀκμῇ πολὺς ὑπὸ τῆς τύχης ἑτεροφρονῶν πλάζεται· ὁ δὲ γέρων καθάπερ ἐν λιμένι τῷ γήρᾳ καθώρμικεν τὰ πρότερον δυσελπιστούμενα τῶν ἀγαθῶν ἀσφαλεῖ κατακλείσας χάριτι.

FRAGMENT 55 (34 cm., 128 cm., 41 cm.)

A wide stone containing the upper portions of two columns with a gap of about 14 cm. between the two and a margin on the right extending to at least 25 cm. It is broken along the bottom and has also suffered erasures.

It certainly seems to be the opening of an address by an older man to his juniors, presumably on the subject of old age. Ph thought that it probably went: 'I am indignant about those who, without having reached old age, attack it; they behave better who have proceeded further with their education so that they not only praise the poet Hesiod but also realize the advantages of old age.' G has tentatively restored col. I on these lines, and finds support for his restoration in Cicero, *De senectute* 2. 4 and D.L.'s life of Bion (iv. 51); in both these passages the point is made that all men wish to attain old age and yet complain when they do. It is a very reasonable proposal but, of course, must remain a suggestion.

II. 4. The possibility of reading Hesiod's name in the strange jumble

[1] suppl. Bailey

of letters first occurred to W. Ph would suppose that the reference is to *Works and Days* 331 seqq.

ὅς τε γονῆα γέροντα κακῷ ἐπὶ γήραος οὐδῷ
νεικείῃ χαλεποῖσι καθαπτόμενος ἐπέεσσιν·
τῷ δ' ἦ τοι Ζεὺς αὐτὸς ἀγαίεται, ἐς δὲ τελευτὴν
ἔργων ἀντ' ἀδίκων χαλεπὴν ἐπέθηκεν ἀμοιβήν.

FRAGMENT 56 (50 cm., 43 cm., 44 cm.)

This is an almost square block containing the bottom five lines of a column (or most of them—the ends are missing) with a blank margin below, and below that again a rather wider scored margin. Only the lower half of l. 5 is on this block; the upper parts of the letters would have been on the stone which held ll. 1–4.

Two interpretations have been suggested for this fragment. W thought the preceding words might have been [καλὸν μέντοι ἐστὶν ἀκεραίοις χρώμενον] ταῖς αἰσθήσεσι κτλ., and that Diogenes is arguing against those who think that the old should withdraw from life when their faculties fail. He adopts Usener's τοῖς οἰομένοις in l. 9 and concludes ὡς ἐξαναχωρεῖν δεῖ ἐκ τοῦ ζῆν τοὺς . . .

Ph, however, proposed that Diogenes' point was that it is wrong to reproach the old with the loss of their faculties since many keep them intact till life's end—hence the introductory words which I have adopted. The writer therefore disagrees with those who blame old age as though it were entirely mutilated. G accepted the opening suggested by Ph and in his 1950 commentary the continuation also, seeing in it a parallel with Juncus *ap.* Stobaeus iv. 1028. 7 seqq., but he gave up the latter in his text and concludes with Gomperz's ἐξ ἀν[άγκης . . . which HK printed.

Ph referred to Juncus *ap.* Stobaeus iv. 1058. 4 seqq., but G pointed out that this must be a mistake, most probably for 1050. 3–5 ἐμοὶ γὰρ δύσκολος ὁ ἐν αὐτῷ βίος καταφαίνεται διὰ τὴν τῶν αἰσθήσεων στέρησιν κατ' ὀλίγον ἀποσβεννυμένων. This is part of a passage which Stobaeus included in the ψόγος γήρως. There are four passages altogether in Stobaeus headed Ἰούνκου ἐκ τοῦ περὶ γήρως, iv. 1026. 10 seqq. in Hense's edition (115. 26 Meineke), iv. 1049. 11 seqq. (116. 49), iv. 1060. 10 seqq. (117. 9), and iv. 1107. 16 seqq. (121. 35). Who this Juncus was we do not know, as nothing survives of him except these four excerpts; he seems to have been a philosophic writer of the early imperial period, possibly second century A.D.

FRAGMENT 57 (37 cm., 92 cm., 27 cm.)

A rectangular block which presents a rather different appearance from those which have so far been assigned to this part of the inscription.

It is only 3 cm. taller than fr. 55 and yet, by having no margin at top or bottom, holds two cols. of eight lines each in lettering which is only slightly smaller than that of fr. 55. It is usually assumed that another block below held two more lines for each column to bring the total up to the usual ten, with perhaps a scored border underneath. But this would have been a very narrow stone, and it is hard to believe that it could have brought the over-all height up to the 80 cm. which we find in the next fragment. Either, then, the columns here were of more than ten lines each, or this part of the treatise was arranged in a different way from, e.g., frs. 55 and 58. The subject-matter proves that it must be part of the same treatise.

The top edge of the stone is damaged along almost all its length, the first line of col. I is completely erased, and the last two largely destroyed. Col. II is incomplete on the right and many letters are badly damaged, with the result that no one has attempted to restore it.

I. 5–6. L.S.J. define ἀμαυρώσις here as 'dulling, as of the mind in old age' and refer to Arist. *De anima* 408ᵇ20, but the meaning must surely be the alternative 'darkening of the eyes' as in Hippocrates, *Coac.* 221; not quite the later 'complete hindrance to sight without any visible cause' found in Galen 14. 776.

8. Diels's proposal for this line is accepted by W and Ph; W translates 'he would shear a sheep with a sword' ('ovem gladio tondeat'); Ph renders 'he would comb a sheep with a spear', i.e. wildly exaggerate. Unfortunately this attractive suggestion cannot be entertained. Not only is it quite unknown as a proverb (and also, one would think, extremely unlikely), but such remnants of letters as can be made out do not support it.

FRAGMENT 58 (33·5 cm., 68 cm., 35 cm., +48 cm., 75 cm., 36 cm.)

The upper block has a margin above, the last 8–9 letters of col. I 1–5, and the first 10–11 letters of col. II 1–5. The lower block has 2–3 letters from the extreme right of col. I 6–10 and the whole of col. II 6–10; it has a margin and striped border below. Though these stones were found in the same area by Cousin, HK were the first to join them to make a more or less complete col. II and a somewhat mutilated part of col. I; see illustration on next page.

There can be no proof that this arrangement is correct; these two blocks could be halves of two entirely separate fragments. On the other hand, it is a not unreasonable hypothesis and no better one is in sight.

I. From ll. 1 and 2 it seems fairly certain that the subject is the elephant and its slowness of movement, and the last word of l. 5 must be μοχθη[ρόν] or μοχθη[ρίαν]. From these beginnings many attempts have been made to restore at least ll. 1–5 of this column. HK assume that the writer is rejecting the idea that anyone could make slowness

the basis for a charge of moral depravity. W thinks that the writer is refuting the critics of old age and its slowness by saying, 'If they hold the elephant to be *wretched* because of its slowness then we must believe them'. But he is not happy about his restoration.

Ph makes no suggestions for the text but thinks that the elephant's *docility* is being opposed to its clumsiness (he presumably understands μοχθηρία in its more usual sense of 'depravity' and assumes that the equation of slowness of body with it is being rejected as absurd). For βραδυκινησία he quotes the similar language of Juncus at 1049. 16, who speaks of the man ἱστάμενον ἐπὶ τῷ γήρᾳ καὶ αὐτὸν ἑαυτοῦ βραδύ-τερόν τε καὶ δυσκινητότερον γεγονότα καὶ ἀεὶ γιγνόμενον τῇ τε ψυχῇ καὶ τῷ σώματι.

For the elephant's docility he refers to Aristotle, *H.A.* 630[b]18 seqq. πάντων δὲ τιθασσότατον καὶ ἡμερώτατον τῶν ἀγρίων ἐστὶν ὁ ἐλέφας·

πολλὰ γὰρ καὶ παιδεύεται καὶ συνίησιν ἐπεὶ καὶ προσκυνεῖν διδάσκονται τὸν βασιλέα.

G¹ altered W's restoration but adopted his understanding of the meaning; he translates '... ma e davvero stolto se accusano di miserabilità l'elefanto per l'eccessiva lentezza di movimento'. But in his later text he limits his restoration to ll. 5–6, κα|[ταγεινώσ]κουσι μοχθη|[ρὸν εἶναι ... (from HK). This is much the wisest thing to do when so little is left of the text.

The Greeks before Alexander knew very little about elephants. Herodotus, who mentions them first, had only heard of the existence of the African variety. But Alexander met the Indian elephant and Aristotle has a great deal to say about both in the *Historia animalium* etc. They then became an important part of all Hellenistic armies and were used by the Carthaginians and even the Romans. It was not long before a body of fact and legend grew up about these extraordinary creatures—about their gentleness, kindness to one another, and docility, as well as their love of beauty (both in girls and boys), and modest and decorous habits. The same stories are repeated in Pliny, *Natural History* viii. 1–13, in Plutarch, *Terrestriane an aquatilia animalia* (The Cleverness of Animals) 959 seqq., and Aelian, *On Animals* (passim).[1]

None of these writers actually mentions their slowness but this is such an obvious characteristic that its omission is understandable.

II. This has also given rise to different interpretations and restorations. HK, who first wrote ἀνθρώ|πων in ll. 1–2, thought that Diogenes was continuing his comparison of man and beast and in this column turning to the discussion of man. But in a footnote they suggested, in view of l. 10, the text for ll. 1–4 which I have adopted; I am not, however, convinced by their interpretation of l. 4. They wrote τοιοῦτος (scil. μοχθηρός, *nichtig*) λ[εκτεός.], which would, I suppose, translate: 'And the argument about feelings of sadness also ... must be called unfounded.' The introduction of μοχθηρός seems very difficult.

W placed a full stop at τοιοῦτος but offers no translation. His interpretation of ll. 4 seqq. (his text) is as follows: 'contra eos qui aegritudines senectutis accusant primum dicendum est, illud non contra senes dici; in universum enim iis quibus cupiditates non insunt, ne aegritudines quidem insunt (senibus autem cupiditates non insunt, ergo ne aegritudines quidem).' For l. 7 he refers to Lucr. iii. 900 seqq. (perhaps 898 seqq. would be better):

> 'misero misere,' aiunt, 'omnia ademit
> una dies infesta tibi tot praemia vitae.'

---

[1] Aelian (xi. 15) even has a story about elephants punishing adultery by killing wives who misbehaved in the absence of their husbands.

illud in his rebus non addunt 'nec tibi earum
iam desiderium rerum super insidet una.'

Ph accepted this interpretation, that in fact old age has less unhappiness because it has fewer desires, but was evidently worried by the
lack of a noun to go with the article in l. 1. He considered that λόγος
in l. 7 should go with it, excluded the full stop in l. 4, and suggested
δηλαδή instead of W's ἀλλὰ τό. This would produce a rather awkward
sentence, with a long gap between ὁ περὶ τῶν . . . λυπῶν and λόγος.

G adopted δηλαδή but puts a colon after it; he does not, however,
in his text restore l. 1, objecting to λυ|πῶν as being too short; he would
prefer τῶν [λυπῶν]‖ τῶνδε κτλ.

What conclusions can be drawn from these differing opinions?
It is a great pity that the first five lines lack their final five letters,
since the restoration of l. 1 is very puzzling. HK's ἀνθρώ|πων is the
right length but does not seem to fit the context; λυ|πῶν on the other
hand leaves a space of three letters unfilled. Fortunately ll. 6–10
are nearly complete and their meaning can be regarded as certain.
'Things that we do not want we do not miss' is the message—cf.
Cicero, De senec. 14. 47 'nihil autem est molestum quod non de-
sideres'. If then these two blocks are correctly joined and do form
one column here, and this seems extremely likely, then it is legitimate
to assume that ll. 1–4 will be an introduction of the topic that the
old are said to suffer from feelings of sadness and loss, the answer
to which begins at l. 5. πρῶτον μέν must be the opening of a new
sentence, and we must therefore assume an anticipatory λόγος with
the article in l. 1. τοιοῦτος I take to mean 'as follows'; it normally
refers to what has gone before but τοιοῦτός τις regularly looks forward
and it is not unlikely that τοιοῦτος alone should occasionally do the
same. As to the last word in l. 4, HK's transcript strongly favours Λ
as the last extant letter rather than A or Δ.

FRAGMENT 59

This small fragment is recorded only by Cousin (p. 27). It forms one
of a group of three which he presumably found together; the other
two are now frs. 63 (part) and 69. Only the part of fr. 63 was found
again by HK, but they were able to join it to two more small pieces
recorded on the same page by Cousin to make an undoubted portion
of the treatise on Old Age—apart from the distinctive lettering one
piece has the distinctive striped border along the bottom. HK therefore included this fragment, together with 69, in this part of the work,
especially in view of Usener's alteration of βηκικά to βηχικά (πάθη).
W for some reason changed this word to ψυχικά and placed the fragment at the end of the ethical treatise.

I can see nothing to justify this change and agree with G in restoring it to the place assigned to it by HK. Since Cousin says of it that it was 'complet en haut et sur les côtés; vide au dessus' (which I take to be a misprint for *dessous*), they thought it might be the lower part of a ten-line block. It is more probable that the column extended over two blocks of which this was the lower.

8. The text can stand if βηκία and βηκίον = βήχιον (a slight cough) in Dioscorides, *Eup.* 2. 31 (L.S.J.).

9. The objection to W's restoration is that there should be one letter before ΧΕ and only one after it. This makes his μο|χθ[ισ]μόν rather unlikely, though G adopts it.

FRAGMENT 60 (47 cm., 34·5 cm., 72 cm.)

A few remains of lines from the bottom of a column; some of the letters have been erased and below a wide margin is the striped border.

Usener's recognition of Homer, *Od.* xxiv. 254–5 has been generally accepted and is convincing, but we can only guess at the context. W thought that the quotation is made by the detractors of old men, who are only fit for sleeping; the refutation of this view would then begin at l. 9. G, on the other hand, was convinced that the whole fragment is in fact in praise of old age. In his commentary he was of the opinion that fr. 65 might have immediately preceded this fragment, especially if ἀλείφωσι is correct in I 6, and that between frs. 60 and 61 there was only one stone containing the end of this fragment and nearly the whole of 61 I. But we have the end of this fragment and it would require at least two blocks to complete 61 I, as the illustration of that fragment shows. In his text he placed fr. 65 *after* this fragment and then 62 and 61 in that order. He does, however, retain his proposed introduction to this fragment, i.e. ⟨"ἐπεὶ λούσαιτο φάγοι τε" κτλ.

With so little left no restoration or interpretation can be anything but very tentative.

FRAGMENT 61 (47 cm., 47 cm., 77 cm.: 34 cm., 33 cm.)

Two blocks first combined by HK as a result of Usener's recognition of Homeric quotations in II 7–9 and II 10–III 1–2. [It is illustrated on the last page of the text—TAB. II.] According to W and Ph, Diogenes is now in his turn quoting Homer (hence ὁ αὐτός in II 6) to show that even if the old are no longer physically active, they can still give valuable advice.

II. 7. *Iliad* ii. 53.

Cf. Cicero, *De senec.* 10. 31 'Videtisne ut apud Homerum saepissime Nestor de virtutibus suis praedicet?' etc.

10. *Iliad* iii. 150.

III. 5. For some fragments from tragedy cf. Stobaeus iv. 1020 seqq., especially nos. 2, 10, 12, 16, 17. All these make the same point as the first (from Eurip. *Bellerophontes*) :

> ὦ παῖ, νέων τοι δρᾶν μὲν ἔντονοι χέρες,
> γνῶμαι δ' ἀμείνους εἰσὶ τῶν γεραιτέρων·
> ὁ γὰρ χρόνος δίδαγμα ποικιλώτατον.

FRAGMENT 62 (38 cm., 38 cm., 41 cm.)

A small square block containing seven half lines, partially erased, with a margin only on the right. This would have been the upper part of a column. The point being made seems to be a continuation of the last fragment, that the old are still strong in counsel.

The reference to Juncus at Stob. iv. 1064. 4 seqq. reads ἐμνημόνευε δὲ τραπεὶς ἐπὶ τὴν Ἑλληνικὴν ἱστορίαν τοῦ Πυλίου Νέστορος, ὃν διὰ γνώμην καὶ γῆρας τῶν συμπάντων ἡρώων προετίμησεν Ἀγαμέμνων ὁ τοῦ πολέμου στρατηγός.

7. ἄρτιος, as applied to soundness of mind, evidently developed from a poetic to a later prose use. It is found in Theognis 154 ὅτῳ μὴ νόος ἄρτιος ᾖ, and Eurip. *Troades* 417 οὐ γὰρ ἀρτίας ἔχεις φρένας, and then in prose writers. Diodorus Siculus has it and W quotes Cyrill. Alex. for τοῖς ἀρτίοις τὴν φρένα.

FRAGMENT 63 (47 cm., 46 cm., 15–25 cm.)

Three pieces were fitted together by HK to make this fragment (cf. on fr. 59); its over-all measurements are given above. There is the usual striped border below a wide margin, so that it must be the lower half of a ten-line column.

There does not appear to be an exact parallel elsewhere to the point being made here. G refers to Cic. *De senec.* 11. 36 but there Cato is saying that just as not all young men exhibit *petulantia* and *libido* so not all old men are victims of 'ista senilis stultitia quae deliratio appellari solet'. In the previous section he has said that feebleness of body is not peculiar to the old but a normal result of poor health (non proprium senectutis vitium est, sed commune valetudinis').

FRAGMENT 64 (38·5 cm., 55 cm., 33 cm.)

A block damaged at the bottom edge containing part of 16 lines arranged in two eight-line columns with a space in the middle. HK, reading ἔρρωσο in I 7, thought it was part of a letter and placed it

between the Letter to Mother and fr. 51, but the appearance of the stone and the script strongly suggest that it came from this section of the inscription.

If the restoration is correct col. II is an echo of P.D. 4 (cf. frs. 38 and 42). The same idea is found in Cicero, *De fin.* i. 12. 40, 'We should not fear pain because it is usually light if long and short if severe, so that when it is intense we have the consolation of a quick end and when it persists the severity diminishes' ('ut eius magnitudinem celeritas, diuturnitatem allevatio consoletur'), and in Seneca, *Ep. mor.* 78. 7 'nos ... natura disposuit ut dolorem aut tolerabilem aut brevem faceret'.

FRAGMENT 65 (43 cm., 51 cm., 38 cm.)

A complete block containing parts of two columns with the usual wide border and striped border below. Unfortunately what can be read of the text is so little that restoration is not possible with any degree of certainty. It seems probable that a detractor is saying that old men are useless in war; G refers to Juncus, op. cit. iv. 1051. 12 seqq. ἐν δὲ πολέμῳ τί χρὴ καὶ λέγειν ὡς ἀστράτευτός τε καὶ γυμνὸς ἀπολείπεται, οὐ πεζός, οὐχ ἱππεὺς τεταγμένος κτλ., but attempts no restoration.

HK's suggestion is not very convincing and the lines they propose are too short; the average length is 17–18 letters.

FRAGMENT 66 (46 cm., 34·5 cm., 39 cm.)

A fragment complete at top and bottom, broken to right and left. Again we have part of the lower five lines of a column with margin and striped border below.

The writer is saying that something is a great advantage, presumably in old age, and there is the word πενία. Ph thought that the advantage was frugality, which it would be wrong to call πενία, but the letter before Υ in l. 10 is almost certainly Λ (it could be Δ or Α but not Ο). G suggested that the advantage is the peace and quiet of the old, which it would be wrong to call πενία, but does not attempt to restore the text.

Juncus (1051. 17 seqq.) has a passage on the miseries of πενία in old age, inadequate food, shelter, clothing, even water, all adding up to a veritable Ἰλιάς κακῶν.

The remaining fragments (67–72) are too small to yield any information.

It hardly needs repeating that this section is the most fragmentary part of the whole inscription; even the pieces that were found, mostly

by HK, contain so little text that it is never easy and sometimes impossible to be sure what the writer was saying. However, it would appear that the following points were made:

1. Even though the old may lose their bodily strength, they retain their mental powers and ability to give good advice (frs. 60, 61, 62);
2. they do not lose all bodily powers (fr. 57);
3. nor do all lose their faculties (fr. 56);
4. it is wrong to condemn old age as a time of misery and sadness.

Cicero (*De senec.* 5. 15) gives four reasons for the opinion that old age is unhappy:

1. It withdraws men from active pursuits;
2. it makes the body weaker;
3. it robs men of almost all pleasures;
4. it is not far from death.

Diogenes, therefore, touches on the first three of Cicero's reasons in some form or other, and if we had more of his text, it is very possible that the parallel would be found to be even closer than it appears now. He does not mention the fourth point—that old age is near to death. This was normally a part of the ψόγος γήρως, as we can see from Juncus, op. cit. 1050. 7 seqq. αὐτῷ τε τῷ πάσχοντι τὴν μεταβολὴν περαιτέρω τούτων ἐνοχλεῖν τὸν περὶ τοῦ θανάτου φόβον ἀεὶ ἑπόμενον αὐτῷ κτλ., and Ph thinks that this topic would have been especially attractive to an Epicurean, and must have been included. This may be so—on the other hand it may not have been. That there is nothing to fear about death is a cardinal belief of Epicurus and a basic teaching at all ages; it might well have seemed unnecessary if not actually irrelevant to introduce it into a treatise specifically devoted to one stage of human life. But see now Appendix, p. 132.

APPENDIX

By kind permission of the editors I am able to reproduce the four new fragments published by Mr. M. F. Smith in *American Journal of Archaeology*, vol. lxxiv, no. 1, Jan. 1970. The text is that read by Smith, except for a few changes I have felt bound to introduce; photographs of varying clarity illustrate the article and he has also, I understand, a squeeze of no. 2.

NEW FRAGMENT I (47 cm., 75·5 cm., 36 cm.)

Col. I   - - -
          - - -

                    ..μ.ο.
                    ἔ]χει - - (c. 3)
5   .χεθεναι
                    που..ο
                    αραιν.ι
                    εινṭ..ι
                    ποιεῖ φό-
10   [βον   δ]οκουν
                        μνου πε-
                    διανιστά-
        [μεθα ἐκ τοῦ φ]όβου καὶ
                    οἷς δ' ἔτι

Col. II   - (c. 10) - μ..οσ
           .....ωσ..υσα.υμι
           τα.οσ...ιασιεναι
           παρ' οὐδὲν ..τιτογα
5   την ἀπ' αὐτῶν εὐφρο-
           σύνην λαμβάνειν
           ὅτι καθεύδομεν. οὔ-
           κουν [εἰδ]η κενὰ λέγει
           ταῦτα ὡς καὶ δύναμις
10   τοσαύτη πρόσεσ[τ]ιν. οὐ
           μὴν πάλιν, εἰ μή ἐστιν
           κενά, αἴσθησ[ιν] ἔχει

Col. II. 3 coniecit Smith ἰέναι   4–5 con. Smith παρ' οὐδέν [ἐσ]τι τὸ μά|την
7–8 scripsi, Smith οὐκοῦν   8 supplevi, Smith [ἔπ]η

καὶ λογισμὸν καὶ τῶ
ὄντι προσλαλεῖ ἡμε[ῖν]

Col. III   .τυπουαυ .ιναορισμε
.ετοις. [ἀμ]ήχανόν γαρ λε-
πτοῖς ὑμέσιν οὕτως καὶ
στερεμνίας φύσεως βά-
5   θος οὐκ ἔχουσ[ι]ν ταῦτα προσεῖναι. οὗτοι μὲν οὖν κα-
τὰ τὸ ἐναντίον ἐπλανή-
θησαν οἵ τε Στωικο[ὶ] κ[αὶ] Δημόκριτος. οἱ μὲν γὰρ Στω-
10   ικοὶ καὶ ἣν ἔχουσι δύναμιν τῶν φαντασιῶν ἀφαι-
ροῦνται. Δημόκριτος δὲ
καὶ ἣν οὐκ ἔχουσι χα[ρί]-
ζεται. ἡ δὲ φύσις τῶν ἐνυ

Col. III. 1–2 dubitans con. Smith [κ]τύπου αὐτοῦ αἰσθανο|[μ]ένοις   14 con.
Smith ἐνυ|[πνίων] vel ἐν ὕ|[πνῳ φαντασιῶν (φασμάτων)

Translation:

II . . . to feel gladness from them because we are asleep. So he says
that these are not empty shapes since so much power belongs to them
as well. On the other hand, if they are not empty, they certainly do
not possess sensation and reasoning and really speak to us . . .

III . . . For it is impossible for these (abilities) to belong to thin
membranes in this way, membranes which do not possess the depth of
a solid nature. So these men are misled in opposite ways, I mean the
Stoics and Democritus. For the Stoics take away from the images even
the power that they do have, while Democritus bestows on them a
power they do not have. But the nature of [dreams] . . .

This is an interesting fragment, not least because it contains no
fewer than five words which occur nowhere else in the previously
known fragments of the inscription. From the height of the stone, the
length of the columns, the size of the lettering (1·4–2·2 cm. high),
and the absence of παραγραφαί it must belong to the physical treatise.
Further, the subject-matter connects it closely, as Smith says, with
fr. 7. This, it will be remembered (cf. p. 47), criticized the Stoic
doctrine that hallucinations and dreams are 'empty figments of the
imagination' (κενὰ σκιαγραφήματα τῆς διανοίας). We now have a
criticism of Democritus' theory of dreams, which is described in col.
III as equally erroneous. In view of this latter remark Smith is clearly

right to place this new fragment after fr. 7 rather than before it, and it may be added that it is conclusive proof that Philippson was wrong to suggest a transposition of frs. 6 and 7. We cannot tell how closely this new fragment was joined to fr. 7 as both 7 III and the first column of this one are heavily damaged.

As to what Democritus' theory of dreams was I cannot do better than quote the standard reference, Plutarch *Quaest. conv.* 735 a–b: φησὶν Δημόκριτος ἐγκαταβυσσοῦσθαι τὰ εἴδωλα διὰ τῶν πόρων εἰς τὰ σώματα καὶ ποιεῖν τὰς κατὰ τὸν ὕπνον ὄψεις ἐπαναφερόμενα. φοιτᾶν δὲ ταῦτα πανταχόθεν ἀπιόντα . . . οὐ μόνον ἔχοντα μορφοειδεῖς τοῦ σώματος ἐκμεμαγμένας ὁμοιότητας (ὡς Ἐπίκουρος οἴεται μέχρι τούτου Δημοκρίτῳ συνεπόμενος, ἐνταῦθα δὲ προλιπὼν τὸν λόγον), ἀλλὰ καὶ τῶν κατὰ ψυχὴν κινημάτων καὶ βουλευμάτων ἑκάστῳ καὶ ἠθῶν καὶ παθῶν ἐμφάσεις ἀναλαμβάνοντα συνεφέλκεσθαι καὶ προσπίπτοντα μετὰ τούτων ὥσπερ ἔμψυχα φράζειν καὶ διαγγέλλειν τοῖς ὑποδεχομένοις τὰς τῶν μεθιέντων αὐτὰ δόξας καὶ διαλογισμοὺς καὶ ὁρμάς . . . i.e. 'Democritus says that images penetrate the body through the pores and when they arise cause visions in sleep. They arise from everything and travel about . . . not only having the moulded outward appearance of the subject—as Epicurus thinks, following Democritus so far but then deserting the doctrine—but they also take up and carry with them impressions of its psychical movements and intentions and character and feelings; and falling on the recipients with all this they speak to them like living things and tell them about the thoughts and reasonings and impulses of those that emitted them.'

As Plutarch says, this theory is nowhere combated by Epicurus, nor does Lucretius mention it, but Diogenes here rejects it just as he rejects the Stoic view of dream images as going too far the other way by denying them all validity.

I. Smith thinks that Diogenes is dealing with fear caused by images in sleep.

II. 4–7. With the virtual loss of ll. 1–3 it is difficult to guess the point being made here. According to Smith, 'Diogenes seems to be saying that it is of virtually no significance that images seen in dreams cause us to experience joy, because we are asleep'—but he admits that the penultimate letter of l. 4 looks more like N than M.

εὐφροσύνη occurs nowhere else in Diogenes and only once in Epicurus, in a sentence from the Περὶ αἱρέσεων quoted in D.L. x. 136 (Us fr. 2, Arrighetti 7).

7–10. I differ from Smith here. He, reading οὐκοῦν and supplying [ἔπ]η, takes these lines to mean: 'So dream images speak empty words,

the reason for their ability to do so being their great δύναμις (l. 10), by which he (i.e. Diogenes) presumably means the extreme subtlety and mobility of the εἴδωλα (cf. col. III 2–3), which enable them to penetrate and stir our minds and, when we are asleep, to deceive them.'

This seems to me to misunderstand the meaning. I regard it as certain that it is the 'images' which are κενά—as in l. 12 (Smith agreeing) and fr. 7. The subject of λέγει must then be Democritus and the sentence needs a negative. Hence my οὔκουν. ἔπη also is not a word one would expect to find in Diogenes; I would not insist on εἴδη but it fits the sense. Diogenes is saying that Democritus denies that sleep images are κενά (rightly), because they have the power to affect the dreamer (and perhaps bring him gladness in sleep, ll. 5–7), but Democritus goes too far in attributing to them perception, reasoning, and speech.

III. 3. ὑμέσιν. ὑμήν is not found in Diogenes or Epicurus, but it is reasonable to regard it as the source of Lucretius' *membrana* which he uses in Book iv (ll. 31, 51, 59, and 95) to describe the thin film of atoms which leave the surfaces of objects and form the *simulacra* (= εἴδωλα) which cause perception.

4. στερεμνίας another *hapax legomenon* in Diogenes. Epicurus, however, uses τὸ στερέμνιον (or the plural) five times in the section of the Letter to Herodotus devoted to his doctrine of sense perception (*Ep.* i. 46 seqq.) to denote the 'solid body' which gives off the εἴδωλα, and he seems to have employed it even more frequently in Book ii of the Περὶ φύσεως. Arrighetti lists 17 occurrences, of which the last two are in fact διὰ τῶν στερεμνίων φύσεων, as here.

7. The nouns πλάνην and πλάνος occur (32 I 6 and 27 I 4), but not the verb.

13–14. χα[ρί]ζεται is another *hap. leg.*

NEW FRAGMENT 2 (62 cm., 45 cm., 40 cm.)

Col. I   . κ . εα
                               . . ον φι-
                               . . ελα
                               . ρου
              5   τατου
                               . εστη
                                ερον

Col. I. 1 dubitans coniecit Smith ['Ἐνπεδο]κ[λ]εα   2–3 idem [τ]ὸν φι|[λό-
σοφον]   4 idem [Πυθαγό]ρου

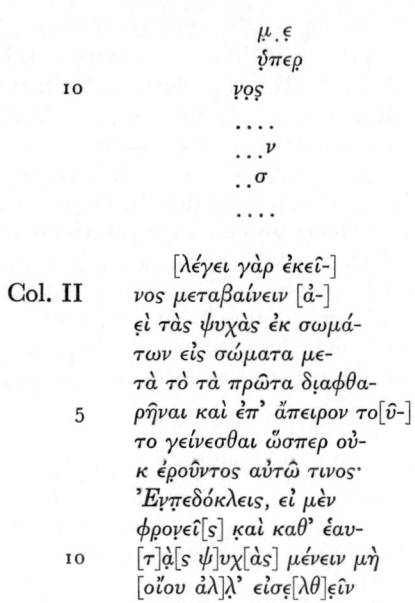

μ.ε
ὑπερ
10   νος
. . . .
. . .ν
. .σ
. . . .

[λέγει γὰρ ἐκεῖ-]
Col. II   νος μεταβαίνειν [ἀ-]
εἰ τὰς ψυχὰς ἐκ σωμά-
των εἰς σώματα με-
τὰ τὸ τὰ πρῶτα διαφθα-
5   ρῆναι καὶ ἐπ' ἄπειρον το[ῦ-]
το γείνεσθαι ὥσπερ οὐ-
κ ἐροῦντος αὐτῶ τινος·
'Ευπεδόκλεις, εἰ μὲν
φρονεῖ[ς] καὶ καθ' ἑαυ-
10   [τ]ὰ[ς ψ]υχ[ὰς] μένειν μὴ
[οἴου ἀλ]λ' εἰσε[λθ]εῖν
εἰς [ζώ]ον φύσιν καὶ τού-
του ἕ[νεκα] μεταφέρει[ς]
[α]ὐτάς, τί σοι δύναται ἡ

Col. II. 4–5 supplevi, S τὸ | {τὸ}   7–8 S τινος, | 'Ευπεδόκλεις.   11 sup-
plevit Skemp exempli gratia, S .εκ.οικλεισευσειν   13 ἕ[νεκα] ego, μεταφέρει[ς]
Skemp; S ει...μεταφέρειν

Translation:

'[Now *he* says] that souls are always moving from one body into
another after the first one has perished, and that this goes on for ever,
just as though no one is going to say to him: "Empedocles, if you are
in your senses and think that souls do not stay by themselves but enter
into a living nature and for this reason you teach their transmigration,
how, pray, is the [transmigration] possible?" '

This is the most interesting fragment of the four, since even without
the help of a 15th line which has unfortunately disappeared it must
be accepted that it stood immediately before fr. 34, and that the
subject of the last line here is the μετάβασις which begins that fragment. We now have the first part of Diogenes' criticism of Empedocles'
doctrine of the transmigration of souls. It was clear from fr. 34 that
he faced Empedocles with a dilemma—if souls can exist in between
bodies, why go to the trouble of moving them from body to body;

if they cannot, how do they survive during the interval between bodies? The first horn of the dilemma occupies fr. 34 I 6–14, beginning εἰ δέ; the gist of the second was reasonably obvious from 34 I 1–6 (hence Grilli's conjectural [εἰ μὲν αἱ ψυχαὶ σώμασι συνοῦσαι ζώου φύσιν ἔχουσιν, ἀδύνατός ἐστιν ἡ] μετάβασις). We now have the corresponding εἰ μέν clause in l. 8 of this new fragment. It is a pity that the lower part of the column is not so well preserved as the upper, and especially that l. 11 looks so desperate, but I am convinced that a tentative restoration is possible which will be on the right lines.

II. 5–6. S thinks that the stonemason mistakenly repeated τό from l. 5 at the beginning of the next line. He suggests that there are similar errors in fr. 8 II 7–8 {πρα}|πράγματα and in fr. 14 I 5–6 {Ταν}|[Τ]αντάλους and 6–7 ἀ{να}|[ν]αγράφουσιν. These three cases strike me as rather different from the present one; in all of them it is virtually true to say that the first syllable of a 3- or 4-syllable word is repeated at the beginning of a line. A repetition of τό would be a different kind of error. There are marks on the stone at the end of l. 5 which I had hoped could be read as Υ. I am assured by S that the squeeze does not support this, but I still feel that to read it is better than an assumption of dittography. We also need a subject for γείνεσθαι.

7–8. I do not know how the passage could be translated if it ended after ᾿Εμπεδόκλεις. The vocative must be the beginning of a new sentence and the gap which S notes after it would be the equivalent of a comma.

8–14. S's comment on these lines is: 'Then, in lines 8 ff., he (Diogenes) argues that, if Empedocles means that souls survive independently of the body and, when separated from the body, do not have a living nature, their transmigration is impossible.' He suggests as a translation: 'If you think that the souls survive even by themselves and [you do] not [mean] to change them into a living nature and [form], how, I ask you, is the transmigration possible?'

I confess that I find this hard to understand and impossible to accept. The supposition that souls *do* survive by themselves is examined in fr. 34 I 6 seqq.—the εἰ δέ clause; we are surely confronted here with the alternative that they *do not* live independent of a body. I originally thought that l. 11 must contain something like δύνασθαι and had proposed to read for it [δύνασθαι] εἰσε[λθ]εῖν, translating: 'Empedocles, if you think that by themselves souls cannot wait to enter into a living nature and for this reason you propose to convey them across, how, pray, is the [transmigration] possible?'

Skemp, however, has very tentatively suggested [οἷον ἀλ]λ᾽ εἰσε[λθ]εῖν as a possibility for l. 11 and μεταφέρεις at the end of l. 13, translated as

above. This, I think, is an improvement on my proposal for these reasons:

(a) it makes the same point;
(b) it retains one more letter of the reading recorded by Smith;
(c) it avoids an awkward use of φρονεῖς in two senses in the same sentence, and also a use of μένειν which is uncommon in prose and not found in Diogenes.

I am therefore happy to adopt his suggestion.

NEW FRAGMENT 3 (40·5 cm., 30 cm., 23 cm.)

Col. I

               ος
               η vac.
               ι   η
            μακά]ριον
5   αι vac.
               νῦν
               .νν
               ονν
                .ν
10   .ι

Col. II

δὲ οὐκ ὠφε[λ
ως καὶ περὶ
φοβεροί.   ὠσ[- - - εἴ]-
πομεν παγ[- - - - τοῦ]
5   φιλοσοφεῖ[ν - - - χρη]-
σίμου τοῖς
καταχρῶ δ[ὲ
τι αὐτῶν
νος.   καὶ τ
10   αν τοσου

The height of the stone and the size of the lettering (2–3 cm. high) prove that this stone belongs to group (c) [cf. Introd., pp. xxxvi seqq.]. This is a small group of eight stones, four of them having 10-line columns as this one has. S reports, further, that this stone is equally lacking in margins above and below. As the original four make up frs. 52 and 53, the Letter to Mother, S may well be right in ascribing this fragment also to that part of the work.

Unfortunately it does not obviously fit in with either of the previously known fragments of the Letter. S guesses that 'the author is emphasizing the necessity of pursuing philosophy in order to dispel

fear (of death and/or the gods?) and attain perfect happiness.' He thinks it might have followed closely after fr. 52, and so, presumably, before fr. 53. With so little of the text left nothing like certainty is possible.

I. 4. if μακάριον is the correct reading it is perhaps significant that this favourite word of Epicurus is found in Diogenes only at 52 IV 6.

I. 10–II. 3. S suggests οὗτο]ι| δὲ οὐκ ὠφε[λοῦνται ῥαδί]|ως καὶ περὶ [θανάτου]| φοβεροί, which he translates, 'These people (i.e. non-Epicureans) are not easily helped (i.e. to see how damaging fear of death is), even when they are afraid of death'. Or perhaps, he thinks, [τῶν θεῶν] should be read instead of [θανάτου].

The restoration seems rather bold and the resultant construction is hardly convincing.

II. 3–6. S regards the restorations in the text as certain, or almost certain, and tentatively proposes further, ὥσ[τε πρῶτον εἴ]|πομεν πάν[τως δεῖν τοῦ]| φιλοσοφεῖ[ν ὄντος χρη]|σίμου τοῖς [ἀνθρώποις].

πάντως does not occur elsewhere in Diogenes.

7–9. S notes here that if the last letter visible in l. 7 is Δ, 'as seems almost certain, we have here an apparently unparalleled personal usage of καταχράω, presumably with the same meaning as χράω'. He points out that Epicurus compares himself to an oracle in S.V. 29, and Lucretius describes his pronouncements as oracles at v. 110–13. It may also be noted, he adds, that the author of the Letter to Mother (whom he takes to be Epicurus) refers to his διάθεσιν ... ἰσόθεον (fr. 52 IV 2–3).

The latter point seems hardly relevant. As for καταχρῶ or καταχρῶμαι Epicurus is not known to have used either; Diogenes uses the middle in its normal sense of 'using' at fr. 2 V 13.

It is a pity that this apparent addition to one of the more important parts of the inscription should after all yield so little of value.

NEW FRAGMENT 4 (37·5 cm., 69 cm., 29 cm.)

Col. I
      .ο
     τεμε
    τ]ὴν σοβα-
  [ρὰν - - -] καὶ ὑπερ
5   ἐπὶ τῶ γέ-
  [ροντι - - τ]οιούτους

Col. II   καὶ ἔτι μέχρι [θανάτου].
            βίου μὲν παλαιοῦ ι..
            μεναι μηκέτ' ε̣ῖ̣να̣[ι].
            ταχὺ γὰρ τὸ τῶν ἀν̣[θρώ]-
     5   π̣ων γένος φθείρ[εται]
            διὰ τὴν συνοῦσαν - -

Col. II. 1 supplevit S   6 con. S [νό|σον, vel [θνη|τότητα

This fragment also belongs to group (c). Its height is slightly less
than no. 3 (37·5 cm. as against 40·5 cm.) but is within the range for
this group (37–41 cm.) and the lettering is of the same size (2–3 cm.
average). The columns, however, consist of only six lines and so it
cannot belong to the Letter to Mother. Of the other four blocks in this
group (cf. Introd., p. xxxviii) one is part of a general introduction
(fr. 49); the others (frs. 57, 62, and 64) belong to the diatribe on Old
Age. It would seem, then, highly likely that this new fragment also
comes from the Old Age, as Smith suggests, and the subject-matter,
as we shall see, supports this attribution.

It must be said, however, that this addition to the diatribe does
not solve any of the problems connected with its arrangement (cf.
Introd., pp. xxxviii–ix). Rather this fragment represents another
difficulty for the theory that it was inscribed on pairs of blocks in 10-
line columns, 5 to a block, with a striped border beneath. Frs. 57, 62,
and 64 had already formed a rather intractable group. Frs. 57 and 64
have parts of two 8-line columns each, fr. 62 one 7-line column, and
none has a margin above or below. This new fragment has parts of
two 6-line columns with a certain amount, perhaps 5 cm., of margin
above the top line. The margin suggests that we have here the *upper*
parts of two columns, but how many lines, if any, are missing from
the lower parts it is impossible to say. It would be very rash to assume
that it is four, plus a striped border, especially as all the lower stones
we do have (with border) contain five.

As to the content, the little that is legible—and it is to be regretted
that no sentence is complete—suggests that the subject probably is
Old Age. But what aspect of Old Age is being discussed is not very
clear. Frs. 57 and 62 seem to be making the point that the old do not
necessarily lose either their faculties or their wits. Fr. 64 *may* be saying
that intense pain does not last long. It seems fairly certain that col. II
4–6 of this fragment mean 'For the race of man swiftly perishes because of the ? which attends upon it', and so Smith thinks that we
now have a reference to a topic not elsewhere discussed by Diogenes,
the nearness of old age to death. This was normally a part of the
complaint against old age (cf. p. 123) and is discussed by Cicero in his

De senectute. Philippson long ago suggested that this topic must have been dealt with by Diogenes somewhere in his diatribe. These last three lines do indeed suggest that this fragment may be part of such a discussion, though col. I is useless and I am not happy about Smith's reading of col. II 1–3. (I agree with him that it is highly likely that some lines are missing from the bottom of col. I so that II 1 does not follow immediately after I 6.)

I. 3–4. For σοβάρος (proud, ? fearless) S refers to S.V. 45. It is otherwise not found in Epicurus or Diogenes.

II. 1. [θανάτου] must be considered highly speculative.

2–3. S translates 'It is the lot of old age . . . to live no longer'. I cannot think what restoration of l. 2 he has in mind; the beginning of l. 3 suggests either a feminine plural participle or an epic infinitive; Diogenes apparently quotes Homer in this diatribe, cf. frs. 60, 61, but this does not appear to be Homeric. Again, βίου παλαιοῦ is a puzzle; would it be a likely synonym for γήρως? Should we not consider reading rather βίου μὲν πάλαι οὐ ι . . ., and even the possibility that βίου is only the end of a word? I also question whether l. 2 is the beginning of a sentence; Diogenes does not normally omit a connecting word. Perhaps, then, we should read for col. II (the average length of line in this diatribe seems to be 17 letters):

καὶ ἔτι μέχρι . . . . ,
βίου μὲν πάλαι οὐ ι . .
μεναι μηκέτ᾽ εἶνα[ι]—
ταχὺ γὰρ τὸ τῶν ἀν[θρώ-]
5 πων γένος φθείρ[εται]
διὰ τὴν συνοῦσαν . . .

INDEX OF PASSAGES QUOTED
OR REFERRED TO

GENERAL INDEX

Academy, xxv
Alexander (of Abonuteichus), xxiv, xxv
Alexander (the Great), xv
Anaxagoras, 5, 7, 44
Anaximenes, 5, 44, 64
Antalya, xv
Antigonus, xv
Antiochus (the Great), xv
Antisthenes, 38
Antonine emperors, xxiv
Apamea (treaty of), xvii
Attaleia, xv
Aristippus, 38
Aristotle, 4, 40–2
Astrology, 51
ataraxia, 31
Atheism, 55
Athens, xx, xxiii, 8
Atoms, 9, 62; (movement), 83; (swerve), 84
Augustine (of Hippo), xxvii
Augustus, xxii

Balbura, xvii
Barigazzi, (on fr. 24), 69; (on frag. 28), 78
Bubon, xvii

Cabalians, xvi
Cabalis, xvi
Causes (of three kinds), 12, 74
Chalcis, xx, 8
χαρά, 30
Christians and Christianity, xxvi, xxvii
Chrysippus, xxv
Cibyra, xvii
Cicero (*De senectute*), 113, 123
Civilization, 53
Colossae, xxiv
Colotes, 41–2, 46
Common citizenship, 70
Constantine, xxvii
Cosmopolitanism, 35, 100
Cousin (G.), xxxi *et passim*
Cynics, 38
Cyrenaics, 30, 38

Demiurge, 57
Democritus, 5, 14, 45–7; (movement of atoms), 83; (on soul), 91; (on dreams), 125–6
Desires (division of), 100
Destiny, 83
Diagoras (of Melos), 7–8; 55
Diogenes (of Apollonia), 5, 44, 51
Diogenes (Laertius), xxv *et passim*
Diogenes (of Oenoanda), (descent), xix; (personality), xx, xlv; *his Inscription*, xix; (arrangement), xxxvi seqq.; (discovered and published), xxxi–ii; (length and location), xxxiii, xliv–v; (peculiarities), xxxv; (present state), xxxiii; (title), 113; (Ethical Treatise), xli, 10–18, 66–96, 128; (Letter to Antipater), xli, 8–10, 59–65; (Letter to Friends), xli, 19, 105; (Letter to Mother), xxxix, 19–20, 108–13, 130; (Old Age), xxxv seqq., 20–2, 113–23, 132; (Physical Treatise), xxxvii seqq., 4–8, 37–59, 125; (on soul), 91; (Various Maxims), xli, 18, 96–103; (Various Writings), 19–20, 103–13; (Will), xxxvii seqq., 19, 104–5
Divination, 82

Earth, 10, 63–5
Elephants, 117–18
Empedocles, 5, 50; (doctrine of transmigration of souls), 85–7, 128–9
Epicureanism, xxii–xviii
Epicureans, xxi–ii, xxv
Epicurus, (doctrines, etc.), xxviii–ix; (on fears), 80–1; (on the future), 34; (on grief), 103; (helped by friends), 112; (Letter to Mother), xxix, xxxviii–xl, 19–20, 106–8, 130; (on perception), 108, 127; (on pleasure), 102; (pleasure/pain doctrine), 78, 79; (on qualities), 46; (on rivalling the gods), 110; (on sight), 49, 108; (on the soul), 91; (on wealth), 68, 101; (*Principal Doctrines*), xxvii, 66; (P.D. no. 1), 10;